Looking for the "Harp" Quartet

Eastman Studies in Music

Ralph P. Locke, Senior Editor
Eastman School of Music

Additional Titles of Interest

Analyzing Wagner's Operas: Alfred Lorenz and German Nationalist Ideology
Stephen McClatchie

The Art of Musical Phrasing in the Eighteenth Century: Punctuating the Classical "Period"
Stephanie D. Vial

August Halm: A Critical and Creative Life in Music
Lee A. Rothfarb

Bach and the Pedal Clavichord: An Organist's Guide
Joel Speerstra

Beethoven's Century: Essays on Composers and Themes
Hugh Macdonald

Beyond The Art of Finger Dexterity: Reassessing Carl Czerny
Edited by David Gramit

Elliott Carter: Collected Essays and Lectures, 1937–1995
Edited by Jonathan W. Bernard

Explaining Tonality: Schenkerian Theory and Beyond
Matthew Brown

Intimate Voices: The Twentieth-Century String Quartet, Volumes 1 and 2
Edited by Evan Jones

Music Speaks: On the Language of Opera, Dance, and Song
Daniel Albright

The Musical Madhouse
(Les Grotesques de la musique)
Hector Berlioz
Translated and edited by Alastair Bruce
Introduction by Hugh Macdonald

Pentatonicism from the Eighteenth Century to Debussy
Jeremy Day-O'Connell

The Pleasure of Modernist Music: Listening, Meaning, Intention, Ideology
Edited by Arved Ashby

Samuel Barber Remembered: A Centenary Tribute
Peter Dickinson

Schubert in the European Imagination, Volumes 1 and 2
Scott Messing

Schumann's Piano Cycles and the Novels of Jean Paul
Erika Reiman

Variations on the Canon: Essays on Music from Bach to Boulez in Honor of Charles Rosen on His Eightieth Birthday
Edited by Robert Curry, David Gable, and Robert L. Marshall

A complete list of titles in the Eastman Studies in Music series may be found on the University of Rochester Press website, www.urpress.com

Looking for the "Harp" Quartet

An Investigation into Musical Beauty

MARKAND THAKAR

UNIVERSITY OF ROCHESTER PRESS

First published 2011

University of Rochester Press
668 Mt. Hope Avenue, Rochester, NY 14620, USA
www.urpress.com
and Boydell & Brewer Limited
PO Box 9, Woodbridge, Suffolk IP12 3DF, UK
www.boydellandbrewer.com

ISBN-13: 978-1-58046-346-1
ISSN: 1071-9989

Library of Congress Cataloging-in-Publication Data

Thakar, Markand, 1955–
   Looking for the Harp quartet : an investigation into musical beauty / Markand Thakar.
       p. cm. — (Eastman studies in music, ISSN 1071-9989 ; v. 82)
   Includes bibliographical references and index.
   ISBN 978-1-58046-346-1 (hardcover : alk. paper) 1. Music–Philosophy and aesthetics. 2. Beethoven, Ludwig van, 1770-1827. Quartets, no. 10, op. 74, strings, Eflat major. I. Title.
   ML3845.T52   2011
   781.1'7—dc22
                                                                          2010033412

A catalogue record for this title is available from the British Library.

This publication is printed on acid-free paper.
Printed in the United States of America.

Some articulation markings from Jonathan Del Mar's urtext edition of Beethoven's "Harp" Quartet have been used in the examples (Bärenreiter, 2008). These are used with the kind permission of Bärenreiter-Verlag Kassel, Basel, London, New York, Prague.

for Victoria, cherished forever

"Beauty is truth, truth beauty,"—that is all
Ye know on earth, and all ye need to know.

John Keats

Contents

Preface

Music can provide a variety of experiences. Most valuable among them is a magical, spiritual, transcendent experience, one in which the sounds absorb us, take us over, one in which we lose our selves and become the sounds. This loss of self is the aesthetic experience; it is, in a word, beauty. The ultimate experience of beauty is available from the most sublime performances of masterworks of Western art music. And it exists on many levels; it is available to a lesser degree from a lesser performance, or a lesser composition. In fact the quality of a composition is directly a function of the degree to which its performance can provide a sublime, transcendent experience; likewise the quality of a performance is directly a function of the degree to which it maximizes the aesthetic experience available from the composition.

Looking for the "Harp" Quartet: An Investigation into Musical Beauty explores how the composer, performer, and listener all contribute to this most magnificent human experience. In the form of five dialogues followed by three related prose articles, the book takes place over the course of a hypothetical academic year. The dialogues are between Icarus, an inquiring student intensely concerned with fulfilling his highest potential as a musician, and Daedalus, an iconoclastic teacher who guides his search for understanding. A student performance of Beethoven's String Quartet, Op. 74, "The Harp," serves as a point of departure and a recurring theme for this inquiry into musical beauty.

The first dialogue, "Looking for the 'Harp' Quartet," explores the question, "What is a composition?" Occurring at the beginning of the school year in September, the dialogue introduces the main issues involved in the pursuit of beauty. The listener's contribution to this highest experience is the focus in December, in "Renoir." February's discussion centers around the composer's contribution in a dialogue entitled "Let's Be Mookie"; and the performer's contribution is explored in April, in the dialogue "Gurus." June brings graduation and a consideration of the future in the last of the dialogues, "First, Last, and Always."

Better than prose, the dialogue format can lead the reader through the step-by-step, question-upon-question process by which understanding can be built. The process is sometimes messy and frustrating, and that can be well reflected in dialogues. Icarus exhibits some youthful arrogance, and Daedalus some curmudgeonly intransigence, for which each occasionally "whacks" the other. Over the course of the school year they approach a mutual understanding. But dialogues by their nature can make for tedious reading, so the book is best absorbed slowly, perhaps a subchapter at a time.

Each of the middle three dialogues is supplemented by a prose article of a technical nature. "Remembrance of Things Future" is a phenomenological investigation of the structure of the listener's consciousness during a transcendent experience of musical beauty. "Patterns of Energy" examines the significance of musical form in the composer's contribution to such an experience. And finally, "Dynamic Analysis" suggests how analysis may aid the performer, as a result of a more comprehensive consideration of a composition than has been traditionally practiced.

The search for the ultimate aesthetic experience of Western art music—a transcendent, loss-of-self experience—drives the book. It brings us inevitably to an understanding that the composition is not itself the aesthetic object, but is a potential for an experience. That understanding—of the composition as potential—in turn leads to an understanding of a listener's experience that is not enriched by knowledge. It leads to understandings of the critical role of the gathering and playing-out of energy for both the composer and the performer. And it is the recognition of the critical, all-embracing, hierarchical patterns of energy, which are the consequence of every single element of the composition and of every single element of the performance, that allows for an effective, comprehensive process of analysis that aids performance, and vice versa.

The considerations in this book are specifically germane to eighteenth- and nineteenth-century tonal music from the European continent—a narrow focus in terms of geography and chronology, but one that encompasses the overwhelming majority of the art music performed, recorded, and listened to. Many of the fundamental issues, though, are completely applicable to music of other cultures and time periods.

To be sure, there are two experiential functions of art. One function of art is to bring us to the transcendent state—a magical, loss-of-self condition. Absorbing the aesthetic object fully and openly, losing ourselves in the object—losing the distinction between the "me" and the "anything that's not me"—brings us into ourselves, and allows us to know ourselves fully in a most profoundly cathartic way. Music can do this, as can visual art.

And there is another function of art, which is to bring us more fully into the world around us. It reinforces our experiences of the world; it makes us think; it gives us new insights; it enriches our experience not of our essential being in and of itself, but of ourselves in relation to our external world. Representative art—artworks that depend for their meaning on understanding the aesthetic object *as* something, such as literature and drama—can do this. Music and visual art can do this as well. To those who seek this kind of experience from music, *Looking for the "Harp" Quartet: An Investigation into Musical Beauty* will prove of little value. The book is a kind of how-to manual for musical transcendence, and not a scholarly resource; it offers a path to achieving transcendence, not enriching information; it presents few citations, and relies on no historical precedents for proof. It asks the reader to come with open ears, it points out possibilities, it leads the reader to experience them, and it depends for proof exclusively on that experience.

Icarus and Daedalus come to us from Greek mythology. Daedalus was the uniquely skilled engineer and craftsman banished to the island of Crete; Icarus was his son. To escape the island, Daedalus constructed wings out of feathers and wax. Icarus, against the cautions of his father, flew too close to the sun; the wax melted, the wings disintegrated, and he fell to his death in the waters named for him, the Icarian Sea. This book is offered in the hopes that readers may enjoy the flight, regardless of the humidity of the landing.

Acknowledgments

Paul Henry Smith was a valued collaborator on the lecture that formed the basis for chapter 6, providing significant input on both content and structure. Not least of his contributions was the title "Remembrance of Things Future." The book owes much to Ralph Locke, whose support made it happen and whose sage guidance made it better. Special thanks are due to Susan Baron, for her meticulous and insightful reading, and to Dr. and Mrs. Robert and Sharon Wahman, for their extraordinary hospitality. And there are no words with which to thank my wife, Victoria Chiang, for her uncompromising search for understanding and growth, her partnership, and her wisdom—Vicky's voice rings throughout.

The dialogues between the younger and older musicians largely reflect my own internal conversations. They also reflect interactions with my teachers, with my own students, and with colleagues and friends. In particular, lessons with Peter Perret were inspirational.

Most of the specific questions and answers were invented for the book, but a few are reconstructed from actual conversations. My students will undoubtedly recognize some of their own questions. Those familiar with the work of Sergiu Celibidache may recognize some of his questions and some of his answers; the same people may also recognize some rejection of, and evolution from, his thought. But my debt to Celibidache far transcends the lifting of a few questions and answers, and any rejection is solely a result of his influence on me to think openly and to listen openly, to be open to that most ennobling, magical, sublime, spiritual, transcendent experience of music that makes life worth living.

Note about Online Supporting Material

This book is accompanied by online supporting material available at www.markandthakar.com/harpquartet (it is also archived at http://hdl.handle.net/1802/11671). The supporting material includes audio realizations of the musical examples from chapters 3, 4, and 7, indicated in the text by the symbol ◀)). It also includes musical examples from chapter 8 that are too lengthy to appear in the printed text; these are available for download, and are indicated in the text by the symbol ⌐.

Part One

Dialogues

Chapter One

Looking for the "Harp" Quartet

September 5

Daedalus: Welcome back!

Icarus: Thanks. I'm glad to be back at school.

D: (*laughing*) We'll fix that. So how did you spend your summer?

I: It seems like all I did is eat, sleep, and breathe the "Harp" Quartet of Beethoven.

D: Why the "Harp" Quartet?

I: I'm performing it this year. And my quartet was able to get together to work on it over the past few weeks.

D: Wonderful. How have you worked on it?

I: Well, we spent a lot of time rehearsing it, and we've listened to a recording of it. Then I did a harmonic analysis of the whole thing, and I stumbled through it on the piano. There were concerts, too—we've heard two performances of it recently.

D: How did you find the performances?

I: One was exquisite—absolutely magical. I was completely transported. In fact, it was after hearing that performance that I knew I had to play the piece. The second was horrendous: technically amazing, but really pedantic, and unmusical.

D: And that recording?

I: Interesting. But it got scratched up so I had to throw it out.

D: You like the piece then?

I: Oh my god, yes. It's an extraordinary piece. It's the best.

D: So after living with a piece as wonderful as the "Harp" Quartet, why do you seem in such a bad mood?

I: Because I want to find out how to play this piece as well as I possibly can. What makes that great performance better than the mediocre one, and much better than the lousy one? And I'm darned frustrated, because I'm not having much success.

D: Ah yes, beauty . . . the reason we all do music. Good luck!

I: And because I have a piano proficiency exam, tomorrow, and the practice rooms are too cold, and I can't play the piano. Why do they expect me to play the piano anyway—I'm a violinist. And those benches are way too low. I started to get a backache. Luckily I had some music to sit on.

D: It wasn't . . .

I: (*laughing*) Yup. The "Harp" Quartet.

D: That's funny.

I: Okay, it's funny. But I'm still frustrated.

D: Let's see what we can do for you. Before you start asking about how to play the piece, you have to answer one question. The "Harp" Quartet—you started by saying you "worked on it." Then you said that your quartet "played it" and "rehearsed it" and "listened to a recording of it," and that you "stumbled through it on the piano." You also analyzed it, heard some performances of it, and you even sat on it.

I: Yes—so—what's the question?

D: The question is this: What is "it"?

I: Huh?

D: What is "it"? What is the "Harp" Quartet?

I: What do you mean? It's Opus 74 of Beethoven.

D: Yes, but that's just another name for it. Can you tell me what it is?

I: It's the piece by Beethoven that goes (*singing*): lah-lala-lah-lah.

D: But you wouldn't say that tune is the "Harp" Quartet, would you? When you say the "Harp" Quartet you mean something different than that tune. Isn't that so?

I: Yes.

D: In fact, you said it's a piece by Beethoven. You even said that it's an extraordinary piece. So, what do you mean when you say "piece"? What is this thing that you say you like?

I: (*frustrated*) I don't know—everyone knows what I mean. You know what I mean too.

D: Yes, I do—and that's the point. Everyone does know what you mean when you use the term "Harp" Quartet—everyone who knows that there is such a piece, that is. Everyone uses the term, everyone understands its meaning, but articulating that meaning is difficult. What is it exactly that is signified by the term "Harp" Quartet?

I: Well, could it be the score? I said that I sat on the "Harp" Quartet, and what I was actually sitting on was the score. So maybe it is the score.

D: Maybe. What do you think?

I: Well the score sure doesn't have much sound.

D: What does it sound like?

I: If you riffle the pages? Whoooosh!

D: Let's get serious. Otherwise, nothing?

I: Right.

D: And what kind of music has no sound?

I: None. But didn't John Cage compose a piece that was just silence?

D: Yes. In fact that brings up an interesting question: is there such a thing in our experience as silence? We know that there is silence in a vacuum, but we don't live in a vacuum. The vacuum is not within our lived experience. Outside of the vacuum there is always the sound of the electric lights, or the wind, or the birds or insects, or—if even those are eliminated—there is the ever-present sound of our bodies.

I: So maybe it was Cage's point that there is no such thing as silence, and by forcing us to listen to performers who are not making any sounds, he would make us hear these sounds that form our environment.

D: Yes, perhaps. And while that's an interesting question, it's not a musical question. But let us accept that music cannot exist without sound.

I: Okay. Done. Music cannot exist without sound. So the score cannot be the piece, because the score itself cannot be heard.

D: Hold on. Not so fast. For that to be true, you must know that the piece is heard. I know that I hear the performance, but I don't know that I hear the piece itself.

I: You lost me.

D: You said that the score cannot be the piece because the score is not heard. That's true only if the piece is heard. In other words, if the piece is heard and the score is not heard, the piece cannot be the score. All we have accepted, however, is that music does not exist without sound; in other words, that music is heard. We are not looking for music, though; what we are looking for is the piece. We haven't touched on the question of whether or not the piece itself— this thing that is the "Harp" Quartet—is heard.

I: That's crazy. Of course I hear it. I hear the piece. How could I not hear the piece? What else could I be hearing?

D: When you go to the concert, what do you hear?

I: I hear sounds.

D: Right. And who makes the sounds?

I: The performers.

D: You go to a concert, and you hear sounds made by the performers. So what you hear—this physical object of your hearing—is the performance. Correct?

I: Yes.

D: But is the performance the same as the piece? Is it possible that you hear the performance, but not the piece?

I: I'm not sure.

D: All right. Imagine an exquisite performance of the "Harp" Quartet. In the middle of the performance, a deafening fire alarm goes off in the hall. The performance is absolutely and completely ruined. Destroyed. What about the piece? Is it harmed, or even affected in any way?

I: No, the piece is—the same as it always was. Unharmed. Unaffected in any way. Hmm. The performance is changed, but the piece is not. So they couldn't be the same thing. The piece is not the performance. Okay, but what about the score. We asked if the score could be the piece.

D: We found out that the piece and the performance were not the same, because we destroyed one without destroying the other. Let's try a similar experiment with the piece and the score. What would happen to the piece if we destroyed the score?

I: Well, I got so sick of performing Schoenberg's *Phantasy* once that I ripped up the score in shreds.

D: That was mature. But did it affect the piece at all?

I: No. The piece came out unscathed. Boy, I sure put that score out of its misery, though.

D: So the score is destroyed, and the piece is still extant, unaffected. Can they be the same?

I: No. So the piece couldn't be the score. Hmm—that piece is a tough bird. We can't destroy it no matter what we do.

D: But . . . what is it?

I: Beats me!

D: Give it some thought, see what you come up with, and if you like we'll talk more about it.

September 8

I: Can I give you a ride?

D: That would be fine, but I live a little out of your way.

I: No problem. I'd like to see that part of town. Anyway, you'll be glad to know that our discussion really helped me. I'm no longer losing sleep obsessing about the "Harp" Quartet.

D: Good.

I: Now I'm losing sleep trying to figure out what that thing is that I had been losing sleep over.

D: (*laughing*) Even better.

I: Easy for you to say. But I have considered the problem a lot.

D: Excellent. In what ways?

I: I started by asking my theory and music history professors for their understanding of what a piece is. My music history teacher said that the piece is a historical artifact. Actually she said an historical artifact. Anyway, she said that we listen to a piece to bring ourselves out of our own world into the world of the composer.

D: And you think?

I: Well I see how that might be possible.

D: How?

I: Because the music was composed in Beethoven's time. When we absorb ourselves in sounds that were composed in Beethoven's time, it might be like wrapping ourselves in a nineteenth-century costume. Or like sitting in a Louis XIV chair. Or holding an Indian arrowhead. In other words, maybe it's a kind of prop to stimulate our imagination. Maybe we can hear the piece and imagine ourselves in the hall, imagine the street scenes and the food. Maybe hearing the piece can bring us to thinking about the culture, or the political climate.

D: That's interesting. What do you think?

I: It certainly seems logical.

D: Let's examine that a little more closely then. You have a recording of the "Harp" Quartet right here. Why don't you pull over and we can listen to it. As we listen, let's imagine ourselves in the midst of a scene in early nineteenth-century Vienna. The music will start; we look around the ornately decorated concert room, excited just to have been invited to this social event. We hear the rustle of the skirts adorning the women of grand society, which is abuzz with the latest news of Napoleon. We are sated with the heavy meal we just enjoyed, and tipsy with wine and brandy, and feel the chill of the drafty high-ceilinged room.

They listen, and imagine as above.

I: Okay. I get it. It was kind of fun, for a while. So it is possible, though? That the piece is a historical artifact.

D: In a sense it certainly is. But not in the sense that interests us.

I: Why not?

D: Where do those thoughts come from? Are they in the piece?

I: What do you mean?

D: I mean this. My immersion into nineteenth-century Vienna depends entirely on my own knowledge. To place myself in the conditions of nineteenth-century Vienna I must have some knowledge of those conditions. In fact, they are not the conditions of nineteenth-century Vienna at all, they are what I imagine to be the conditions; they are more precisely *my* conditions. The political situation in my fantasized experience is my understanding of the political situation; the social conditions in my fantasized experience are my understanding of the social conditions, etc. It comes from me, not from the piece. The piece serves only as a stimulus to my own imagination.

I: But isn't the piece one of the things that allows us this kind of historical fantasy? Hearing the piece, knowing the costumes, the interior decorations, the political climate, and so on?

D: In this case, yes.

I: Then—theoretically—to fully enjoy a piece, wouldn't I have to know everything there is to know about the conditions of the world in which it was composed?

D: Why?

I: Because none of that stuff is in the piece itself. And we've just seen that my experience will be wonderfully enriched if I know about all those things.

D: Will it?

I: We just saw that it would. Won't it?

D: Okay, let's try to clear things up. How much do you know about nineteenth-century Vienna?

I: (*grinning*) I know that the concert rooms were ornately decorated and chilly.

D: In other words, next to nothing. How much did you know about nineteenth-century Vienna when you heard that wonderful performance of the "Harp" Quartet last week?

I: Practically speaking, nothing.

D: And yet you described that experience as magical. I think you said you had been transported.

I: Yes, it was the most incredible thing I've ever heard.

D: How would you compare that experience to the kind of historical fantasy we just had.

I: Well this was . . . interesting. But the performance I heard was—I hesitate to say this—like a spiritual experience.

D: Like a spiritual experience?

I: Well, in a way it really was a kind of spiritual experience.

D: Let me try to express those thoughts another way. The experience you had at that performance of the "Harp" Quartet was an experience of musical beauty. It was exhilarating, it was sublime, it was transcendent. The experience of historical fantasy was enjoyable, it was enriching, it was rewarding, but it was an experience of the intellect. The historical exercise enriched your understanding of the world and your place in it. The experience of music took you out of the world, and allowed you to be in touch with the essence of who you are.

I: But wasn't it the piece itself that stimulated that intellectual experience? Isn't that a valid function?

D: Yes, certainly. But the same performance could serve as the stimulus for thinking about a day at the beach.

I: How?

D: Suppose that the first time I studied the piece intently I was on the beach. The piece and that experience at the beach have become associated in my mind. So when I hear the piece, I am easily brought back to the sun and the sand . . .

I: So the piece has about as much to do with nineteenth-century Vienna as it does with fabulous babes on the beach.

D: That's not entirely correct, because the piece came into being in nineteenth-century Vienna. It's true to the extent that you use the performance to enhance your connection to the world. But neither the beach nor nineteenth-century Vienna is part of your consciousness when an aesthetic experience results from listening to the "Harp" Quartet.

I: And the fact is that this is why I'm involved with music to begin with. That's why I'm a musician, I guess, and not a historian. I want to do music to have a musical experience. As the means to a musical experience, then, the "Harp" Quartet can't be a historical artifact. Not even an historical artifact. Okay. But then I asked my theory teacher. He suggested that a piece of music is the sum total of its performances, scores, and recordings.

D: What do you think?

I: I don't see how it could be.

D: Why not?

I: Because first of all we already determined that the piece isn't the score.

D: Yes. And . . .

I: And I'm not sure, but somehow it just doesn't seem possible that the piece is all of the performances and recordings.

D: When you play the "Harp" Quartet, does it feel like you're playing the tiniest fraction of all of the performances and recordings, or does it feel like you're playing an entire thing—the whole piece?

I: Certainly the whole piece.

D: Not just the tiniest fraction of it?

I: No. No, not at all. We are playing the piece. The whole piece.

D: And imagine the first performance in Beethoven's time of the "Harp" Quartet. Do you think that the piece that was first performed in 1809 was less in any way than the "Harp" Quartet as it exists today? Let's hypothesize that there have been fifty thousand performances and recordings of the "Harp" Quartet since 1809. Was that piece as played in 1809 1/50,000 of the piece as it exists today?

I: Possibly, if the performance was out of tune, or not together.

D: Now you're talking about the performance. And we know the performance doesn't affect the piece itself. Was the piece, the "Harp" Quartet, a lesser piece? Was it different in any way?

I: I don't think the piece itself could have been different. That seems absurd to me. I think that in 1809 they were also playing the whole piece, and not $1/50,000$ of the piece as it exists today.

D: It seems absurd to me also. And this thing that you worked on, analyzed, lost sleep over, etc.—it wasn't all the recordings and performances, was it?

I: Please! I'm having enough trouble with just this one.

D: Seriously.

I: No, seriously, the "Harp" Quartet that we're working on really seems to be a single thing; something entire in and of itself. It doesn't seem at all to be the sum of anyone else's performances, or recordings.

D: And what happened to the piece when you threw out that recording.

I: Nothing. Not one thing.

D: So, the piece is unchanged by its performances or recordings, and you see no reason to imagine that any future performances or recordings could change the piece. Perhaps this is why you say that in your experience, what is understood by the term "Harp" Quartet couldn't be the sum of all the performances and scores and recordings.

I: Perhaps.

D: But what if he meant something else. What if he meant that for me, the piece is the sum of all the scores, and performances, and recordings that I have heard, much like my concept of a particular human being is the sum of all the contact I've had with them and everything I know about them.

I: We've already established that it couldn't be.

D: It couldn't? When you think of your mother, is what comes to mind an impression of her as she was the last time you saw her? Or is what comes to mind a composite of impressions and feelings and associations gathered over years of contact? Is your understanding of your mother simply the person you had dinner with two weeks ago, or is it also the woman who raised you, who took care of you when you were sick, punished you when you were bad, the person to whose skirts you clung, etc.?

I: Well, all of those things.

D: Precisely. And if you think of what the music school signifies, is it just what you experienced the last time you were in the building, or is it again a composite of your impressions of your classes, and teachers, and colleagues, and good times, and difficult times; memories of all the images and feelings associated with the music school?

I: Again all of those things.

D: So when you think of the "Harp" Quartet, does it not signify, point to, bring out, associate with all of your experiences with the piece—the performances and recordings you've heard, the people you've played it with, the backache that you got trying to stumble through it on the piano, and so on?

I: Yes it does. So you're saying that's the "Harp" Quartet? It is what he said it was . . . the sum of all the performances, recordings, and scores that I experienced?

D: Let's hold off again. If that's the case, then is the "Harp" Quartet different for me than for you?

I: It must be.

D: Yes, it must be, because I have a quite different set of experiences with the "Harp" Quartet than you.

I: So the piece is a different thing for everyone?

D: Yes, if your theory teacher is right. But I thought you said way back when we started talking that I knew what you meant when you said the "Harp" Quartet. Not only that, but you said that everyone knew what you meant.

I: So then it isn't true that everyone knows what I mean by the term "Harp" Quartet?

D: Not at all. In fact, I agreed with you completely. Everyone does know what you mean by the term "Harp" Quartet. Anyone who is aware that there is such a piece knows what is meant by the term. The problem here is simple. Your theory teacher did not answer the question that you asked. Your question was "What is the piece?" He answered by describing the significance the piece had for him. Perhaps he was saying that we cannot define what the piece itself is, or perhaps he thought he was defining the piece. In either case, his answer is a description of the piece as a sign of something. By taking the piece not as an object but as a sign, he has a cumulative, associative, composite notion of the piece as it exists in its infinite variations. What we are after is something quite different, something opposite. We are after the object that is the continuity across those infinite variations. We are after the essence of the piece itself. Your theorist answered the question, "What does the piece signify to you?" by adding all the experiences and associations. We are instead asking "What is the piece?" What is left after subtracting the variations; what is at the core of what we all understand as the "Harp" Quartet?

I: And I for one have no idea. We know it's not the score, and we know it's not all the performances, and recordings, and scores. We know it's not all the things it signifies to me. And we know it's not a historical artifact. Well this is great timing. Here's where you get out, and I'm more confused than ever. Now what?

D: You're doing fine. When you go back, keep directing your attention to your experiences, and keep asking questions. Go after your experiences, without fear of what you discover. We'll talk some more.

September 12

I: I'm still thinking about this stuff as much as ever.

D: Good. Let's go for a walk and we can talk about it. What have you come up with?

I: I saw our chamber music coach and our orchestra conductor standing together, and I asked them what they thought the piece was.

D: And they said?

I: They seemed to agree that it was the composer's intentions as indicated in the score.

D: What do you think?

I: I don't know. I'm sure it does have something to do with the composer's intentions.

D: What do they mean by "the composer's intentions"?

I: They agreed that our job as performers is to serve the composer. He gives us precise indications, and we serve him by following his requests. For instance, at our last session with our coach he said, (*imitating him*) "Can't you read music? Staccato!! Staccato!! Beethoven told you how long to play those notes—pay attention. He precisely marks staccato because he precisely in-*tends* staccato!"

D: You impudent punk. But did he? Did he mark his intentions? Did he indicate to you how long he intended those notes?

I: Well . . . actually . . . sure, I guess. By staccato markings—dots over the notes.

D: You guess? If you play staccato notes, isn't it up to you to match your articulations with those of the rest of the quartet?

I: Absolutely. But you can't deny that the articulations are dictated by the score. It's right there: dots mean staccato.

D: Okay. Let's take . . . for example, that spot in the first movement. The first violinist, violist, and cellist play a staccato chord, and you answer one quarter note later. Imagine that in a given performance, the length of your note is different from that of theirs. Your double stop was also staccato—somewhat separated—but it was notably longer than theirs. Why might that have happened?

I: Probably because I wasn't listening. It's up to me to match their note length.

D: It is. But when you played your chord longer—was it staccato?

I: Yes. You said it was.

D: Just not the same staccato as the previous chord.

I: Sure.

D: So where was Beethoven's precise indication?

I: Oh boy. Another trap. Well, I guess in the case of articulations it's somewhat general.

D: General enough so that you can both be following his indications faithfully, and yet the result is noticeably different.

I: Okay. I see that. But dynamics? Dynamics are indicated in the score. Aren't they?

D: Again, though, isn't it possible for two instruments to be playing *forte* at quite different volumes?

I: As a matter of fact, yes. It happens all the time, especially in orchestra. The conductor says "Everybody just play what's in your part." So the brass players play *forte* and they blast us out. Obliterate us completely. My stand partner jokes with me, "Make sure you let me know if I'm covering the trumpets."

D: So again, you are all following Beethoven's dynamic indications faithfully, and yet you produce dramatically different volumes. So again, where is Beethoven's precise indication for dynamics?

I: Okay, okay. But anyway, he indicates pitches precisely.

D: I'm not so sure that he does. Have you ever heard the expression "playing in tune with himself, but not with the group"?

I: Yes, but that usually is just a nice way of saying someone's playing out of tune.

D: That may be the case, but is it possible for you to have an idea of the pitch of a tone, which you play in unison or octaves with someone else, whose idea differs?

I: Sure. We spend excruciating hours matching pitches. Actually it usually is so that we learn to play in tune, but maybe—well—okay—we're also probably doing that so we learn to play in tune in the same way.

D: So Beethoven indicates pitches, and dynamics, and articulations, which we've seen are all relatively imprecise suggestions. Now your conductor and coach said the piece was indicated in the score. What, exactly, is indicated in the score?

I: Hmm. Exactly? Not sure. But general suggestions.

D: And they also said that the piece was the composer's intentions. How do they know the composer's intentions.

I: Because they've got the score. Well that's stupid. We know that the score makes only general suggestions. And the precise demands for how to play the tones are made by the tones themselves? What's going on. I don't know how to play the tones until I hear the tones which tell me how to play themselves. Now you've got me more confused than ever. And what does this have to do with where the piece is? I thought you were supposed to clear this up for me.

D: Here—let's stop in here for something to drink. We can gather our thoughts.

They order coffee. After a while Daedalus continues . . .

You have a question. You said you want to learn how to play a certain piece better, and I asked you what you meant by the term "piece of music." You thought it was a simple question, and the more it involved you, the more complex it became. Now you are looking to me for answers, and you are disappointed. The most you can hope for from me, or from yourself for that matter, is well-pointed questions. "Live the questions now," as Rilke said. Then maybe you can live your way into the answer.

I: Okay. Maybe I'm not looking in the right place. Where do I look? How do I look?

D: If you want coffee, where do you go?

I: To a restaurant, a coffee shop.

D: Why?

I: Because that's where the coffee is.

D: And if you want to know about music theory?

I: To a theory book. Or to a theory teacher, because they're both containers of facts about music theory.

D: What an arrogant little jerk you are! Have some respect!

I: Well, some of my theory teachers have been just that: containers of facts. How does harmonic analysis help me? I did it, but it didn't help me play the piece any better. That's what I want to know. Why does it matter to me if I can describe an entire movement of the "Harp" Quartet as $\hat{3}$–$\hat{2}$–$\hat{1}$ over I–V–I? This is valuable only to the music theory students who study music theory so they can teach music theory to students who can teach music theory, and so on. What value is that to society? Where's the relevance?

D: Who says there needs to be relevance? And what gives you the right to say that a life dedicated to the study of Rameau's theory of harmony or Schenker's theories of voice leading isn't valuable? Is it less valuable than one spent buying and selling stocks? Than one spent racing horses?

I: Of course not. But stock trading and horse racing are not part of the core curriculum in instrumental performance, so I don't have to spend time studying them.

D: (*to himself*) Never try to argue with a music student about the relevance of music theory.

(*to Icarus*) You may yet find some value in studying music theory. In the meantime I suggest that you be a bit more courteous and respectful, and say that music theory books and teachers are sources of information.

I: Okay.

D: Then, if you want to find out facts about music history?

I: I go to a music history book, or a music history teacher, because they are sources of information about music history.

D: All right. And finally, if you want to find out about music, where do you go?

I: Well, to where the music is.

D: Yes, yes, and where is that?

I: Maybe—to another musician—a more experienced one maybe.

D: Ach! Use your brain! When you hear the "Harp" Quartet, how do you know that the succession of sounds that is the "Harp" Quartet is all the same piece?

I: What kind of question is that? Of course it's the same piece. It doesn't stop. Well, the movements stop, but I know from reading the program that there are four movements. But within the movement, I know it's the same piece because it doesn't stop.

D: Doesn't it? What about the first four staccato chords of the first movement *Allegro*? Each chord sounds, and then stops. There is sound, and then silence. The sound is not continuous. Is the piece continuous, though?

I: Yes.

D: The sound is not continuous, but the piece is. What is it that makes it continuous?

I: Hmm. Boy. That's a hard question. I absolutely do not experience the piece as stopping. It's inconceivable that I could experience the piece as stopping and starting, stopping and starting. I really don't know why—I just hear it that way.

D: As it happens, that's a perfect answer. There is a complex answer for that question that involves the structure of our consciousness of temporally extended events, but we can get to that some other time. For now the simple truth is that the piece is continuous because it comes to us—to you and to us all—as continuous. You know the piece is continuous because you hear it that way. In other words, the piece exists in your consciousness as continuous, even though the sounds that you are experiencing stop in physical reality. What makes it continuous? Your hearing of it as continuous. So, where is the music?

Icarus pauses . . .

I: In . . . me. Hmm. In reality, the sounds are out there, but the music—this—connection of the sounds—it's in me. In my consciousness. So the music isn't out there. There is no music out there, it becomes music only in my consciousness. Only in my experience of sounds.

D: Precisely. So where do you look to find out about music?

I: Inside me. In my consciousness.

D: Now you're on the right track. Let's say that again, because that understanding is critical. In the physical world there are sounds. When we hear them as music, though, the music is in our experience of them—in our experience of the sounds in relation to each other. We have seen this from the simple fact that while the sounds in the physical world stop and start, they can be experienced as an unbroken continuity. The continuity—what we experience as the music—exists only in our perception—in our consciousness.

I: But doesn't that bring us back to the question of different strokes for different folks? Doesn't that mean the music is different for everyone?

D: In one very real sense, that is true. But . . . sorry to change the subject, but that woman I just saw passing us . . . I think she looked like your orchestra conductor.

I: Are you kidding? That woman didn't look anything like the maestra.

D: (*smiling*) We just did a little experiment. We both passed a woman. I saw the woman, and you saw her too. When I asked you about the woman *I* saw, you talked about her. I didn't ask about the woman you saw, but the woman I saw. Even though you disagreed with my view of her appearance, your answer was grounded in the assumption that we both saw the same woman. Both of our experiences of that woman are unique. Your sight of her was definitely not my sight of her, and in fact from your angle of vision you perceived different images than I did from mine. But along with our individual sights of her, we both know that the other had a similar perception. When I hear music, not only is my perception of the music different from yours, but—because the music exists only within my consciousness—I hear a different music. Along with my experience of that music, though, I know that it is possible for you to have a like experience . . . that you, too, can hear essentially the same music. Clear?

I: Clear? No. But maybe I'm beginning to get the picture.

D: Good. Now let's work our way back to the original question. Here you are, listening to the "Harp" Quartet. The music is in you, in your consciousness. Out there are sounds, which allow you to have your experience. Who is responsible for the sounds?

I: Beethoven.

D: No, certainly not. Beethoven's dead. He couldn't have made those sounds.

I: Right. In fact, we've already established that it's the performers.

D: Yes, exactly. The performers. The music is in the consciousness of the person who experiences sounds. The performers create those sounds. What is the composer's contribution?

I: He makes general suggestions for the sounds.

D: So the composer makes general suggestions for sounds, which can lead to an experience of music. Is there a difference between the suggestions and the sounds?

I: Of course. The suggestion is unrealized. It's only a suggestion. The sound is actual.

D: Then the composer . . .

I: (*interrupting*) The composer composes a piece. A piece is a set of unrealized suggestions for performance.

D: And performance is what?

I: The performance is the realization of those suggestions.

D: To what end?

I: What do you mean?

D: By itself, the performance—the production of sounds—is what?

I: Oh. It's just sounds, it's not music. The music comes from the experience of those sounds. The performance then results in the experience of music.

D: So the piece is ultimately . . .

I: The piece is the potential for an experience of music.

D: Absolutely. It is. But isn't the performance also the potential for an experience of music?

I: Yes. Well, the piece is the idea—the plan for the performance.

D: Yes, but a suggestion to play with greater articulation would also be a plan for a performance, and that suggestion is not a piece. More specifically you would have to say the piece is the design for the sonic relationships.

I: But that's not quite right, either, because the directions for church bell ringers is also a design for sonic relationships, and so are the words for a speech, and they're not necessarily pieces.

D: Excellent. So what do we add?

I: Well, we could add that the sonic relationships exist for the purpose of allowing a musical experience.

D: Yes. That's good. So what we have is a design for sonic relationships that exist to allow a musical experience. But it's not a precise design. It's approximate.

I: That's important?

D: Approximate is critical. You said you heard two performances. Both of the piece. Both within the range of playing what the composer wrote. But one you hated, and one you loved. You loved it so much you wanted to find out how to do it . . . how to go from any possible unfolding of this piece to one that provides an optimal experience.

I: Hmm. An approximate design. An approximate design for sonic relationships that exist to allow a musical experience. So that's it? That's all it is? So what's the big deal?

D: What's the big deal indeed! That was the easy part. You've arrived at a definition—that a piece is an approximate design for sonic relationships for the purpose of allowing a musical experience. Now you get to think about what that might mean.

I: Okay, I'll do it tonight. At least I'll try.

September 13

I: I know it's been only a day, but I've been cogitating something powerful, and I think I've got it nailed down. Do you have time to discuss this with me?

D: I'll be surprised if you have anything nailed down, but I could be pleasantly surprised.

I: (*laughing*) Zing! Let's get out into the fresh air, though.

They walk and talk. Icarus continues . . .

My original question was: how can I make the best possible performance of a piece? I've got a definition of a piece; it's a design, an approximate one, for sonic relationships for the purpose of allowing a musical experience. Now if that's true, a great piece must be a design for sonic relationships that allow a great experience. And my experience comes from hearing the performance, which is a realization of that design, so a great performance must be a realization that likewise allows for a great experience.

D: (*smiling*) You really have it nailed down, eh? The piece allows something that the performance allows too? The piece then is a potential for a potential?

I: *Gulp . . .*

They walk further.

Okay. We know it's not a thing in and of itself . . .

D: Of course it's a thing, it's the thing we're trying to define.

I: But we know that we want to understand it in terms of its potential. If we understood it as a historical artifact, or we took it as a precise record of the composer's intentions, the question "what is the best way to unfold it" would be moot. And likewise if we understood it as the sum of our experiences, because we'd pretty much then want to play it in all different ways, because then the piece would be that much richer. So this thing that we're trying to define, for us must be a potential.

D: For a potential?

I: (*deflated*) I guess I haven't nailed anything down.

D: Ah, but you're on the right track. The composer writes a piece. The performer plays it. And the listener perceives it. The end result—*if* the composition allows it, and *if* the performance allows it, and *if* the listener allows it—is a magical experience:

beauty. The magical, transcendent experience of beauty. Now before you can make any headway in understanding how to make it, you might profit by a better understanding of the goal, of this thing you're trying to make: this magical experience.

I: So what can I do? How can I learn? Are there books I can read? What's the next step?

D: *Lento. Lento.* You have much to learn, but you have much time. And some things you cannot rush. I'm going to a lecture this evening on the structure of our consciousness during a musical experience—it's called "Remembrance of Things Future."[1] You're welcome to join me.

I: Okay, I just may. Shall I bring my hammer?

Chapter Two

Renoir and the Survival of Classical Music

On the Listener's Contribution

December 1

Daedalus: It's good to see you. How are you?

Icarus: Discouraged.

D: Discouraged?

I: You heard us on the big end-of-semester concert. It was exhausting. We worked very hard.

D: And you don't feel good about your performance?

I: Well, yeah, maybe the performance went okay, but it's the story of my life: an artistic success and a public failure.

D: Why do you say public failure? I thought the audience reaction was quite favorable.

I: Sure, all six of them. Geez, there were almost as many people on stage as there were in the audience.

D: Yes, I'm sure that was disappointing.

I: You work hard and you want to share it with people—so the fact that no one particularly cares is a little discouraging. But it's also frightening. I mean, we're going to have to earn our living somehow, and there just doesn't seem to be any market for classical music. I went to the symphony concert last week and the hall was only a third full. Orchestras are folding left and right, and even big-time orchestras are in deep trouble. Eventually I have to think about putting bread on the table, and it's scary to think about what's going to happen.

D: Have you thought about law school?

I: Oh sure, you can joke—you already have a job. But I'm talking about survival here.

D: Well, you're right. There just is not as much interest in classical music as we would like. Audiences are aging, attendance is uncertain, private contributions are insufficient, corporate support is shrinking, and government support is almost nonexistent.

I: Yes, it's our lousy government. They spend more on military bands than they do for all the arts. No wonder we're struggling.

D: They? Who's "they"? You're forgetting about government of the people and by the people.

I: You mean that we elected the jerks, so if we want to change things we have to elect other jerks who will support the arts more?

D: Actually, I mean something even more discouraging than that. I mean that the government *is* the people—our government and, ultimately, any government.

I: Are you saying that our people don't value the arts, so the government won't support them sufficiently?

D: Right. Can't support them more than the people want—couldn't possibly.

I: Okay. So we're trying to fix this problem.

D: We are? No, you are. I'll go along for the ride, though.

I: If we can't get the support of the government until we get the support of the people, then we have to find a way to increase interest among the people.

D: And how do you propose to do that?

I: Well, I've been reading the reviewer's complaints about stale repertoire. Maybe audiences are not interested in hearing one more performance of the old warhorses: Beethoven, Brahms, et cetera. Maybe we could solve the problem by playing more contemporary music.

D: But doesn't the symphony perform a new piece on just about every program?

I: True. And my symphony friends told me that every time a big new piece is programmed it takes money out of their pockets, because people just don't show up. Maybe we just need better marketing.

D: Ah, the American solution. Market your way out of the problem!

I: Sure, promote, and educate. In fact it's the same thing, isn't it? Just like Coca-Cola educates consumers about the benefit they can derive from drinking the stuff, maybe we can begin to educate our potential audiences about the benefit they can derive from our concerts. We have to start the cycle going somehow, don't we? I mean, if the German government supports classical music, it's probably because Germans are trained from birth to love it. And therefore they support it. And Japan too. I've heard that in Japan people can't get enough classical music. Here we support professional wrestling and monster-truck races.

D: Then maybe you should start studying Japanese. Or monster-truckery.

I: (*somewhat dejected*) You know, I'm disappointed because I thought you might be helpful. This really isn't a joking matter.

D: No, of course not. And I am quite serious about it. In a free-market economy the product must go where the buyers are, and the buyers largely determine what the product is. If the only market for your product is in Japan, then go to Japan. If you want to serve the American market, drive a monster truck or become a professional wrestler.

I: But wait a minute. If you believe that, why are you in the business of training classical musicians?

D: Ah, the great moral dilemma. (*smiling*) Maybe I do it to improve the musical life of the Japanese.

I: Come on.

D: Look, you're troubled because without popular interest in what you do, you are rightfully concerned about being able to earn a living. Of course if not enough people are interested in what we offer, we will not have sufficient financial support: we will not have ticket income, we will not have donations from individual music lovers, we will not have corporate support, and we will not have government support. How do we increase financial support for classical music? Obviously by increasing interest on the part of the people. So of course we have to market—to present ourselves to the public—and it's critical that we do it well. But there's something else we can do.

I: Yes?

D: It's simple.

I: Yes?

D: Make better listeners.

I: Better listeners? And how do we do that?

D: One way you do it is to play better concerts.

I: Make better listeners by playing better concerts? Hmmm. But playing better concerts is really what I want to know about! So how . . .

D: I'm going to the Renoir exhibit first thing tomorrow morning, and I have an extra ticket. If you'd like to join me, we can pursue this further. I'll be there when the exhibit opens to avoid the crowds.

December 2

I: (*waving*) *Hello! Over here!*

D: Why, hello. I'm glad you could come.

I: Yeah, well, it was either practice or try to figure out my financial future.

D: Perhaps you could help your financial future more by practicing.

I: Yeah, okay. *Touché.* But you made me an offer I couldn't refuse. Renoir *and* the survival of classical music.

D: Good. Well let's start with Renoir. (*approaching a painting*) Now who composed this painting (see plate 2.1)?

I: What do you mean, composed?

D: If we make a parallel with music, who composed it?

I: I'm not sure what you're getting at. Renoir, I guess—he was the artist.

D: Okay let's try a different question. Who is the performer?

I: Huh? I don't know. Us? The viewers?

D: *Aaiiigh!* Use your brain!

I: I am using my brain. You have to ask clearer questions!

D: (*smiling*) We discussed what a composer does in writing a piece of music—the composer contributes a plan for how combinations of tones can unfold to yield a sublime musical experience. And the performer brings that plan into physical actuality by creating the sounds. So in terms of this painting, whose plan was carried out?

I: I guess it was Renoir's plan.

D: Yes, Renoir made the plan. And who carried it out? Who brought the plan for visual images into physical actuality?

I: Well, Renoir did too.

D: Of course. In classical music there are generally three components of the experience: composer, performer, and listener. But in visual art there are only two: artist and . . .

I: Viewer.

D: Right. And how does the viewer participate?

I: Participate?

D: Participate in this artistic experience. What is the viewer's contribution?

I: Is this a trick question? The viewer looks at the thing—he views it.

D: Well we're on the right track. No doubt. But let's take it a little farther. We have a painting here. *The Skiff.* What are you experiencing?

I: Experiencing? Well I see a red boat and some women rowing, and a blue river, and some houses in the distance.

D: And what does it do for you?

I: It's . . . pretty. I like it. But . . . well, I don't know . . . I guess I don't know enough about art.

D: So you think that if you knew more about art you would have a better experience? How so?

I: Well, see, if I were more educated as far as the significance of the boats or the river, maybe . . . I would have a better experience. Or if I knew what he was thinking about at the time it would be more meaningful.

D: What about the painting process itself?

I: Yeah, that too. If I knew more about the brush strokes, or how he went about the process of painting this picture, or even maybe the significance of his technique in the history of painting, I think that the whole experience would be . . . somehow . . . richer.

D: Like knowing about nineteenth-century Vienna made your experience of the "Harp" Quartet better?

I: Ah . . . you're saying it's an intellectual experience, not an aesthetic one.

Plate 2.1. Auguste Renoir, *The Skiff (La Yole)*, 1875. Oil on canvas, 71 x 92 cm. National Gallery, London. © National Gallery, London / Art Resource, NY. Used by permission.

D: Precisely! The impetus for this kind of intellectual experience is the work of art, and the thoughts may involve the work of art. But the experience itself is not artistic. The conscious activity involved in an expert viewer's intellectual experience of a painting is essentially similar to that of a botanist studying a flower, or an archaeologist studying ancient ruins.

I: And the flower is beautiful! And the ancient ruins are beautiful!

D: Sometimes they are.

I: They change?

D: They don't change. We change. And that's precisely the point: the experience of beauty is quite different from the intellectual experience. In other words, in an aesthetic experience of a flower, the nature of our consciousness is quite different than it is in an intellectual experience of the same flower. Any aesthetic object—any object such as a performance or a painting that allows an aesthetic experience—can also be experienced intellectually, nonaesthetically. But the intellectual, nonaesthetic experience of an aesthetic object—in other words, the ever-expanding network of thoughts of the educated perceiver who experiences a work of art *as* something—will never be sufficiently rewarding for enough people to make a significant difference in our popular acceptance. Therefore, training more educated perceivers is just not the long-term answer.

* * *

They walk slowly around the room, taking in paintings.

I: So what can I do to become a better listener, or viewer—perceiver of art?

D: Nothing.

I: Huh? You mean I can't have the experience? Of course I can.

D: No, what I mean is that you can do nothing.

I: Oh . . . you mean that I can't do anything—that it just will happen if it wants to?

D: No. Listen carefully. I said you can do nothing. That's what you can do. You can come to the object—the sounds—empty, with a consciousness filled with nothing, a consciousness devoid of all intellectual activity. You can come to the object empty of all thoughts, thoughts of taxes or food or housing or children, or thoughts of Beethoven or Renoir, of how the work was created, of other art works. You can come to object completely . . . empty. Completely . . . free.

I: That's kind of Zen. Wow. Cool, baby. Do I do incense first, and wear beads? And when does the chanting start? How about if I smoke dope—does that help?

D: (*not amused*) Look, you came here to talk to me. I am happy to exchange knowledge and experience with anyone who is genuinely interested in sharing the journey. But if you already know the answers—if you have your own questions—different questions . . . well, let's just go our separate ways.

I: (*to himself*) Touchy, touchy. (*to Daedalus*) No, wait. Really, I'm sorry. I do want to learn what you think about this. I am ready to be convinced.

D: (*shaking his head*) I have no interest in convincing you. In fact, I cannot convince you. I can only put you in a position to convince yourself. I can only point you to the experience and suggest how you can find it. The finding, the convincing, the believing, the understanding, these are all your jobs.

I: Okay, I see that. So point the way. What do I do?

Daedalus is silent.

Oh, not talking eh? Oh yeah—nothing. I do nothing, I empty my mind. But . . . how do I start? Really—how do I go about this?

D: (*nodding slowly*) *The Skiff*—the painting you wanted a better experience from. We'll start there.

They walk back to "The Skiff."

First of all, stand at a distance that allows you to absorb the whole painting and nothing more than the painting.

I: I'm not quite sure what you mean.

D: What I mean is that if you are very close, only parts of the painting can be seen; some portion of the painting is outside of your realm of vision. And if you are too far away, your focused consciousness must include not only that painting but other percepts around it—other paintings, people, lights, and so on. So try this: stand directly in front of the painting. Slowly walk toward the painting and then away from it, until you are far enough away that you can focus your attentive consciousness on the entire continuity of component images that make up the painting, but not so far away that you have to include anything but the images of the painting in your attentive consciousness. In other words, the whole painting and nothing but the painting.

Icarus walks slowly forward and then backward, and then forward again, finally coming to a stop.

I: I think—right about here.

D: Fine. Now, relax your body, and free your mind from extraneous thoughts, so that your entire being becomes taken up with the continuum of visual images. Absorb the images; allow them to work on you; allow yourself to become the painting.

Silence . . .

I: Wow . . . nifty. I mean, very nifty. Magnificent.

D: So, what happened?

I: I don't know. I don't know, but I like it.

D: Well try it again.

Silence . . .

I: I like this. I love this painting.

D: So what does this painting do for you?

I: It's beautiful. It's magical, thrilling. I lost myself in it. It's like . . . being in another world. But I can't put my finger on it.

D: I don't think you can define it. I don't think anyone can, and I'm not sure it's worth trying. But this experience—this otherworldly, transporting, sublime experience, this experience of pure consciousness, this is the transcendent aesthetic experience.

I: Transcendent aesthetic experience? Okay, first off, what do you mean "pure consciousness"?

D: A conscious experience without the judgment that establishes a dualism between us and the external world. An experience in which the conscious act does not include subject or object.

I: You're kind of losing me.

D: It's not that opaque. Let's think about our ordinary experience of the world. Ordinarily, our conscious activity has three components. There is the subject, who is doing the thinking. And there is the object, the perceived thing or percept that is thought about. And then there is the nature of the consciousness itself; in other words, the way the object is taken in: by looking at it, by remembering it, by imagining it. Ordinarily, we judge the objects of our perception as something.

I: Judge them? As good or bad?

D: No, in this sense the term judgment is not at all qualitative. For the purposes of our discussion of the activity of the consciousness, the term judgment means the consideration of an object *as* something. If my focused consciousness includes an object that I am also conscious of as a thing, I am judging that object. For example, I see a tree. I judge it to be a tree, to be green, to be tall. In considering it as a tree, out there, I am also necessarily establishing a me, here— a me that is apart from the tree.

I: That's clear. But what if I don't know what it is? I'm not judging it as a tree then.

D: Not as a tree, but you are still judging it. You are conscious of it as something, different from yourself. Any awareness of an object, there, that is apart from me, here, is an act of judgment. By judging any object to be an object I necessarily establish that subject/object dualism: the object there and me here.

I: And the aesthetic experience then is . . . without judging?

D: Exactly. An act of consciousness that does not involve judging does not require a subject to judge, or an object to be judged. In other words, as soon as we stop considering the object *as* something, we need not ourselves be in the process as apart from the object. What remains is purely the experience, the pure consciousness. In your aesthetic experience of *The Skiff* your consciousness was fully absorbed by the visual image, which had no external significance. In fact, it had no significance whatsoever, and that was the point: it did not mean anything outside of the interplay of its components in your consciousness. And thus you did not have to judge them as anything. They came together, they absorbed you, you became them, the distinction between your self as subject and their being as object disappeared, along with the distinction between your being and the external world. You were transported, you transcended our physical world of time and space. That is an aesthetic experience.

I: But in my experience of the painting, did I not judge the paint as the image of a lake, and a boat, and rowers, and trees, and so on? Or are you suggesting that it just came to me as an amorphous blob of colors?

D: If you had the most sublime aesthetic experience, and I believe you did, in the moment of that experience, an awareness of the blue as a lake and the red as a boat was not part of your focused consciousness. It may have been part of your consciousness on some level, but not as part of your focused consciousness.

I: Focused consciousness?

D: Imagine you are driving down the road, listening to a baseball game on the radio. It's exciting. It's a World Series game, and your team is in it. You are focused on the game. The road is clearly part of your consciousness, otherwise you would have driven off it, but it is in the background. You're concentrating on the man on third with one out. A large truck in the next lane begins to weave. Your focused consciousness immediately shifts from the game; it is now on making sure that you navigate your vehicle safely around the truck. All the while you are conscious of your name, that it's October, that you are in a car, that you are alive, and so on. All the innumerable elements of consciousness are there, but receded into the background, giving way to what you are focusing your attention on—in other words your focused consciousness.

I: Could I have an aesthetic experience by being fully absorbed in something else? This really does sound awfully Zen. What about from meditating?

D: We're calling it the aesthetic experience to differentiate from other types of experiences available from art. But you can certainly achieve a transcendent state through meditation. I even think that athletes may, in rare moments at the top of their form and at a peak of concentration, have this kind of transporting, pure consciousness experience. For example, a tennis player at the very peak of intense concentration, beyond awareness of footwork, or spectators, or opponents' strategy, it seems likely that this person has achieved a state of oneness with the ball; he or she for moments becomes the ball. Consider the language of sports. A basketball player who has a stretch of uncanny shooting accuracy is said, in the parlance of the streets, to be "in the zone" or "unconscious." Even something as comical as Yogi Berra's philosophy of batting, "Think? How the hell are you going to think and hit at the same time?" suggests a transcendent level of consciousness at the highest level of athletic competition.

I: Not for spectators, though.

D: No, not for spectators, who are judging the contest from the outside. And not for the athlete who is focused on the score, on anything but the object to the exclusion of every else so that he becomes that object—within his conscious act the subject and object are unnecessary and all that remains is the consciousness, transcendent.

I: Isn't any athlete focused on the score?

D: Yes, necessarily. The athlete must return his focused consciousness to the circumstances of the competition: the score, the other athletes, his physical condition, and so on. So no athlete could have this experience throughout a contest. And not being a top athlete, I can only surmise. But I surmise that there are moments, extended moments, in which it is possible for an athlete to become one with the object—the tennis ball, the basketball hoop, the baseball. For the duration of those extended moments, the athlete can be involved in a loss-of-self experience, similar to meditating, similar to the highest experience available from the arts.

I: So why not just meditate? Music is hard. Tennis is hard.

D: Have you ever meditated? To the point of achieving a transcendent state of pure spirituality? Music is easier. Music takes you there, music helps you and guides you. It's a magic carpet and all you have to do to ride it is to open yourself up to the sounds.

I: So the arts are an aid to spirituality?

D: Among other things. But at the highest level, yes. In the highest functioning of aesthetic object and aesthetic perceiver, yes, the object is an aid to a spiritual, transcendent, loss-of-self state.

I: Beauty.

D: Yes. Beauty, of the most exalted kind.

Silence.

*   *   *

I: I'm struggling with this. When you say it, it seems logical . . . losing the subject and object to achieve beauty. But if I just listen to your words, it seems like a bunch of mystical nonsense, some kind of philosophical wordplay that does not conform to reality. Because how can you say that the object did not participate in the process? Or that I did not? I mean, here I am, standing *here*. And there's the painting, hanging *there*. I can see it, I can touch it, I know it's there. Of course there's an object, it's that painting, and of course there's a subject, it's me watching the damned thing, and without either one there would be no experience at all.

D: Yes, of course, in physical reality there is a painting there, and there is of course a you here. You do not physically become the painting, neither you nor the painting physically dissolves or disappears. But the aesthetic experience is an act of the consciousness. And a meaningful study of art is a study of how artistic objects work on our consciousness. Under the highest of circumstances, they absorb us so that—within our consciousness—no subject and no object participate.

I: So are you saying then that all we need to do is to focus our minds, emptying them of all extraneous thoughts, and absorb music?

D: Yes.

I: And then we can all have this fabulous experience?

D: Yes, depending.

I: Here we go. Depending?

D: Depending on the aesthetic object. The object itself must allow such an experience. For example, we just had a wonderful experience from that Renoir. But instead of using a painting as the object of your perception, let's consider the space framed by that window. Go through the same procedure that you did with the painting. Walk back and forth until you have the area completely and exclusively within your focused consciousness.

I: (*walking*) Okay.

D: Now empty your mind of all extraneous baggage, so that you are completely free to absorb the images within that window.

I: (*concentrating*) Okay.

D: And . . . what does it do for you?

I: Well, really . . . nothing. The different images seemed so . . . awkward, so discomforting. So . . . could it be that the aesthetic object must be an artwork—something composed for the purpose of giving off an aesthetic experience?

D: It could be that, but it isn't. Let's try another room in this museum. Pick a lesser painting . . . here, this one.

Icarus finds a spot from which to absorb the painting, and focuses on it.

I: This is different from the window. Parts of the images seem to join, but on the whole it seems unconnected.

Still concentrating on the painting . . .

In fact, it gets a little frustrating, because I can't completely slide into this painting. It doesn't allow me to absorb myself fully in it—it keeps pushing me away somehow.

D: Okay. Then let's return to the Renoir.

I: Great. Because I'd like to do that again. It was magical. It was transporting. Let's go.

D: (*looking down the corridor*) I'm afraid we'll have to leave that for another day. Or another museum. Or another great painting that is a bit less popular right now. Because with this mad crowd, we just are not going to get back into the Renoir room today. Let's continue this conversation as we walk.

They leave the museum.

What struck you most about this trip to the museum?

I: *The Skiff,* hands down. That was an amazing experience. I would do that any day.

D: And what else?

I: Well, the other painting that was less rewarding. I mean, when I came to these two paintings completely open, the difference in my experience was remarkable. I really was annoyed by how the lesser painting kept—somehow—distracting me. That never happened to me before from looking at a painting.

D: Good. Possibly. Because realizing more fully the magnificent experience available from great paintings requires that you be disappointed with the experience available from lesser paintings.

I: Gee thanks.

D: But what about the people?

I: There sure were a lot of them.

D: Exactly. And why are they here? Why are they at the museum and not at the symphony concert?

I: Hmm. Good question. Aw, they're probably here to tell their friends that they went to the museum, or just to be seen.

D: The fur coat crowd? Maybe at an exhibit opening, with a champagne reception. But not these people. In fact, on the whole this is a very middle-class crowd. These are middle-class consumers, consumers of the aesthetic experience. The same middle-class consumers who work for a living, who go to plays, who eat in restaurants, who buy books, who attend movies, who watch television. And who don't go to classical music concerts in sufficient numbers.

I: Okay, well maybe they go to the museum because a particular painting by Renoir is the only one that exists, and this is the only chance people will have to see it. But they can hear the "Harp" Quartet performed three or four times in this city this season alone.

D: Possibly. But they won't line up like this to see a painting by Gnerpshnorts, even if it's the only Gnerpshnorts in the world and they might not get a chance to see it ever again.

I: Maybe because the Gnerpshnorts is not publicized. Nobody knows about it, so they can't know whether or not it's good, they can't know if they want to see it. In fact, speaking of publicity, maybe the people are lined up to see the Renoir exhibit because it's been so well publicized, because it's the thing to do. I mean, this is a major exhibition that's toured all over the world with tremendous publicity.

D: Well, that's a good point, and there is something to it. And here we are, back to your advertising solution. But any advertising professional will tell you that advertising can only introduce the product. Ultimately the quality of the product itself is the biggest determinant of sales. So it is *de rigueur* to see an exhibit of Renoir's painting after a hundred-plus years because the inherent value of the paintings is the quality of the experience they offer. If these paintings did not offer valuable experiences—better and more valuable experiences than other paintings—they wouldn't be this popular after so long in the public eye.

I: Sort of like, you can fool some of the people all the time, and all the people some of the time, but you can't fool all the people all the time?

D: Right. No amount of great advertising can sustain substantial sales of a poor product.

I: But, what about beer? What about cars?

D: Precisely the point. What about cars? Let's look at the American automobile industry. It found itself in deep financial trouble. Why? Simple economics: Japanese cars gave more for the money. Americans bought Japanese cars because they offered better-made cars, a better value. No quantity or quality of advertising will change that. The auto industry tried more advertising. It didn't work. So they tried to get trade tariffs enacted, to make a better value out of their own cars by making other cars more expensive. But the bottom line is that for the American car industry to thrive, it had to make a better product. And as the product has been improving and the value increasing, more people have been buying it.

I: But music is not a car. Music is not a product. You're talking about business, about a product, about consumers, about a free-market economy, but the arts are different from business. We're not selling a product here, we're engaging in art, in the pursuit that separates us from the animals.

D: What is it that separates us from the animals? What is it that we are pursuing?

I: Music. You know, Bach, Beethoven.

D: Again, I'll point out that Beethoven is dead. We have no interest in Beethoven. But what *are* we pursuing? Yes, music. Where's the music?

I: Okay, it's in my consciousness. So . . . well . . . I guess we're back to the experience.

D: *Yes!* The experience. So there is a product—the product is an experience. In fact, the economic equation at work is exactly analogous to industry. We are selling an aesthetic experience. The listeners are our consumers; they go to concerts in the hopes of having an aesthetic experience. The cost to the listener is the price of the ticket and the time invested. And the cost to the public at large includes the private donations and the corporate and government grants for the arts that are not available for other worthy causes. Right now we're looking to increase the consumer demand for our product, and I am saying to you that one very important tool that we have is to play better concerts. Now, the assumption of musicians that the public owes us support because the concert poster says "Beethoven" or "Famous Orchestra" is every bit as arrogant and unrealistic as the auto industry's assumption that the public owes it to them to buy a car because the logo says "Cadillac." And, like the auto industry, if we want more consumer demand for our concerts—and more ticket income, more donations, more corporate and government support—then we will make a better product—we will make better concerts, we will provide the opportunity for better experiences.

I: And audiences will come if we play better concerts?

D: They'll come more often if they have greater expectations of being rewarded, and they'll be more rewarded if we consistently play the most sublime possible concerts. Yes. Play better concerts.

I: And that's what I'm trying to do. But the fact is that not all concerts are without imperfections; in fact, virtually none of them is. You're not saying that these can't be valued, are you? Audiences come, they're excited, they're moved.

D: Yes, there is beauty on all levels. A passage may unfold an electrifying accelerando. It may be gloriously in tune. It may come in a celestial balance. It may present a progression that grabs and melts. Or it may simply offer a seductive beat. In fact, it is not true that Americans appreciate music less than any other culture. Because commercial music is a multibillion-dollar industry in this country.

I: But that isn't the same experience that classical music offers.

D: To some degree it is. What does commercial music or any music offer? At the most basic level it offers a relief from our everyday experience of time, which is chaotic.

I: But our experience of time is not chaotic. Actually I believe the temporal aspect of our experience is highly ordered.

D: (*amused*) Oh?

I: For example by the relation of the earth to the sun—in other words, the seasons. Or by the relation of the earth to the moon—months—or by the earth's rotation—days. And more.

D: Yes, go on.

I: Our lives are also ordered artificially by us or by society or by our institutions. I mean, we have a workweek—that's something completely artificial that we have invented. I guess though some might say that the week was given to us by God, who created the world in seven days. But then not all gods gave that to all people, because there are plenty of cultures in which people haven't had a seven-day cycle of work and rest. So it seems reasonable to accept that the seven-day workweek is an artificial invention. And other things too, like a school schedule of hour-long classes, or changing the oil in the car every three months, or an annual checkup at the doctor. So I think our existence is highly ordered in a temporal sense, because everything that we do is related to a system of temporal landmarks.

D: In what way?

I: Okay. Let's take cooking dinner. We cook dinner once a day, so the cycle of days and nights is a temporal referent for cooking dinner. It occurs every day in a temporal relation to the sun's rotation. Or we could go farther. Let's say that every Sunday we eat ice cream for dessert, but only on Sundays. The week then is a temporal referent for eating ice cream. Or what if we cook a goose for Christmas dinner and only for Christmas dinner. Then the cycle of the seasons is a temporal referent for an annual event like cooking a goose for Christmas dinner. At school every event comes to us in relation to the schedule of classes that is highly ordered and defined. So our lives are not chaotic in temporal sense. In fact, every event is highly ordered; it stands in relation to a complex network of temporal landmarks. Bingo. Gotcha!

D: (*head in hands*) Yes, congratulations. Wonderful, as far as it goes . . . on a most elementary level. Now listen. On a different level, the temporal aspect of everyday human experience is entirely random. Here's what I mean. Human experience comes to us as our consciousness. Experience is, in effect, our consciousness. To be sure, the consciousness brings us our experience of the world very much in relation to these temporal signposts you described. But our daily existence is characterized by constant activity of the consciousness, which undergoes continual and random change. The rhythm of the consciousness is shaped by the material of our everyday experience—cars driving by, the air conditioner coming on, a rain shower passing through, clouds blocking the sun, bodily functions, conversations. Let's return to that Christmas dinner. I may be worrying about the peas I am cooking for Christmas dinner. My consciousness shifts to consider the guests who are arriving. A train whistle blows; I wonder which train it is. I, the subject, have undergone three conscious acts, three separate acts of my consciousness, each with a different object: *worrying* about the peas, *considering* the guests, and *wondering* about the train. Each conscious act begins at a random point in time and has a random duration. The temporal aspect of these acts of consciousness—when they begin and how long they last—is created by the changing object of my focus.

I: Whoa, whoa, and whoa. The changing object of my focus?

D: When the object of my consciousness changes I am engaged in a new act of consciousness. Like shifting from the baseball game to the weaving truck: two different acts of consciousness. Or, back to the Christmas dinner, my consciousness is engaged in a single act when it is focused on the peas. The shifting of the object of my consciousness to the train brings about a new act of the consciousness. In fact, the shifting of my consciousness to several different aspects of these peas brings about several separate acts of consciousness: from the color of the peas (one conscious act), to the shape of a particular pea (a second act), to how long the peas need to cook (a third), to the taste of the peas (a fourth), to the taste of the peas as it complements the taste of the other dishes (a fifth conscious act).

I: So the temporal aspect of my experience of the world is shaped by the changing of its object.

D: Actually the temporal aspect is much more complex than that. For example, if, while I am worrying about the peas, the wind begins to howl but my consciousness does not shift to consider that howling, the howling still colors my consciousness that is focused on the peas. That coloration also has a temporal element—a beginning and a duration—that participates in the rhythm of my consciousness. So while it's true that the conscious acts that make up daily existence are highly ordered in relation to a broad temporal reference system, their temporal relation to each other is very much random.

I: Okay. That makes sense. But what then is the significance for music? For beauty on all levels?

D: On its most fundamental level, music offers a temporal reference system that brings a degree of order and unity to this random temporal aspect of human experience. Each component sound has a temporal aspect—a beginning, a duration, and an end. The conjunction of the component sounds, each with its own temporal aspect, results in a hierarchy of temporal referents: pulse, meter, phrase, and so on. The musical experience is ordered to the extent that each component sound has a specific position relative to the system of temporal referents. While changing the order of the objects of my everyday consciousness—the peas, the guests, the train—does not fundamentally alter my everyday experience, changing the order of the sounds changes the essence of the musical experience. And it brings unity to the extent that it makes my experience of the sounds simultaneous—the experience of any component sound is shaped by the experience of any other sound within that conscious act.

I: I understand that my experience of music brings order because changing the order of the different elements of a musical experience changes the experience fundamentally. But I don't understand this unity-simultaneity stuff.

D: Let's imagine a melody. The sounding of a melody has temporal extension—duration. To experience it as a single melody and not a succession of unrelated tones it comes to us as a simultaneity, all at once in an extended present.

I: You've lost me. Of course it's not all at once—it takes time. Each tone comes to us one after another. How could it be a simultaneity?

D: Again, don't mistake the object for the way that we experience it. These are two different things. The object is unfolded one different tone after another. Each component tone has temporal extension—it is extended in time. But we experience the entire object as a simultaneity, all at once. Although we do not hear the initial tone concurrently with the final tone, our experience of the initial tone shapes our experience of the final tone. Likewise, although we do not hear the final tone concurrently with the initial tone, the final tone shapes our experience of the initial tone—the initial tone would be essentially different without the context of the final tone. Our consciousness of the first tone of the melody and that of the last tone—and, in fact, the entire continuity of consciousnesses of the tones in between—are united in a single, simultaneous experience.

I: Okay. I understand that the consciousness doesn't stop. But simultaneous? I mean, it's not simultaneous. It doesn't happen at the same time.

D: The first and last tones are simultaneous to the extent that they shape the experience of each other.

I: I don't understand. If I run a marathon, each step is governed or affected in some way by the fact that I am running twenty-six miles. The experience of the first step is shaped by the experience of the ones to come, and the experience of the last step is most definitely shaped by the steps preceding it. But the first and last steps are not simultaneous.

D: No. No they're not. But if you consider both the first step and the last step, if you think about them and compare them, you have a simultaneous consciousness of the two—they must both be in your consciousness at the same time. In a musical experience there is only consciousness. Although the tones are not sounding at the same time, they exist in my consciousness for the duration of the transcendent musical experience, both, simultaneously.

I: Okay. I'm beginning to get that. So you're saying that pop music provides a degree of what the best classical music offers, and that is a kind of temporal order. And is that the reason that pop music is so . . . ummm . . . popular?

D: Yes. That's the principal reason. Of course there are other reasons for the popularity of popular music: an attachment of meaning to the words, or as a vehicle for dancing, which of course is just a physical manifestation of the search for temporal order.

I: But in terms of music for music's sake, as I understand it you're saying that there is a range of the value of the experience available. Theoretically, wouldn't the popularity of a piece of music, commercial or classical, rest on the quality of the musical experience?

D: Yes, to the extent that the popularity is a function of its musical value. And ultimately it is. But let's examine what we mean by the quality of the musical experience. Essentially what we are talking about is the ability to unify and order our experience, with the highest level being a spiritual, transcendent state in which the consciousness is one, indivisible. And we also have to include the openness of the listener. A particularly banal rock tune with a pounding beat and a limited harmonic palette may ideally suit the needs of the listener who is not open to a higher experience.

I: But at a rock concert you can't say that people are not open.

D: Open to the experience? The lights, the movement, the costumes, the people, the societal bonding, the rhythms, the volume of sound, the pharmaceutical enhancement? Absolutely. But they are not open to the extended musical object. Because when the musical object has no hierarchy of sounds, no higher connection, no dependence of one musical event on another, the listener who is open to a higher, spiritual experience that transcends time . . .

I: Whoa! Transcends time?

D: In the highest, most sublime, spiritual experience of a temporally extended object that comes to the perceiver as a simultaneity, the element of time in our experience is transcended, just as in your sublime, spiritual experience of *The Skiff*, the element of space was transcended—the space between you and the painting, the space taken up by its component percepts. The listener who is open to that experience will be disappointed, annoyed, even, by the particularly banal rock tune.

I: Wouldn't the listener who is closed to the higher experience be bored by even a sublime performance at a classical concert.

D: May well be.

I: But I thought you said better concerts made better listeners.

D: Yes, good point. But full stomachs make better listeners too. Let's stop for a sandwich.

*　*　*

I: So . . . better concerts make better listeners, exactly how?

D: Let's take a step back. For most people at an ordinary concert, musical experiences come as a "shish-kebob" of conscious acts that follow each other in succession. There may be a moment of sublime beauty, a thought about the timpanist, a pleasant melodic line, a thought about the conductor's gestures, a guess at the soloist's fee, another moment of sublime beauty, and so on, all attached to the skewer of a continuing musical experience with a continuing temporal reference system. Of course the specific content of these successions of thoughts will vary depending on the listener; for instance, those of the more educated listener may include thoughts about the extramusical program, about historical considerations, about mechanical aspects of the performing process, about structural considerations of the work—it may include comparisons with previous performances, and so on and so on. Even someone who appears completely engrossed in the concert may have experienced a similar succession of acts of focused consciousness.

I: So are you saying that in a performance that is not so thrilling, like that not-so-great performance of the "Harp" Quartet, that's what happened? My consciousness was divided?

D: I would assume so. Possibly from your own lack of openness to the sounds, but possibly by the sounds themselves. We search for oneness. Finding it is satisfying. Our highest experience of music comes to us undivided, singular, one—simultaneous. It is satisfying on the highest level of human experience. But we are not always rewarded with that highest degree of satisfaction. If the experience is not of a single, undivided consciousness, but of a consciousness divided into multiple conscious acts with different objects, it may be satisfying, but to a different degree, on a different level. The more divided the conscious activity, the more the receiver must provide the conscious understanding of the connections that create the musical continuum, and the less satisfying the experience.

I: I don't understand that.

D: The musical object comes to us as a continuum. We understand the object to be continuous. However, if the continuum comes to us in such a way that our consciousness cannot absorb it all in the same, single act, then the listener must provide the connections in an act of judgment, and no loss-of-self experience is possible. The more frequently we must provide connections, the less satisfying the experience. Eventually we will most likely use the musical object as a background for other thoughts rather than continue a frustrating search for unattainable spiritual experiences.

I: And conversely if the connections are made for us, they suck us in.

D: Yes.

I: But if the listener is not open, playing better concerts, playing sublime concerts will have no effect.

D: Yes. But that's a big "if." Eventually, the person who attends sublime concerts will become more and more open. And the better the experience they have as they become open, the more open they'll become. They'll be invited in. Consider the process of buying an instrument. The best thing you can do when buying a better instrument is to play on better instruments for some time, so you understand what they can do. If you've never played on a better instrument, you are unlikely to appreciate the qualities that make it better. A better violin makes a better violin consumer.

I: And better concerts make better listeners.

D: Yes. More open listeners.

I: And an open listener is one who focuses exclusively on the sounds.

D: Exclusively on the totality of the sounds. A listener whose attentive, focused consciousness is directed on all of the sounds and only the sounds.

They leave the café.

I: Some questions as we go?

D: By all means.

I: You're saying that anyone can have this aesthetic experience—without any kind of training?

D: Absolutely anyone. Anyone with open ears.

I: And how will they know? How do I know if I've had this loss-of-self experience?

D: You yourself told me about experiencing a sublimely beautiful performance of the "Harp" Quartet. You said you were quite moved, transported, I think. And how did you know? How do you know you like ice cream? How do you know that you're eating ice cream? How do you know that you're alive?

I: *Cogito ergo sum?* And the same for the aesthetic experience?

D: (*eyes twinkling*) Yes, but for an aesthetic experience it would be *Non sum ergo sum*—I lose my self, therefore I am. Seriously, though, we may never know for an absolute certainty whether or not we are alive. Unlike Professor Descartes, we may have to accept that we don't need to know that, probably because we accept that we cannot know it. What we know for an absolute certainty is that we intuit our aliveness; our dealings with the world are unavoidably accompanied by the assumption that we are alive. So it is too with the aesthetic experience: we may never know to an absolute certainty whether or not we had this experience; we simply know by our intuition that we had an aesthetic experience, an experience of beauty, a sublime, transcendent, loss-of-self experience. Simply—we know we have undergone such an experience because we know it.

I: Okay. But what about literature? According to you, literature will never provide the same ultimate aesthetic experience that music can, because any cognition of words means a judgment of the sounds we hear, and that involves the subject, and that prevents a loss-of-self experience. But that couldn't possibly be true. We have great literature—we know that. But according to this theory that sublime aesthetic experiences involve a loss of self, there is no sublime literature.

D: Yes, that's true. There's no literature that can provide the level of transcendent experience that you can get from music or visual art. I may find a great novel stirring, and moving, and thought-provoking, and many, many good things. It may even in a sense transport me to a different place. But it cannot provide the same transcendent, spiritual, loss-of-self experience.

I: This is true of any art form that uses words? Fiction, theater, opera, poetry?

D: It's true of any art form in which the object is a sign.

I: A sign?

D: Something that depends on meaning. As you point out, words require us as subject to participate in the process.

I: You're not saying it's not art.

D: Certainly not. It's the intellectual function of art, it's the art that brings us into the world, that broadens and enriches our understanding of our place in the world. It defines the world around us, the world that is not us. The more the world that is not us is defined for us, the more we are defined for ourselves. That's supremely valuable.

I: But less so than the aesthetic experience?

D: The aesthetic experience lets me experience me. Me separate from the world that is not me. Me in my essence. My soul, if you will.

I: Are you saying music and the visual arts can't do this?

D: Oh, but they can. Any work of art that depends on external meaning for its value provides an intellectual experience. Consider a painting like Andy Warhol's *Campbell's Soup Can*, or a piece of music like John Corigliano's Symphony No. 1, the "AIDS" symphony. Each depends for its essence on its power to make us think . . . to bring us more closely into our world. In purely aesthetic terms the soup can is not a particularly engaging piece, and without the context of excruciating loss, the "AIDS" symphony would provide a far paler experience.

I: What about program music?

D: To the extent that your experience of it is taken up with the program, yes. If you listen to Beethoven's Pastoral Symphony and think about a day in the country . . .

I: Or about nineteenth-century Vienna . . .

D: Or about nineteenth-century Vienna, you'll have that intellectual experience. Not a bad one. But pale in comparison to the experience possible from the aesthetic experience of that work.

I: But look at all those people who were walking around the museum with audio players that explain the paintings. Those players weren't saying "Stand back, empty your mind, and absorb the image and nothing but the image." They were saying "Renoir was thirty-eight years old, this is a view of the Seine, he had such-and-such relationship with the woman in the boat, and consider how the brush strokes differ from his earlier paintings." They were increasing the intellectual component of the experience. Some people might find that a worse experience, but clearly others find it better, because they pay to rent those players. Hasn't museum attendance increased with the popularity of the audio tours?

D: Hold on. First of all, the museum says "Pay us more money to rent this machine and you'll have a better experience." So people do, because they want to have the best experience, and the museum tells them how to do it. Now if the museum said "Stand back, empty your mind, absorb the image and see how it works on your consciousness," and then afterwards encouraged them to buy the books if they wanted more information, people might do that too. And they'd get an overall better experience than thinking that the value of viewing the painting comes from knowing about the brush strokes.

I: It's harder to open your mind; it's easier to have someone tell you about the painting. So if museums get more attendance by offering more enhanced information viewing, you would think it would make sense for symphonies to adopt some of those practices—informative movies, and high-tech lecture concerts. But I've seen some of these—heck, I've participated in some. On stage we all find them a huge distraction.

D: Unfortunately, unlike the museum audio tour, which may lead an individual viewer away from an aesthetic experience, the "visually enhanced" concert limits the possibility of a sublime aesthetic experience for *all* listeners. Once you put up a screen you are telling your audience: this is how to experience this music; this is what we think you find valuable, this is what to include in your consciousness. And you are guiding them firmly and effectively away from open listening. A restaurant could suggest that their customers pay extra for ketchup on their crepes. People are used to ketchup; they think it's good; they're told to buy it, so they do. That's the museum audio tour. Now imagine the same restaurant slopping ketchup on all the dishes. That's the visual or high-tech informational "enhancement" at a concert. For every person that it attracts—which is a good thing—it limits the possibilities of the highest possible transcendent experience for all.

I: Sure, but the museum attendance . . .

D: Museum attendance studies attribute increased attendance to blockbuster shows.

I: More marketing?

D: Perhaps, but blockbuster shows means exhibits of the works of Rembrandt, Monet, Vermeer, Degas, Van Gogh . . .

I: Renoir.

D: Exactly. And these artists are in the pantheon not because of marketing; they are revered because their works can provide better experiences. As the "performers" of their initial plans they are ultimate masters. And that's the parallel with music that you might take.

I: Play better concerts?

D: Play better concerts.

I: And you'll help me figure that out?

D: (*smiling*) Keep at it, and you'll work it out yourself. As Ben Franklin said, "God helps those who help themselves."

Chapter Three

Let's Be Mookie

On the Composer's Contribution

February 1

Icarus: (*knocking on the window*) Good morning!

Daedalus: Why, good morning. Come in. It's cold out there. What are you doing out this early? And on such a morning.

I: (*shivering*) Oh I was just out for a walk, and saw signs of life in the greenhouse, so I thought I would say hello. Working on your flowers?

D: Yes, just trying to give these buds an even chance in an inhospitable world. My, that must have been some walk. So . . . something is troubling you?

I: As a matter of fact, I've been busy being humbled by the world. Humbled and a bit confused.

D: This is probably a good thing! How so?

I: Well I was quite taken with my experience at the Renoir exhibit; it was clear, for example, that *The Skiff* was a magnificent painting.

D: There is nothing wrong with that.

I: No, but I began to think about what makes some paintings better than others, and then I began to think more about what makes some pieces better than others. For example, why is Beethoven a great composer—better than, say, Cherubini?

D: Yes . . .

I: And I began to ask friends, and teachers.

D: (*knowingly*) Good. And?

I: At first people explained patiently that Beethoven was more inventive than Cherubini, more dramatic, that his compositions were more exciting, more interesting, that they had interesting textures, attractive passages—artful use of harmony. Some people said they were emotionally rich, they had compelling stories, they were expressive, they were convincing.

D: And you asked what they meant.

I: Yes, I asked what they meant. I said I thought it had to involve more than interesting textures. I asked how a piece involves the emotions, because— hey you don't necessarily get sad if you hear a sad piece. In fact you might become elated. I said an awful lot of pieces have more compelling stories than the Pastoral Symphony—some peasants have a picnic, they dance around, it rains, they dance some more. Or what about pieces with no stories at all, like the "Harp" Quartet? I asked them what expressive compositions expressed; I asked what convincing compositions were supposed to convince me of. My friends just sort of ignored me after a while—they think I'm a little nuts. But they got someone else to play a gig I was supposed to do. That was disappointing. Faculty members, though, got angry. I even argued with the dean about it. She reduced my stipend for this semester.

D: (*incredulous*) She reduced your stipend? Because you argued with her about what makes a great piece of music?

I: Yeah, well, I was a bit obnoxious, I'm sure. Anyway, I have now been shown the folly of my ways. I'm trying to be good and not raise too many difficult questions, because it seems to be detrimental to my financial health. I had to sell my car, which makes life a little bit more difficult. But I'm also thinking that if everyone seems to think in a particular way that's different from the way I've been seeing things, then there must be something that I'm missing. If everyone says you can't explain what makes a great piece, then they may well be right, and if I'm going to find my way in this world I will have to fit in—I will have to learn to see things as they do. So, here I am, humbled and mute, and curious, and mostly confused.

D: It's important to follow your curiosity. As Mark Twain said, "Loyalty to petrified opinions never yet broke a chain or freed a human soul in this world—and never will."

I: He also said, "Be respectful to your superiors, if you have any."

D: No wonder your stipend was reduced. Now if you're not serious, I have more important matters to attend to.

Daedalus returns to the flower pots.

I: Umm . . .

D: (*not looking up*) Yes, next question.

I: Well, umm, I mean . . . I guess it comes down to this. The fact is that I'm a little apprehensive about this subject, because I've been burned by it. But I still would really like to know more about the quality of a musical composition.

D: (*turning toward Icarus*) What about it?

I: Well, in my heart of hearts I'd really like to be able to know what makes a great piece great.

D: It allows great experiences.

I: But why it is that a great piece of music is great? What determines compositional quality? I want to know what it is about a great piece that makes it better than a lesser one.

D: Oh you do? *Not in three hundred lifetimes can one find an answer to this question!* But perhaps you . . . with your curiosity and intelligence . . . perhaps you will find an answer. Yes, perhaps. But if you do find one, keep it to yourself because it will be wrong.

I: (*shivering*) So they are right? I shouldn't ask about quality?

D: Ach! You must be freezing. Come into the house and we can try to warm you up.

I: (*to himself*) Said the spider to the fly.

They sit by the fireplace.

D: Now what is this business about Beethoven being a better composer than Cherubini? Is he?

I: Of course he's better. He wrote better music. That's common knowledge.

D: So popular acceptance determines quality? What everybody likes must be better?

I: Well, uh, yes, in a sense. Isn't it?

D: Wonderful! Popularity as determinant of quality. Hundreds of millions of people around the world would rather drink Coca-Cola than water. Which is better, then?

I: (*laughing*) Clearly the caffeinated bubbly sugar-water. No, just kidding. So now you're saying that if it's popular it can't be good? What about Renoir? You spent a lot of time last semester convincing me that Renoir's art is popular because quality will out—because his paintings are better than others'.

D: And I think I wasted my time if your conclusion is that it must be good because it is popular. I did not intend to imply then that something must be good because it is popular, nor do I now intend to imply that something could not possibly be good if it is popular. There is, to be sure, a rough correlation between the quality of an aesthetic object and its staying power. But it would be most erroneous to assume that any piece of music that is popular must be good.

I: Okay.

D: So what then is the proof that some compositions are better than others?

I: That I believe it?

D: *Dio mio!* What a world we live in. Anything you believe is true because you believe it! Anything everyone believes is true because they believe it! So . . . the earth is flat because everyone believes it to be flat?

I: No, I guess not.

D: But in fact, there is a sense in which if you believe the world to be flat, it may as well be so.

I: Oh no, here we go again. You've lost me.

D: Well let's try to find you. Why do we theorize?

I: Theorize?

D: Make theories. Why do we make theories?

I: I guess to explain things.

D: Yes, to explain things. To connect our thoughts and perceptions. And how do we know if a theory is valid?

I: I guess we can prove it. We can do experiments. And if they are successful, the theory is true.

D: True?

I: Yes, true.

D: Hah! I admire someone with the courage of their ignorance. Let's take an example. Let's consider the shape of the earth. Two cavemen, Oog and Goog, are walking along, talking—theorizing, much as we have been. Oog says, "Hey Goog, you know, I've been thinking about the shape of the earth here that we're walking on." And Goog says, "What are you talking about, the shape? It's got a few hills and valleys, and some flat parts. That's the shape." Oog continues, "But I'm thinking a bit more generally, Goog. I'm thinking, sure, it has some hills and valleys. But overall? Overall don't you think that fundamentally the earth must be flat, one long stretch, with the hills and valleys just slight variations? Because that's the way it feels like to me." And Goog says, "Well, yeah, Oog, I guess that's right, because we keep walking and walking, and as far as we go we're still standing up straight, and as far as we look it's just pretty much flat, so, dadgummit, I'll bet you're right. The earth has got to be flat."

I: (*to himself*) The man is insane. I knew I liked him. (*to Daedalus*) Okay, sure. Oog and Goog. They think the earth is flat. This is important exactly why?

D: Don't make fun of Oog and Goog. Quite respectable scientists. What's important about their theory? They wanted to explain the information they had—to accommodate it in a higher truth. So they devised a theory. Their information was that they could keep walking and walking, on what felt unquestionably like a flat plane. Not only that, but as far as they could see it looked like the earth was flat. They had information derived from their visual perceptions at a fixed point, and they compiled that with additional information—the visual perceptions and physical sensations from their wandering. And all of their information was accommodated quite effectively by their theory that the earth is flat.

I: So what?

D: So what? So they proved their theory. So, they theorized that the world is flat, and they performed experiments, and they found it to be true—a law of nature. The earth is flat.

I: But it's not true. Of course the earth is round, not flat.

D: How do you know that the earth is round?

I: Mmmmm, probably because I read it in a textbook in—like—second grade.

D: Fine, that's all right. We get a lot of information from books. And some of it is even true. But how do the authors know? How did someone else come along and determine that the earth must in fact be round?

I: I'm not sure.

D: Neither am I. But here are some ideas. What if someone noticed that as ships sail over the horizon, the masts are the last to disappear? What if someone noticed an arced shadow on the moon during a lunar eclipse? Let's say that the next generation of scientists, Mookie and Wookie, noticed the ships disappearing over the horizon, and saw an eclipse of the moon. So Mookie says, "You know, Wook, those guys Oog and Goog just can't be right. I know they're famous scientists and all, but the earth can't be flat, because it makes an arced shadow on the moon. It must be a sphere." He had new information about the shape of the earth that was not accommodated by the earlier theory: the arced shadows visible occasionally on the moon. If the earth were flat, it could not block the light on the moon in that way. But Wookie was able to accommodate the new information with the old theory. He says "But Mookie, don't you see? That's just the nature of the moon. Sometimes it gets in a bad mood, turns dark, just because that's the nature of the thing to do every so often . . . like the sky . . . like your wife . . . your boss . . . the moon. Same thing. Just happens." Or maybe he modified the old theory. "Sure, that's because the earth is a flat disk. And when it gets between the sun and the moon just right, well, there you go—it makes those shadows on the moon. No problem." Seems perfectly plausible. But then there was this other information, the disappearance of the ships on the horizon. "Wookie, my friend," says Mookie, "that's not sufficient. Because that does not explain why ships disappear on the horizon, with the masts disappearing last. No, the only explanation for all that is that the earth must be round, it must be a sphere. It just has to be." Mookie absorbs new information, the shadows and the disappearing ships. What does that do to the "earth-is-flat" theory?

I: I guess it invalidates it. It can't be reconciled with the new information—the information and the theory come into conflict.

D: Exactly. To accommodate the new information, Mookie has to alter that theory, or scrap it entirely and devise a new theory. But it's dangerous to contradict these famous scientists. Wookie stops talking to him, Oogites by the hundreds dismiss him, his professional prospects take a decided turn for the worse, but he has no choice—he's in too deep. He now has four bits of information to accommodate: (1) that we sense from looking around us that the earth is flat; (2) that as far as we can go in any direction we still have that sensation; (3) that outgoing ships gradually sink from view until they disappear; and (4) that the earth makes an arced shadow on celestial bodies. So he devises a new theory, that the earth is in fact round. But it is also enormous. With a theoretical earth as a sphere, Mookie can accommodate first the disappearance of the ships, and second the arced shadows. Because the size of the sphere is so great, the part of the earth that we experience in our wandering has such a subtle curve as to be unnoticeable.

I: But this is simplistic. Okay, so the earth is round.

D: How long did this theory last?

I: Last? But it's true. It's still operative.

D: Actually not—and it hasn't been for three centuries. More information—about gravitational pulls and orbiting bodies—contradicted a theory of the earth as a perfect sphere. Newton theorized that the earth is an oblate spheroid—that it bulges somewhat at the equator. And this theory has since been bolstered by measurements from space.

I: Okay. I guess theories evolve to accommodate our information.

D: Yes, to the extent that a theory stands in harmony with all the relevant information, the theory is valid. It serves its purpose. Now if you are an Oogite, and you are satisfied to exist within the same few hundred square miles, then believing that the earth is flat is absolutely fine for you. Your understanding of the world—the theories to which you subscribe—accommodates the extent of your limited information. But if you are Mookie? If you are Mookie and you have new information, and you want to expand your world—you want to know more, go further, discover, evolve, advance, develop, make a contribution to your society, then you cannot settle for the earth being flat. That would be death. If you are Mookie you opt for life; you must continue to grow, to struggle, to learn, to risk not knowing the answers to your questions. If you are Mookie, you say, "I accept the new information, and the world must be round, and so I bet there are other kinds of people out there, and I would like just maybe to meet them, just to say, 'hey.' Just to make contact. Just to find out what they are like, how they live. And I bet I can find some magical potions that will heal the sick and revive the dead; wouldn't it be great if I could find them and bring them back here. Charts be damned, if my life is going to have meaning, if I am going to contribute, if I am going to have influence, if I am going to leave my world a better place than I found it, then there is no choice. The earth must be a sphere, and, by God, I am going to sail a little further to see just what is over that horizon." To you, my young friend, I say: don't be afraid to take a chance. Don't be afraid to be Mookie.

I: And sail around the world to find a nonexistent magic potion?

D: And consider all our information, so that we can expand, develop, advance, contribute to our society. If we are open to a magic potion, we may actually find one, like penicillin, like pasteurization. Let's not be afraid to explore areas that are out of bounds in our society of musicians—to ask questions like, "What makes one piece better than another?" Let's not be afraid to consider all of our information; let's scrape away ideas that hold us back, no matter how commonly accepted they might be. Let's be Mookie.

I: (*thoughtfully*) Okay . . . Okay. But wait a minute. First I came to you and said that I wanted to know what makes a great piece. And you said I can't know that. Now you say, "Let's be Mookie. Don't be afraid to ask difficult questions." What gives?

D: You came to me and asked how you could know what it is about great music that makes it great. I don't know what music is, and you don't either. Music is nothing. There is no thing that is music. Connections of sounds, connections in my mind, which result in an experience, that are an experience.

I: But there is an objective thing: the sounds . . .

D: . . . to the extent that even the sounds exist.

I: Do you mean: does a falling tree make a noise if no one hears it?

D: Yes, exactly. But we can accept that whether or not the sounds actually exist is unknowable, and—if so—therefore uninteresting for us. What we can know is that they come to our consciousness with the understanding that they do exist in physical reality. These things, these elements of physical reality, can—under certain circumstances—become music. But music itself? What is it? Pfffff! We cannot know and we cannot say.

I: So if we can't answer this question, why are we wasting time talking about it?

D: Ah. Because just maybe we can answer a different question. Just maybe—contrary to what your society of musical scientists tells you—you *can* discover something meaningful about the quality of a composition. We cannot divine the true nature of reality; at very best we can introduce better, closer approximations. Now, although we students of the musical experience may be very, very far from any certain knowledge about what we do—what music is, what great music is, and so on—there is no reason that the question of musical quality cannot be broached. And open, intelligent thinkers, I believe, may be able to come closer than the notion of interesting textures or dramatic expression. Mookie did not discover the meaning of life, but he may well have found a distant island, or a cure for disease, or untold wealth. We may not discover the answer to the question "What is music?" But we may be able to nudge just a bit further our understanding of the essential nature of a masterwork of musical composition.

I: Okay. I'm with you.

D: So now that we're sufficiently warmed up, let's go for a little stroll.

They leave the house.

* * *

D: So where are we, then, we two scientists, standing together?

I: I'm hoping we are about to make a theory. I'm hoping we are about to tighten our approximations of what determines the quality of a composition.

D: Very good. And how might we do that?

I: We should probably begin by taking stock of the information that we have so that we can accommodate it all. Maybe we can begin by accepting that some pieces are better than others.

D: Accepted.

I: Then we can examine those better pieces and find out what attributes they have that the lesser ones do not. For example, I know for a fact that the "Harp" Quartet is a great piece because it provided me with a sublime experience.

D: Now there's a leap of faith. How do you know that?

I: Because it was the most sublime experience. I can't imagine it gets any better than this. Or do you think I can't trust my experience enough to be sure that the piece is great?

D: Can you trust your experience? What else do you have? Where else do you find music but in your experience? Of course you can trust it—you can and you must.

I: Okay. But on the other hand don't you risk setting a dangerous course when you allow your experience to be the sole determinant of some kind of objective quality? In fact, you jumped on me for saying something may be so because I believe it. Because doesn't this invite anyone to say, "Well, for me it is not that way, but this way. And thus it must be so."? In other words, "I know what I like, and so according to you, it must be of a high quality."

D: Of course. And ultimately to us that is irrelevant. We can only know what we know.

I: So if there is no objective reality, and we can only know individually what we know, then for Pete's sake, what is the benefit of a theory?

D: The benefit is that if it has validity then we may build on it, and further the good that we do in the world. The benefit is that others will eventually find it comports with their experience, and will benefit from it and build on it. Consider the radical theories of Galileo, or Darwin, or Schenker, which initially generated scorn and worse. But they gathered momentum as their inherent validity became recognized. And of course they are essentially universally accepted today, and today they serve as the foundation of other profound discoveries and inventions.

I: So we *can* depend on our experience.

D: Our open experience. That's ultimately all we have. Only after an open experience of music free of prejudgment, followed by a consideration of the experience with a free and open mind, can a seeker progress in his understanding. That said, let us begin with the proposition that yes, the "Harp" Quartet is a sublime piece of music; it allows sublime experiences; it is a better piece of music than other pieces; it has an extremely high degree of quality. Now, why could that be?

I: Maybe we can examine what people say, which must be based on the information they have, and then we can determine if there is other information that their theory does not accommodate. For instance, people say that what makes a great piece great is that it is more exciting or interesting. From how people describe exciting pieces I gather that exciting means viscerally striking, sparkling, stimulating. And from how they describe interesting pieces, I gather that interesting means varied material.

D: Are those necessary and sufficient to a great piece?

I: I think neither. I started to think about pieces that are not masterworks, but are tremendously exciting, like *Pines of Rome* or the theme from *Rocky*. Or ones that have extremely varied material, like Boulez's *Pli selon pli*. I also thought about some pieces that are masterworks but wouldn't be considered exciting or interesting in those terms, like a Bach dance movement—say the first Gavotte from the first Orchestral Suite (ex. 3.1◔◀)). So I don't think exciting or interesting is the answer.

D: So you're dismissing these theories? All right. Go on.

I: And I'm certain that it's not a question of how thought-provoking the composition is, because thoughts about things stand in the way of a sublime experience.

D: Yes.

I: Then I thought about this question of emotions. Some people say that a great piece is emotionally fulfilling. But this emotion business I think is more complicated than it might seem. The association of music and emotions seems to be pretty powerful, and pretty common. But it is confusing. How does a piece express emotions? Like I said before, I don't understand where the emotion is, or what it is, or what is expressed, or how. I think about, say, the second movement of the "Harp" Quartet, and it seems to be associated with some kind of a poignant sadness. Where is the sadness? Well it has to be in me, in the listener. There must be something in the sounds that evokes in me that feeling of sadness. But it is my sadness; there is not sadness in the piece. And if I listen to a sublime performance of this work that has the character of a poignant sadness, I'm not sad. On the contrary, I'm elated, energized, moved, thrilled. So I'm wondering, then, could that be the beauty of a musical composition—just the very fact that it touches emotional parts of the listener's being? Is it like taking in a great play, which illuminates for me aspects of my life, and stimulates me to think—that it illuminates the human condition?

D: My God. You sound like you've been reading program notes or some other pornography. We come back to the two possible functions of art. There is that function that stimulates and illuminates—that brings me closer to the world around me. And then there is the possibility of aesthetic beauty. It is aesthetic beauty that we're after, which allows me to touch my own, pure, unadulterated self. And in the aesthetic experience of music sounds may well be associated with characters. But it is similar to the way in which our experience of a car involves the color of the paint. We cannot experience the car without also experiencing the fact that it is red, or blue, or black, and so on. But the quality of the car— the degree to which a certain car is valued—comes from its power, handling, comfort, efficiency, and styling. Its redness or blueness or blackness has nothing to do with the essential quality of the car. Likewise the experience of a sublime masterwork is colored by the character of the music. Consider your experience of a masterwork like that Bach Gavotte; your consciousness is colored with a mildly buoyant character. Contrast that to the deeply tragic character that colors your experience of the final act of *La Bohème*, which is lushly beautiful, but doubtless inferior as a purely musical composition.

I: So it seems unlikely that the quality of a composition is contingent on the degree to which it manifests characters or human emotions. But now that I'm thinking about it, I have to admit that I'm not completely comfortable with the idea of eliminating the importance of character or emotion in the quality of a composition. Because in better compositions, the emotions are deeper, more sincere, more profound, more poignantly drawn.

D: More sincere? More profound? More poignantly drawn? What does this mean? Anything? Once again, the characters or emotions that may be associated with a piece are not determinative of the essential quality of that piece.

I: Says you. Maybe I can be more precise. I'm thinking that the Bach Gavotte has the general character of joyous buoyancy, as you said, with maybe a darker splash of irritation at the opening of the second strain. Would you accept that, or is it more meaningless words?

D: (*frustrated*) Of course meaningless words! What's the relevance?

I: Let me finish. We talked about a piece like *Pines of Rome*. It has a certain character, too. In fact, it has starkly drawn characters: exuberant elation in the first movement, foreboding in the second, maybe wistfulness in the third, and I might describe the final movement as mysterious foreboding transforming to triumphant exhilaration.

D: Yes?

I: But they don't seem as sincere to me as the Bach Gavotte, which is far simpler. They seem shallow. Or there is the Gavotte by Rameau that I had to learn for piano class (ex. 3.2). It has a similar character of buoyancy, and I found it cute when I first heard it. But after practicing it for a little while I began to find it tiresome and pale. Do you think it's me or is it the piece?

D: I think that would be an expected reaction.

I: Then couldn't the honest, sincere expression of emotions or characters somehow be at the center of this issue of compositional quality?

D: Look, it's clear that some more overtly emotional or character-expressive compositions are of a lower quality—provide a lesser aesthetic experience. So we have to give up the notion that any kind of "illumination of the human condition" by painting emotions or characters is in any way determinative of the quality of a composition as it concerns the experience of beauty. And the fact is that if we are consciously in touch with our emotions—if our emotions are part of our focused consciousness we have lost any opportunity for the highest possible experience. Sincere? That's a meaningless adjective. The question for us is this: can we identify any property of great works that is lacking in lesser ones?

* * *

I: One more idea down the drain. Well there is another issue that keeps jumping out at me: unity. People talk about the value of unity. For example, I have heard often that a piece like the *Symphonie fantastique* is unified, because the themes recur from movement to movement.

D: Yes, the U-word. Unity. Well let's explore that. What does the word "unity" mean?

I: Unity is oneness, singleness. Unifying is becoming one. So to say a piece is unified means that it is in some way one, single.

D: Is the "Harp" Quartet one? Is it unified?

I: In the sense that it all makes sense together, I guess it is.

D: But what, exactly, is unified?

I: The piece.

D: Let's consider the first movement. Is it one, indivisible, single? Or is it easily divisible into sections, and periods, and phrases, and even individual notes?

I: It pretty much divides into component parts.

D: And the material itself—is it unified, one, single, or is it fairly diverse?

I: It's all a string quartet, and it's all in a tonal, classical style.

D: Within that context . . . ?

I: Quite diverse.

D: Can you think of any music in which the material is more unified—more one with itself?

I: What about the minimalist composers?

D: Minimalist composers? What do they do?

I: Well, they take sound . . .

D: Yes?

I: and they turn it into noise.

D: (*smiling*) Ah, a music critic. But quite seriously . . .

I: They use a minimal amount of different material within a composition. Hence the name. These pieces kind of lull you into submission with endless repetition and slight variation. So as a result the material is very much unified. And it is also fairly seamless—generally these pieces have relatively few discernible sections.

D: Do you find this minimalist music to be good music?

I: Basically I find it irritating. Fence-post music, I call it.

D: Fence-post?

I: Yeah. If you're riding along a highway, say in Texas somewhere, and for miles on end you see a fence along the road. Every few yards there is a fence post. Mile after mile after mile, nothing but prairie and fence posts. Sometimes you stare at them for a while and try to focus on them, but you always lose concentration, and begin to think about other stuff. Then you'll come back to the posts every so often. But if you try to concentrate on them you've got a continual series of shifting thoughts, to other stuff, back to the posts, lose concentration on them after a while, think about other stuff, go back to the posts, and so on. Same with this minimalist music. I listen to this stuff, Philip Glass and Steve Reich, and other stuff like that, and I try to absorb it, and I simply lose concentration. My mind begins to wander, and I find myself thinking about other things, and then it wanders back to these sounds, and I just wish that they would stop, so I could think in peace. Either that, or absorb me in some way. Fence-post music.

D: But it is unified.

I: Yes. I think we have to say that according to how we've been defining the term unified, this kind of music tends to be unified.

D: More unified than, say, the "Harp" Quartet?

I: Very much so. But now I'm really confused. Because it does seem clear that these minimalist compositions are more unified than other, better, compositions, and yet at the same time I can't escape the idea that unity is valuable, that unity is some kind of key to quality.

D: Yes, I think you're right. It is about unity. But you've also fallen into a common trap. Let's return to the question of what, exactly, is it that is unified?

I: The piece. But it couldn't be the piece, because we've considered compositions that are very unified but are not of particularly high quality.

D: So what is unified?

I: The performance?

D: A performance is sounds. How can a performance be unified? Let's put it this way. With this minimalist music that you find irritating, that you find not to be very good music, what was unified?

I: The piece.

D: And what was not unified?

I: Huh?

D: We are working on the assumption that unity is a good thing, and we are also working on the assumption that a composition with a higher quality will yield a better experience. Here we have been discussing a piece that is unified but the experience it yields is not a particularly good or rewarding one. We must accept, then, that the unity of the composition itself, in the sense that we understand unity, is not relevant to compositional quality. But if unity is a good thing, as we both think it is somehow, wouldn't it also be true that disunity—multiplicity—is a bad thing? What if we found some element of disunity associated with a less than desirable musical experience—in other words, maybe if we found what was disunified in a bad composition, we could also find what is unified in a good composition. In your disappointing experience of minimalist music, what was disunified? What was segmented, fragmented, unwhole, disunified?

I: My consciousness. My conscious experience. Yes, my experience was quite divided and inharmonious. So—maybe in a great composition the experience is unified.

D: Of course. It's the experience. And this is a critical point, one that has tripped up many better theorists than you and me. Let's be crystal clear about it. Unity of the piece in terms of its material—in other words some kind of unity deriving from recurrent themes or motives—is not relevant to quality. The piece is a design for relationships, but unity of the relationships—in other words how similar the material is—isn't relevant to quality either. Compositions of the highest quality may have quite a range of different material, and consequently different and varying relationships between the component sonic elements. Unity of the piece in terms of its being seamless is of course not relevant either. But unity is important: unity of the experience that the composition can provide. A great piece of music can, under the right circumstances, yield a unified, singular experience. If a piece of music is a design for sonic relationships for the purpose of allowing a musical experience, a great piece of music is a design for sonic relationships that can allow a sublime, transporting, loss-of-self experience, one in which the consciousness is focused wholly and indivisibly, one in which you become the sounds. A great piece of music can come to you as a single, uninterrupted simultaneous experience, an indivisible experience, all in one extended now.

I: Indivisible?

D: One indivisible experience in which every component event gives meaning to every other. One experience in which the first note remains present in the same, singular conscious act to shape and be shaped by every note that follows.

I: In contrast with the minimalists . . .

D: Oh let's leave the minimalists alone—in contrast to your conscious experience of any music that is less than the highest quality. You mentioned Cherubini. When you listen to music of Cherubini what is the nature of your experience?

I: Again fragmented.

D: In the same way?

I: Actually, yes, in very much the same way. I attempt to become absorbed in the sounds, and yet I am led to other thoughts.

D: And how would you describe the activity of your consciousness?

I: Like I said, fragmented. A thought, back to the music, a thought about something else, a beautiful progression, noticing the hall, or the audience maybe, maybe smelling someone's perfume.

D: Your experience is segmented, divided?

I: Yes.

D: So, what about the concept of the first note being present in all that follow?

I: Well in a great work the first note sounds and it doesn't stop . . .

D: No! No, no, no, no, no. The first note is gone. It begins and it sounds and it ends. In the worst pieces of music ever conceived and in the most sublime. The note is gone. But in an indivisible, singular, uninterrupted experience, what happens to the first note? Where does it live on?

I: Ummmm . . . my consciousness. It stays in my consciousness.

D: Yes. *Bongiorno*! It stays in your consciousness. For how long?

I: Until the act of consciousness ends—it remains over the course of the act of the consciousness in which it is perceived.

D: Yes. Now . . .

I: Now if I perceive the first note in a certain act of consciousness, that act in which, say, at the beginning of the performance I am focused fully on the sounds—and then that act of consciousness is ended when I focus on another object—the first note, and every other note in that act of consciousness, is not there to shape my experience of notes that follow; I am not conscious of it concurrently with my perception of other notes in later acts of consciousness.

D: Yes, more or less. Somewhat like that last sentence. Perhaps I would understand it if I could have retained the opening words by the time the sentence ended. In all seriousness, though, you are close. But there is another level of complication that we may attack at some later date.

I: Okay. But let me get this straight. If I listen to a performance of something by Cherubini and I find it to be a less good composition than something by

Beethoven, it is because my consciousness is fragmented, it cannot be held, so that when I return my focused consciousness to the sounds I do not have the original sounds still in my memory . . .

D: *Aaiiigh!* Not memory. Not memory. This process has *nothing* to do with memory. It has to do with retention. Memory is something quite different. Memory is a mode of consciousness. I can perceive a sound, or a group of sounds, say a single performance. I (the subject) hear (the mode of consciousness) the totality of the sounds (the object). If the subject changes from the entire piece to—say—the vibrato of the cellist, the conscious act is a different one: I (the subject) hear (the mode of consciousness) a particular portion of the sounds (the object). If the subject changes to—say—my neighbor's perfume, the conscious act is again different: I (the subject) smell (the mode of consciousness) the odor (the object). If the subject changes to—say—the sex life of the conductor, the conscious act is different yet again: I (the subject) imagine (the mode of consciousness) unimaginable acts (the object). I could not perceive tones in the middle of the piece and remember tones from the beginning of the piece in the same act of consciousness. The act of remembering would involve me (the subject) remembering (the mode of consciousness) the initial tone (the object). No, memory is simply not part of the process, no matter how many famous scientists say it is.

I: I read a book recently in which the author discussed our consciousness of music, and he stated that we could only retain musical sounds in our memories for a few seconds.

D: You believe what you read in a book? That's your first mistake. Go out and experience things. And think about it. That's how you know something. Not from a book!! But this points out the very value of music—the extent of our retention in a single act of consciousness is as great as the piece and its performance allow to us. If it's just a few seconds in a twenty-minute movement, that's a terrible shame. If it's through the course of the entire movement—then we have something magical. But it's a question of retention, and not memory.

I: But—humor me please—it happened in the past. The present sounds are sounding, and the earlier sounds are no more—they must be in the past.

D: *Physical reality is different from consciousness! Physical reality is different from consciousness! Aaach!* We are studying music; we are studying the experience; we are studying how sound acts on the consciousness. Music exists in the consciousness, not in physical reality. So physical reality is important for the purpose of this pursuit to the extent that it affects the consciousness—*only!* In physical reality the tone is past. No question about it. In music it is present. And this is not mysticism—it is simple fact that if my conscious act is uninterrupted, then the objects perceived at the beginning of that act are still present, they still shape and give meaning to my experience of other tones. Just so, if my conscious act is uninterrupted, the tones that come later shape and give meaning to my experience of the tones I hear at the beginning of the experience. Just like if I say, "Icarus" or if I say, "If you are going to the store, please buy me some beer." The initial "ih . . ." sound is the same in both utterances, but the meaning is vastly different, and there is no confusion. The ". . . carus" sound shapes the initial "ih . . ." sound in the first utterance, just like the ". . . f you are going to the store please buy me beer," shapes the second "ih . . ." sound, because in each case the consciousness is one, in each case we are conscious of the entire utterance in a single, undivided act of the consciousness.

I: But this request for beer can't provide the ultimate experience of beauty. Nor can the "Icarus" sound. Right?

D: Right. Because?

I: Because they're signs of something. You need to be judging to understand that the sound "beer" signifies that bubbly, alcoholic liquid, or that the sound "Icarus" signifies that bubbly young scientist.

D: (*shaking his head*) Oof!

They near the house.

I: Question. You are calling this loss-of-self experience indivisible. Why is it indivisible? Wouldn't it be more accurate to say undivided, not indivisible—in other words, to say that it wasn't divided instead of saying that it couldn't have been divided?

D: No. The aesthetic object is divisible, to be sure. It could be conceived of in parts, it could be constituted in the consciousness in parts. But we are speaking of the highest, most sublime experience of musical beauty. In this experience, the consciousness is one, unbreakable, indivisible. It cannot be broken.

I: Sure it can be broken, if I think of something else. If in my consciousness I focus on a component only. Or if a plane crashes in the middle of the concert hall. Then of course it's broken.

D: Certainly, but then you no longer have the highest, most sublime experience. Singularity is a defining characteristic—an essential attribute—of the experience.

I: But what about the opposite notion from unity? What about the common idea that a great piece is an unlimited font of variety? People say the mark of a great piece is that you can hear it over and over and hear something new each time.

D: Quite frankly, there is an abundance of weak compositions in which you might still notice new things if you heard them repeatedly. But how often you would be inclined to listen to them is another question. And the fact is that if a listener is hearing different things in different performances of a truly great work, then either the performers aren't doing a maximal job, or the listener isn't coming with a naked consciousness, open to the totality of the sounds. So the highest experience is not available. And of course there may be some people who say that a great piece allows for something new at each experience of it, meaning that it allows a new, stimulating, sublime experience at any listening, regardless of how many times you have heard the work.

I: In other words, that a great piece is one that allows a great experience, not necessarily a different experience.

D: Precisely.

I: (*pensively*) Let me try to put this together. First of all, we know that some pieces are better than others. What makes them better is that they allow better experiences. We dismissed the notions that the experiences are better because the compositions are more dramatic or exciting, or more emotionally rich, or more interesting, more expressive, or more thought-provoking. We have theorized that the quality of the experience depends on the degree to which the listener's consciousness can be indivisible—the best experience is one in which the listener's absorption of the sounds is uninterrupted and unadulterated. A listener can have that experience only if the object—the actual performance— allows it; the object can allow it only if the composition allows it.

D: So far so good. Now, our question is how does the composition allow it. Can we discover anything about how—on what basis—tones can combine to yield that unified, indivisible, loss-of-self experience? Here we are, back at the house. Well we've gone far enough for today anyway. Why don't you think about this issue, and we'll get together when you've come up with some ideas. I'll give you a ride home if you like.

I: Thanks, but the sun's come out a bit, and I like the walk.

February 14

I: Were you leaving? I was hoping to bug you with the question of the day.

D: As a matter of fact, I was getting ready to go home, and looking forward to it. But I can spare a few minutes. Come into my studio. Now—the question of the day. Which is what, exactly?

I: The next step is to nail down how a composition can lead to a great aesthetic experience.

D: (*shaking his head disappointedly*) Yes, wouldn't that be wonderful. Wouldn't it be wonderful to know the meaning of life. Yes, wonderful. And to have eternal peace. And, for that matter, to have breakfast in bed every Sunday for the rest of my life. Yes, that would be quite wonderful. (*starts for the door*) Now, if you do not have a more serious question, I will be going.

I: (*confused*) But . . . but wait. That is a serious question. You said at your house that it would be the next question.

D: Tsk. No. No, I'm sorry. Not at all. Ach, the arrogance of youth. Or perhaps it's just the stupidity of one particularly arrogant youth. You want to know what a great composition is? It is one that can allow a great experience. Next question.

I: I'm so confused. But how? Why? That is the next question. You said so yourself.

D: Sit down. My dear young colleague, you will never define wholly the attributes of a great piece of music. Mr. Schenker wanted very badly to do that. He said a great piece of music unfolded a soprano line descent to the tonic over a consonant harmonic progression. Do sublime tonal masterworks do that?

I: As far as I know, yes.

D: Do all masterworks do that?

I: I'm not sure.

D: Are there any great nontonal works? Bartók? Stravinsky? Berg? Shostakovich?

I: Yes, I think so.

D: Are there any works that prolong a soprano line descent to the tonic over a consonant harmonic progression that are not sublime masterworks?

I: I would guess there might be.

D: Then did Mr. Schenker in fact have his answer for the secret of all music? Of course not. Now he was not wrong about the hierarchy of musical elements. And his work has been and will continue to be extremely fruitful and valuable to anyone who thinks about music. But this urge to answer the question with any degree of completeness is only foolishness. You are curious about how a composition can lead to a sublime experience. Yes, so am I. And I do not believe you can answer that question.

I: But . . .

D: But maybe, just maybe, you might be able to come a little bit closer than "interesting," "thought-provoking," "dramatic," "expressive," or even than "$\hat{3}$–$\hat{2}$–$\hat{1}$ over I–V–I." Mookie cannot know the meaning of life; he cannot know the extent of the universe; he cannot know why we were put forth on this earth. But he can use his resources to determine that, yes, there might be a magic potion like aspirin, or some spices that preserve meat, or some gold over that horizon, and by God he's going to find it and bring it back to help his society.

I: I'm with you. How do you know it's unanswerable if you don't try to ask it? How did Ponce de León know that there was no fountain of youth if he didn't look for it? So it can't be bad.

D: Is it bad to steal gold, rape women, slaughter men and boys, and decimate a thriving population by spreading disease?

I: Aw . . .

D: He had no idea that he would do that, at least the spreading disease part. And that may not necessarily have been the outcome of looking. And for all we know, there may be a fountain of youth that just has not yet been discovered. But what may be bad about looking? Only the very real likelihood that you might convince yourself of an answer when none exists. Like many better music theorists and scientists and explorers before you.

I: Like Columbus, who convinced himself that he discovered India.

D: Precisely. So our interest is not in the secret ingredient that is the final answer to musical quality. Rather it is in bringing a bit further our necessarily incomplete understanding of how a great piece yields a sublime experience.

I: Okay. And I've been thinking about this issue since we spoke last. Don't get mad now, but . . . don't you think that what we were discussing about the experience of a weak composition as not holding the attention—don't you think that comes down to being interesting? I know that we dismissed that idea, but if the piece doesn't hold our attention, and as a result our conscious experience is multiple, don't you have to say that this is because the piece is not interesting.

D: Yes, that's so. But there are many levels of interesting. A nude centerfold can be interesting, but not to lead to a loss-of-self experience. Not as an aesthetic object separate from the sexual associations someone might have from viewing a naked person in an alluring position. Renoir's *The Skiff* is interesting to a more profound degree; it is interesting in that it captures our attention—draws us in, not from the limited aspect of a boat and two women and what significance they may have to the viewer, but from the interplay of the forces created by the lines, the shapes, the colors—what Arnheim calls the "*activating and balancing forces.*"[1]

I: I'm not sure I understand.

D: Every visual image comes with component parts, each of which has its own attribute of color, size, shape, and location. Each also has as an attribute its relations to the other components of the image. These are not static relations; rather the relations between the components of the visual image are dynamic. They involve forces, the give and take of energy. The component parts give meaning to each other through the interplay of the forces. Here, let's consider an elementary example.

Daedalus draws a square on a piece of paper. Then he takes a coin and places it, some-what off-center, within the square.[2]

Look at this image. We perceive the coin as part of the whole image; we perceive not just a circle and a square, but the entire image with its attendant forces of attraction and repulsion. The image seems unbalanced; the circle seems unsettled, floating, pulled toward the center. Now you take this second coin and place it in the square, so that it balances the first one.

Icarus places another coin somewhat off-center in a symmetrical position to the first. He then slowly absorbs the image.

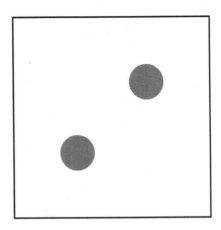

I: There, I think that might do it.

D: I think it just might. The forces that seem to pull the upper coin are balanced by the forces at work on the lower coin—and by the forces that result from the relation between the two coins. Now, we've barely scratched the surface of what kinds of forces are at work when we perceive visual images. For our purposes it is enough to recognize that such forces exist.

I: Do they, though? Do they exist? They don't exist in the paper, or the coins, they are not physical properties of the objects that we are seeing.

D: Did you see the forces? Look again. Do you see them? Do they exist?

I: Yes. I see them. So, I guess they do exist.

D: Can you take in that visual image without also perceiving the forces at work within it?

I: (*peering thoughtfully*) No. No, I can't.

D: If they are not physical properties of the actual material objects, but they are necessarily present when we take in the image, then where are they?

I: They're in the image. Oh, I get it—the forces exist in my consciousness—in my consciousness of the image.

D: Exactly. The marks—the lines and circles, and whatever other differentiable components of the image—they exist in physical reality. But the forces, because they result from the relations between the components, exist in my consciousness.

I: Can I ask a stupid question?

D: You certainly cannot. There are no stupid questions.

I: What about paintings that are formless?

D: Formless? Ach, I was wrong. That is a stupid question. If you spit tobacco juice on the canvas blindfolded, the image has a form. What is formless? There is no work of art that is formless. The components of the image, of any image in any work of visual art, result from the differentiation of colors, in different sizes, and shapes, and positions. There is no painting that is without form. Even if the canvas is completely white, the image has form.

I: Okay. Sorry. But didn't Beethoven say that the slow movement of the Fourth Piano Concerto was formless?

D: I never heard him say that. But if he did . . . is it? Use your own brain. Did Wagner say he was indissolubly fusing music and text and action and scenery? Yes. Did he? Is such a thing possible? Of course not. Does the slow movement of the Fourth Piano Concerto consist of tones, and phrases, that unfold in relation to each other?

I: Uh, yup. If you are open to it in that way.

D: If you are not open to it in that way can you be listening to that piece? Certainly not. Then is it formless?

I: Uh, nope. Okay, I get it. I won't believe everything I hear.

D: Nor should you disbelieve it. But healthy distrust might be a good way to describe a good intellectual stance.

I: All right. Then I healthily distrust the notion that balance of forces can affect my aesthetic experience of a work of art.

D: There is a difference between healthy distrust and stupidity. If you have had a spiritual, transcendent experience from a work of art in which the forces are balanced, and have not had any from works in which the forces are not balanced, then it is simply stupidity to assert categorically that they cannot affect it.

I: That doesn't prove a thing. How do I know that the forces were balanced in that Renoir? And if they were, I still don't know that this is the reason I could have such an experience.

D: Fair enough. First of all, the consciousness is one.

I: Come again?

D: The consciousness is one. The human consciousness can encompass only a singular object.

I: I don't understand this. What about the things on this table, what about the forks in the drawer. What about the orchestra members. Can't we be conscious of all of these at the same time?

D: Absolutely. But in each case we raise the multiplicity to a unity that we can absorb. We do not focus on eight forks as eight separate and unrelated objects within the same act of consciousness. We raise them to a group, a singular unit, namely, the group of forks in the drawer. Likewise with the things on this table. We raise them to a group—the singular group of things that are on the table. We could not have a simultaneous consciousness of two entirely unrelated objects. Radiation and love. What is the relation? The flu and an alto clef? Can you, in the same, singular conscious act, focus on both objects?

I: Sure—as objects that we can conceive of.

D: Only in the absolute broadest commonality of objects that are conceivable by humans. What kind of useful relation is that? What kind of group do they participate in? The group of all conceivable objects. Can you raise a group of objects to this level in your consciousness in any meaningful way?

I: No, I guess not.

D: The consciousness is one, seeking one. We seek to join multiple objects in a single, unitary act of consciousness. When the component percepts of a visual image can come together in a conscious act, we reduce the many objects to a single object, we raise them into a higher group, we transcend the multiplicity. The coins in the square come to us as component parts of a single image. They come to us with dynamic forces only because they stand in our consciousness as part of the entire image. Remove the parts from the image, focus on the part alone, and you remove the dynamic forces that give meaning to the image. And it is critical that you are clear about dynamic forces. If an image is unbalanced, out of equilibrium, we can perceive the component percepts as parts of the same larger image through an act of judgment. We judge the circles and square to be a part of the same image. We consciously make the connection. Through the act of judgment, the subject is required as part of the conscious procedure. When the images are in balance, in a state of dynamic equilibrium, so that the forces of activation—the forces that create energy—are neutralized or played off by other, balancing forces, then the subject is not needed in the process to judge the image as one. The image comes as one, all together. And so the subject stays out of the process; the viewer becomes the image in an act of pure consciousness. Loss of self. The highest artistic experience.

I: If this highest experience is indivisible, then how can you talk of component parts? It would have no component parts.

D: Excellent question. But once again don't get caught in the trap of equating the physical object and the experience. We are discussing the experience, the conscious act. It is the conscious act that, as a result of how the component parts of the image relate, may be singular, indivisible.

I: Isn't it possible that the artist might intend some kind of imbalance?

D: Is it possible that a string quartet intends to play out of tune?

I: Wait—are you saying that it could never be the intention of the artist to create some kind of unbalanced image?

D: Could it be the intention of a chef to make a bitter dessert? Surely. Is it bitter? Yes. Could it be the intention of the quarterback to throw the ball into the stands? Certainly. Is it still an incomplete pass? Of course.

I: So an artist *might* paint badly on purpose.

D: No, not at all, Of course, intending an artwork to be unbalanced, or intending to play out of tune, or intending to compose a piece that is annoying, any of these might make a political or social statement of some kind, and might do so quite effectively. If, for example, the purpose of a composition about a mass genocide is to raise social consciousness, this might be accomplished quite effectively by calling the piece "Mass Genocide." Then if the composition annoys the bejeezus out of an audience, the composer may well have made them more aware of the ugliness of the inhuman acts. Undeniably, this might be effective. But this is an intellectual experience. It is not an aesthetic experience; it is not a loss-of-self experience; it is not as high or rewarding an experience as is available from music. Take careful note, though: this notion of intending a nonartistic goal is more commonly heard from the commentator and not the creator, from the art historian or the musicologist attempting to explain deep inner meaning, and not from the composer or the artist. The artist doesn't generally intend to create a nonaesthetic object.

I: I can't say I've ever heard anyone claim to play out of tune on purpose. But an underlying program . . .

D: . . . is the source, not the goal. The composer may be inspired by some extramusical consideration, but generally the ultimate aim is aesthetic beauty. And the fact is, whether or not it's the ultimate aim of the composer, the potential to move us listeners is the ultimate determinant of quality.

I: All right, but going back to balance, how do I know that the forces were balanced in *The Skiff*? How can I be sure that this explains my experience.

D: How did Oog and Goog know that the earth was flat? How did Mookie know that the earth was round?

I: They accumulated their information and explained it.

D: Yes. They considered information that they were told, and that they learned from their experiences, and partly through intuition and partly through concentrated thought they arrived at a theory that encompassed and connected it all.

I: But . . . but . . . they were *wrong*! Oog's and Goog's earth wasn't flat. And Mookie's wasn't round. So what good is that? Their theories were bad.

D: Their theories were absolutely excellent! Oog's theory allowed him and his society to travel miles and miles to hunt for food, because they knew that with the earth being fundamentally flat they would always be able to maintain their bearings, and thus would be able to find their way home. Mookie posited that because the earth was round he could sail over that horizon to bring back a magic potion or riches or spices, without ever falling off. This is a process, a very positive process, and the best one that we have. For us, we have information derived from our conscious experience of art. And through our intuition and a great deal of thinking, and discussing, and arguing, and questioning, we have come to a certain understanding of the process. If it fits all the information we have, our understanding is valid.

I: Okay. But can it help us advance our society? Our society is one of musicians. Can we help our society—the society of musicians and listeners? What can we know about how tones come together? Of course there must be some connection with the visual arts. What about musical forces? Interplay of forces of energy?

D: (*laughing*) Slow down. What we are after is to further our own under-standing. If any narrower approximations that we might propose prove to be beneficial or fruitful to performers, or theorists, or composers, that would be a wonderful thing to be able to contribute. Musical forces? Energy? Yes, it's there, and we'll get to it. But this is enough for today. Tomorrow same time?

I: *Hasta mañana.*

February 15

D: Where were we now? Ah yes. Musical forces. Let's start with single tones and their attributes—the properties that differentiate them from other tones. Any sound in and of itself—in other words considered alone, without reference to any other sound—has attributes in and of itself. Let's call these original attri-butes. In and of itself, a sound has the original attributes of pitch, of duration, of timbre, of volume, and of temporal placement—the point in time at which the sound begins. A sound in a musical context also has other attributes that derive from its relation to the other tones within the musical object, so we will call these relational attributes. One such attribute is linear function. Imagine two tones of similar pitch, duration, timbre and volume, each of which participates in a melodic line. The two may sound fundamentally different simply by virtue of their relations to the other tones in the line. For example, listen to the G♯s in these two fragments (ex. 3.3◀》).

In the first fragment the G♯ is approached by leap, and is part of the foun-dation of stepwise motion C♯–B–A–G♯–A. In the second fragment the G♯ is approached by step, and is not part of the foundation of direct stepwise motion; it is approached and quit by step, but it participates in the F♯–G♯–A stepwise ascent that embellishes the indirect B–A step. Listen again.

Daedalus plays the two examples again.

Assuming that the two G♯s have the same volume, timbre and duration, they differ only in terms of the relational attribute of linear function. Now let's take up another relational attribute, that of scale degree. Listen to the first fragment again, and let's have the tones participating in the key of A major (ex. 3.4◀》).

But if the same tones played in exactly the same way participate in the key of C♯ minor they sound fundamentally different (ex. 3.5◀》).

This difference is due to the attribute of scale degree: the C♯, B, A, and G♯ function as scale degrees 3, 2, 1, and 7 in the key of A major, and scale degrees 1, 7, 6, and 5 in the key of C♯ minor. Another relational attribute is that of harmonic function. When tones of similar pitch, duration, timbre, and volume participate in different harmonic contexts they sound fundamentally different. Listen to the A in each of these chords (ex. 3.6◀)).

Each A had the same volume, duration, and timbre, and of course pitch, yet each of the four sounded fundamentally different simply because of the relation to the surrounding tones in a harmonic context.

Tones in a musical context also have a rhythmic attribute, resulting from the relation of the duration of the tone to the duration of other tones; and a metric attribute, resulting from the relation of the temporal location of the tone to the meter, and a dynamic function.

I: Dynamic in the sense of energy, right? Not as in volume?

D: Correct. Remember volume is an original attribute of any sound. But here we're talking about energy. Every musical articulation is defined by a creation of energy and the release of that energy.

I: Every articulation? What do you mean by articulation?

D: Every discernible musical entity is an articulation. For example, a single unit of the pulse, or a phrase, or a section. Let's begin at the beginning. The medium of music is silence. Silence is not only the background; silence is the ineluctable destiny of sound, the natural state out of which all sound emerges and to which all sound returns. Sound exists only to the extent that it successfully struggles against the eventual return to silence. That struggle is energy. Energy is required to create the sound, energy is required to keep it alive, energy that comes to the listener experiencing sound.

I: Energy is required to keep it alive?

D: Imagine a pendulum. The pendulum sits in its natural state of equilibrium, at rest, motionless. To set the pendulum in motion I apply a force to it. It swings back and forth describing an arc; it swings to rid itself of the energy. Each arc described by the pendulum is shorter than the one before as some of the energy is converted by friction to heat. Eventually all the energy is dissipated, and the pendulum returns to a state of equilibrium or rest. To keep the pendulum swinging at a constant level, just a tiny bit of energy must be applied with each swing—precisely the tiny amount that is dissipated by conversion to heat.

For the arc of the pendulum to increase, even more energy must be applied than was lost to heat. As soon as no additional force is applied, the pendulum will succeed in its efforts to return to equilibrium.

I: And you're saying sound is like the pendulum?

D: Sound is very much like the pendulum. Sound is created when a force is applied to an object. To rid itself of the force, the object vibrates. The vibration of the object causes waves in the air—densification and rarefaction of air molecules—which register on the eardrum and are converted into sound in the consciousness. As with the pendulum, without additional applications of force each vibration is shorter and shorter, until all the energy has been dissipated and the object returns to its state of rest or equilibrium. So we can say that sound exists only to the extent that it successfully struggles against the return to silence.

I: Wouldn't any sound come to us with this struggle inherent in it? Not just musical sounds?

D: Yes. Any sound is a struggle against the return to silence. Musical sounds are generally produced by vibrating strings, or air columns, or plates, media that dissipate energy slowly and evenly, giving duration and pitch to the sounds. So the struggle in musical sounds is generally more gentle and uniform than in nonmusical sounds. But it comes to us as energy. When we hear a sound, we are not only perceiving a pitch, duration, timbre, and volume, but an attendant play of energy as well.

I: So isn't the energy in the sound an original attribute, not one given by its relation to other tones?

D: Yes and no. Each sound has its own original dynamic property, which is a consequence of the other attributes. In other words, it resists silence on the basis of its pitch, duration, volume, and timbre, and thus is not an attribute independent of them. But musical sounds also have an additional relational attribute of dynamic function, an attribute that derives from the relations between the sounds. I think we can grasp this idea most clearly if we return to a single sound. For example, listen to this tone on the piano.

Daedalus plays a C on the piano and holds the key down until the tone dies out.

The hammer strikes the string, displacing it from equilibrium and injecting energy into it. The string vibrates back and forth, releasing the energy bit by bit, so that each vibration is somewhat smaller than the previous. The size of the vibration determines the volume: the bigger the vibration, the louder the sound. As the vibration diminishes in size, the sound decreases, until the string stops vibrating altogether and the sound stops. The energy that gives life to the sound we can call *impulse,* and the playing out or releasing of that energy we'll call *resolution.* In the single piano C that we heard, the initial attack was the impulse; it provided the energy. The resolution or playing out of that energy began immediately; virtually the entire sound consisted of that resolution. So this single sound consisted of the creation of energy and its playing out, or an impulse and its resolution. What determines how long the sound lasts?

I: Assuming we just let it ring? Well, gee, the volume. If I play the C louder it will take longer to die away.

Icarus plays the same C louder, and holds the key down. After a considerable time . . .
It's still ringing!

D: Yes. In terms of energy, how would you describe the louder tone?

I: If I play the C louder, that would be the attack, so I would be creating more energy. And if there is more energy, then it takes longer to release.

D: Very good. And in terms of the dynamic forces of impulse and resolution?

I: The greater the impulse, the larger the resolution it requires.

D: Now imagine a car sitting in the road, in neutral gear and without brakes. A truck comes along and bumps it from behind, and the car rolls. The bump is an immediate injection of force into the car; the force is continually released as the car rolls until all the energy is released and the car returns to a dead stop. The greater the force of the bump, the farther the car rolls, because it needs to release more energy.

I: The greater the impulse, the larger the resolution it requires.

D: Right. Now, instead of a sudden injection of impulse with an immediate release, imagine that the impulse grows. Imagine that same car sitting in that same road. This time you get into the car, start it up, and accelerate up to—say, five miles per hour, and then release the gas pedal. Again the car rolls to a stop. If you do this again, only this time you accelerate even more—say to ten miles per hour before releasing the gas—the car rolls further. The more you accelerate the further the car rolls, continually releasing the energy that was built up through the acceleration. Luckily a car has brakes, which increase the resistance to the initial force, so that we can control when that force is completely released.

I: Okay, so what does that have to do with music?

D: It illustrates the difference between dynamic activity of a sound and dynamic activity in a musical context. The dynamic activity of sound is like the car as a hunk of metal on wheels, hit by the truck and rolling freely until it releases the energy. The same principal is at work in the car with a variable-speed engine and brakes; however the injection of force can be built up, and varied—in other words controlled—and its release can be controlled as well. Just so in music, the particular succession of tones controls the way impulse is created and resolved.

I: How?

D: Consider that same C we played before. Just like we use the engine to accelerate the car, what might we do to effect a growth in the impulse?

I: (*moving to the piano*) We could increase the volume. Maybe . . . like this (ex. 3.7◀»).

D: Good, and now we have tones in relation to each other within a whole . . . a musical context. What is the dynamic structure: the structure of impulse and resolution?

I: The impulse grows to the final tone.

D: We call the height of the impulse the *climax*—the point of greatest tension. So why do you say the climax came on the final C?

I: Well, the energy seemed to grow through the first four Cs as they grew louder, until the loudest—the last one. But if the final C was the climax, then where was the resolution?

D: Think. Listen and think.

I: Umm . . . also the final C. Confusing.

D: Specifically the climax was the attack of the final C. The remainder of the final C—and remember we're in a musical context here—released the energy that was gathered in the first four tones. Now, how might you create even more impulse?

I: With a bigger crescendo?

D: Certainly, that would do it. But what about a different way. What about with rhythm?

I: Oh, maybe we could get a kind of a running jump into it (ex. 3.8🔊).

D: Good. As the rhythmic density increased, the impulse grew even more than in the first example. How might you increase impulse using melody?

I: Well, how about if we add a D♭, like this (ex. 3.9🔊)?

The impulse begins with the first C and extends through to the D♭, which is the climax of the impulse. The final C forms the resolution.

D: (*taking over at the piano*) Yes, although more precisely the final C participates in the resolution, which begins immediately after the initial attack of the D♭. Good. And harmony can effect impulse too. Listen to this example (ex. 3.10🔊).

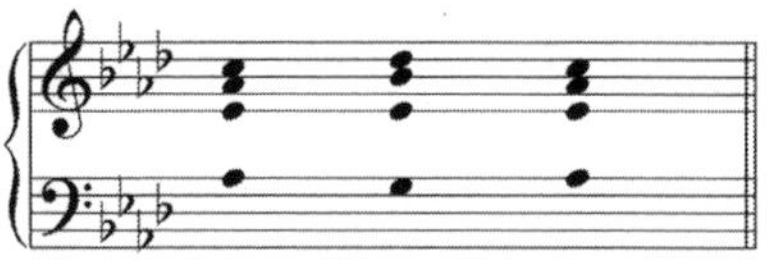

I: The middle chord, the dominant seventh, creates a lot of impulse. Much more than just the melodic line.

D: Now we've encountered the attribute of dynamic function. The two Cs are identical in every original attribute but temporal placement, with the same harmonic function, the same scale degree and the same linear function. But they have a different dynamic function.

I: The dynamic function of the first C is creating energy, that of the second C is playing it out.

D: Exactly. Now what is the dynamic structure of this four-chord progression (ex. 3.11 ◀))?

I: The impulse seems to climax with the new subdominant chord, the IV^6. It creates even more impulse than the dominant seventh chord did in the three-chord progression.

D: And now what is the dynamic function of that dominant?

I: Now it's part of the resolution. It's playing out energy gathered by the subdominant. Is it possible though that the melodic ascent is giving this impulse—that the impulse is not brought about by the harmony?

D: The melodic ascent may contribute to the impulse, but rest assured the harmony is creating impulse. Here—essentially the same four-chord progression with a slightly different bass line has a completely different dynamic structure (ex. 3.12◀)).

By changing the final chord to a dissonant diminished seventh it becomes filled with energy, more than any of the other chords.

I: I hear it. So a more dissonant chord creates more impulse than a more consonant one.

D: Not necessarily, but usually. There are some tendencies, but there are no rules.

I: Then ascending lines have a tendency to create impulse, right? And increasing rhythmic density, and increasing volume do the same. Isn't this so?

D: Yes, it's so, but there is no formula. Again, there are no rules. Impulse is created with a complex network of factors: linear, harmonic, rhythmic, metric, intensity, and so on. Ascending melodic lines tend to add impulse; we've heard that. But some ascending lines play out energy. We've also heard that increasing rhythmic density tends to create impulse. But again . . .

I: . . . there are no rules.

*　　*　　*

D: Let's consider some passages from the "Harp" Quartet and hear some of the ways that a composer builds up impulse. Let's listen to the opening theme of the second movement (ex. 3.13◀》).

I: Hey—we just heard that.

D: Yes, the four-chord progression that we heard earlier (ex. 3.11) forms the backbone of this 4-bar phrase, here with the addition of a final dominant harmony. Just like the earlier four-chord progression, the impulse of this passage climaxes with the sounding of the subdominant on the downbeat of the fourth bar. The remaining bar resolves that impulse. Now let's find a phrase in which impulse is generated by increasing rhythmic density. How about this passage from the end of the last movement (ex. 3.14◀》).

I: It grows. It seems to grow as a result of the increasing rhythmic density, as well as the increasing volume.

D: Yes, and the accelerando.[2] Now that we've created impulse, let's consider some of the factors that go into resolving it. Here's a passage from the first movement. Listen very carefully to the gathering of energy (ex. 3.15◀﹚).

I: The impulse grows with the increasing volume and the expanding register through the first four bars, and I think even into the first sforzando.

D: Fine. Now I'll play the passage again. This time focus on how Beethoven resolves that impulse.

Daedalus repeats the example.

I: The resolution takes place primarily through the decreasing volume and the descending register.

D: Yes. Notice that he gradually lets out the energy over the course of these eight or so bars with injections of smaller and smaller impulses with the offbeat accents. Now I'm going to add some extra bars to the resolution. Pay attention again to the gathering and playing out of energy, and this time raise your hand when you feel that all the impulse has been resolved (ex. 3.16◀﹚).

I agree. The impulse ended at some point shortly into the extra bars. The music continued but the energy was done. Finished. How about this version (ex. 3.17◀﹚)?

I: Not enough resolution.

D: Right. There was more energy left at the end of the music.

I: Let me understand this. Within a section, or phrase, or some articulated unit the tones combine to create impulse, and then a resolution of that impulse.

D: Yes.

I: What happens if there is no resolution?

D: Then it's not a unit. The beginning of the impulse defines the end of the previous unit and the beginning of the new one. The beginning of the resolution defines the end of the impulse. But with no resolution, just imagine: energy grows, grows, grows, to where? Where would the unit end? It wouldn't.

I: Then does the impulse need to be resolved completely within the section?

D: It needs to be played out to the right degree. We may touch on that later.

I: Wait a minute, though. Aren't sections also largely delineated by differences of texture . . . or material? If the texture changes or the material changes, then don't you have a different section?

D: In one sense that's true, in a similar way that each new pitch is a separate and definable entity. It is possible to understand a piece of music as a succession of several thousand pitches or pitch configurations—harmonies—of different durations. But the aesthetic value comes in the experience of transcending, which is allowed by the relation of those events in our consciousness, which in turn is allowed by the network of energy.

I: But what about a piece like *The Rite of Spring*, which is built of section after section. Don't we understand this as a succession?

D: To some extent we may. But again, we value the piece for its aesthetic possibilities to the extent that all its component tones, and sections, combine in our consciousness in a way that allows us to transcend—allows us to come to one. Now we have arrived at a critical issue, which we will need to take up some other time: hierarchy, the key to Western art music.

I: Hierarchy?

D: Yes. The end in the beginning and the beginning in the end.

I: The end in the beginning and the beginning in the end?

D: Give it some thought.

I: (*getting up to leave*) End in the beginning and the beginning in the end. Hmmm. Okay, I'll think about it. Well—Hello, I must be going!

February 29

D: Good evening. Nice to see you today. And on Leap day, a day that comes by only rarely.

I: Yes. What better day to talk about the end in the beginning.

D: So what have you understood this to mean?

I: Clearly it means that in some way the end of the piece is part of my experience of the beginning, and vice versa. Just like in any temporally extended act of consciousness. The first note present with the rest of the notes.

D: Yes. The enormous challenge is to compose an extended work in which all the component parts can be present in my experience simultaneously.

I: And that has to do with a hierarchy of dynamic structure?

D: Exactly. We've heard how small sections of a piece are articulated as units by the impulse and resolution. Now let's go to the most basic level—the pulse. What is the pulse?

I: Yes, I remember what you said about pulse—the smallest unit of time that characterizes the motion.

D: I give up. I just give up. Not time. *Not time!! Time has no relevance to music!! Time is an aspect of the physical world . . . in the world of music we are not concerned with time . . . we are not concerned with stopwatches; it is of no relevance to us how long something takes to play!!!*

I: Yeah, yeah, yeah. Okay, are you finished yelling?

D: (*calming down*) Music . . . takes place . . . in the consciousness. How long is a four-hour date with a boring person? How long is a four-hour date with a stimulating person? So how long is four hours?

I: Yeah, energy.

D: I beg your pardon?

I: Energy. The pulse is the smallest unit of energy that characterizes the motion.

D: *Bongiorno!* And what does that mean?

I: I believe it means that the pulse is that smallest unit that describes the character of the motion.

D: And what is the pulse of the first movement Poco adagio?

I: (*walking and humming*) A pulse comes every quarter note.

D: Good. So intone the pulse (ex. 3.18◀᭙).

Icarus hears

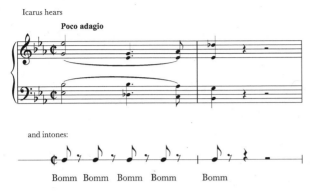

and intones:

Bomm Bomm Bomm Bomm   Bomm

Now intone the pulse of the first movement Allegro (ex. 3.19◀)).

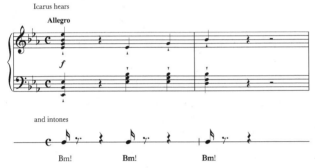

Icarus hears

and intones

Bm!   Bm!   Bm!

Yes, but go on. Hear the first several bars. Yes, now. Just listen to them in your mind.

Icarus focuses intently on the first seven bars.

Now intone the pulse of the first phrase (ex. 3.20◀)).

Icarus hears

and intones

Bm! Bm! Bm! Bomm   Bomm Bomm Bomm Bomm Bomm

Yes! Absolutely. So what happened?

I: The pulse was different in the legato passage than in the staccato passage at the opening.

D: Yes. It's different. How so?

I: It's . . . umm . . . slower.

D: Slower? No. What is the frequency of the pulse? How often does it occur?

I: Twice in every bar. Every half note.

D: Yes. The pulse has the frequency of the half note. That is the beat; the beat is given by the half note—in both the staccato and the legato passages. So the pulse isn't slower.

I: No, but it's . . . longer.

D: What's longer?

I: The energy. The impulse. Within the beat. Wait, I'm confused. What's the difference between beat and pulse?

D: The beat is a metric phenomenon, an issue of frequency. Pulse, on the other hand, is dynamic. A single pulse has the same duration as a single beat, but a pulse has a dynamic component. The pulse is a unit of energy on the smallest scale, consisting of an impulse and a resolution. The difference between a staccato pulse and a legato pulse is the relation of the impulse to its resolution in terms of energy. In a staccato pulse the energy is compacted into a brief spurt at the beginning of the beat, with very little energy left for the remainder. In a legato pulse the energy is spread essentially evenly over the course of the beat.

I: Okay, I get it.

D: So, what concerns us today is the dynamic structure. On the lowest level of dynamic structure, then, we have the pulse. The continual injection and discharge of energy. Now, do you remember the passages we heard in our last meeting—units defined by impulse and resolution?

I: Of course.

D: Imagine a pulse within one of those resolutions. The pulse itself has an impulse and a resolution; that impulse of the pulse is part of the larger resolution. The musical event is generating impulse on the level of the pulse, and resolution on the level of the larger unit.

I: Thus the hierarchy.

D: Thus the hierarchy. But let's carry it further. The unit itself participates in a larger section. The larger section is a singular entity on the basis of a single overriding gathering of energy and release—one impulse and one resolution.

I: And the next level, and the next.

D: Until . . .

I: Until the level of the whole piece. So if a masterwork is a piece that can allow the highest, most sublime, transcendent experience, it does so by allowing its perception as an indivisible object. What makes a great piece then is that it is unified on the basis of a single, large-scale impulse and a resolution of that impulse. So that's it! So we know!

D: We can't know. We'll never know definitively what makes a great piece. But we know that energy is a component of our experience of sound, we know that singularity is essential to the highest experience, and we know that in terms of energy, singularity results from impulse being resolved consequently. So a great composition—one that can provide the highest experience of musical beauty—is one that can allow a performance in which a single overarching impulse is consequently resolved.

Icarus ponders this for a few moments.

I: And this is being Mookie? The end in the beginning?

D: Yes, this is the theory that will earn scorn and ostracization, pain and heartache.

I: (*smiling*) Or perhaps untold riches.

D: Good luck with that. As for being Mookie, what we've uncovered about what makes a great piece is not only the end in the beginning, but the totality of the piece at any moment within it. And if we have listened openly, and if we have thought openly, perhaps we can contribute a small advance in our understanding.

I: The totality of the piece at any moment within it? Now you definitely lost me.

D: In a simultaneous experience of a work of music, there is a very real sense in which the totality of the piece is found at any moment within it. Remember the attributes of tones?

I: Of course. Original attributes of pitch, duration, timbre, volume, and temporal placement. Relational attributes of linear function and harmonic function and dynamic function.

D: This is the critical part. Consider a given tone in a composition. Imagine that within its motive it is creating impulse. If the larger phrase in which it participates creates impulse, then on the level of the larger phrase the tone is also part of the impulse. Say that phrase stands within the resolution of its section, which itself is part of the global impulse on the highest level. The tone itself then carries within it impulse on one level, impulse on the next higher level, resolution on the next, and impulse on the highest. The dynamic function of the entire complex of tones is present within each of them.

I: The dynamic function at every moment has a universal implication.

D: Yes, exactly. Because the totality of the critical pattern of energy is implicit in every note.

Icarus begins to pace.

I: The beginning in the end, the end in the beginning, and the whole piece at every moment, because the piece can become a simultaneity, depending on its performance and the listener.

D: Yes.

I: But how? How does he do it? How does a composer create the possibility for this indivisible experience? To create one overarching impulse—building energy over the course of five, ten, fifteen minutes is extremely tricky, no? Does he do it with volume? With rhythm? Melody?

D: With those things, but also primarily with structural harmonic activity. By bringing us farther and farther from home, before returning us there. But this gets quite complicated and somewhat theoretical. There is an article about it called "Patterns of Energy" that you might find interesting.[3]

I: Okay, I'll look it up. But for now, to make sure what we're saying: one of the necessary elements for the sublime aesthetic experience of music is that the composition must allow it, which it does on the basis of enabling the performer to create energy and resolve it consequently.

D: Yes.

I: But then doesn't this theory about what makes a great composition depend on the performance?

D: Most definitely.

I: So isn't it then at best incomplete, and possibly even worthless?

D: On the contrary, since a composition is in itself a potential for a performance, any study of the composition as a thing in itself, without reference to the possibilities in sound is necessarily incomplete. Now it's getting late, and for me this has been quite exhausting. Stimulating, but exhausting.

I: Creating energy and playing it out all at the same time. Well, good night, Mookie.

D: (*smiling*) Good night.

Chapter Four

Gurus

On the Performer's Contribution

April 1

Icarus: To what do we owe the honor? Or is this some kind of April Fool's trick?

Daedalus: No, I really was here at the Symphony concert tonight.

I: Troglodyte! What's the occasion?

D: Guilty as charged. But every so often I have to see how the real world lives, just to know I'm not missing anything. So you're subbing in the orchestra this week. Did you enjoy it? Did you *really* enjoy it? Did it move you?

I: It was certainly rewarding financially. It's a great orchestra; we played well, and there were two or three stunningly beautiful moments. And the audience loved it—that was rewarding.

D: What makes you think the audience loved it?

I: Well, they all clapped like mad. Like for the new piece. I was skeptical, but in the end I was glad to have done it. . . . I thought there were some nifty sounds. How did you find it?

D: Let me ask you—did it provide you with a sublime musical experience?

I: Not totally, but I was busy scrubbing away trying to find those notes.

D: Well it didn't provide one for me either, and I was just listening.

I: Maybe it would have helped if you heard the composer at the preconcert lecture.

D: There are only . . .

I: Yeah, yeah. (*imitating Daedalus*) "There are only two things that can happen, and both of them are bad. Either they lead you to fill your mind with non-musical baggage that prevents the open consciousness required for any kind of higher, aesthetic experience, or you ignore what you heard and are open, but you wasted the time and effort to listen to the lecture or read the program notes." But that's just not true. A good preconcert lecture or good program notes can lead you to open up to the possibility of an aesthetic experience. You're hopeless. But you might have been entertained if you'd come. I certainly was when I heard the composer tell us he thought his piece would take its place next to the great symphonies of Mozart and Brahms.

D: And maybe he's right . . . who knows? In any case, when I rule the world we're not going to have program notes or preconcert lectures . . . only postconcert lectures. Oh, you think I'm crazy, but hey—Henry Ford was crazy, too. So were the Wright brothers. So was Lister, the first surgeon who washed his hands before surgery to kill these tiny invisible evils called germs.

I: So was Charley Manson.

D: *Touché.*

I: Seriously, though. Why did the audience respond so enthusiastically if this piece didn't move them?

D: (A) Emperor's New Clothes syndrome. Everyone else around you is applauding, so you think it must have been good and you don't want to seem stupid. (B) You've invested a small fortune to come to this concert, so you better like it. (C) The composer has a very large family.

I: Boy are you grouchy. I wouldn't ever go to concerts either if they put me in this bad a mood.

D: And (D) There is beauty on all levels. There was something in this music that did move people. Just like there was an occasional sublime moment in the Beethoven symphony performance. And people responded to both of those performances with great enthusiasm. But just imagine if an entire movement of that Beethoven symphony had allowed one extended, indivisible, uninterrupted moment. That would have been life-changing. With regular performances like that there wouldn't have been a ticket available for love or money—certainly no freebies for old curmudgeons, and then maybe the orchestra could afford to hire you permanently.

I: And maybe then I'd even want the job!

D: And I would gladly pay to come to the concerts.

I: Okay. It's a deal. So what do we do?

D: You know the answer to that question.

I: Yeah, yeah, we unfold the sounds in such a way that they can be absorbed in one indivisible act of consciousness. But what does that mean? What do we do? How do we do that?

D: And do you want the secret of life while we're at it?

I: I just want to know . . . We have an amazing thing here—this music stuff—and when we do it at an ordinary, routine, pretty good level like tonight, we provide people with a wonderful and valuable experience. But we know that there is even more, and I want it. I want the max. I want to play concerts as if my life depended on them. I want to be transformed by the sounds. Now you got me into this mess; you have to help me through it.

D: I have to? No. It's your mess. You get through it. If you need an occasional push, I'll be happy to assist you, but you need to figure your own way out. Otherwise you don't have your way out—you have my way out. Listen, think about it, Listen, and then think some more. You work on it, and if you want to check in with me from time to time you know where to find me. Besides, I have great faith—I think you're very much on the right path. (*raising his glass*) Cheers.

April 15

I: (*calling after Daedalus*) Hey, excuse me. I've been thinking for the past couple of weeks.

D: What is it? Come here. You say you've been drinking for the past couple of weeks?

I: (*out of breath*) No, no. Thinking. I wonder if I could run this by you. What I've been thinking is this. A sublime masterwork is a sublime masterwork because it allows a sublime experience—a single indivisible experience. But it's possible to play even a sublime masterwork in a way that does not allow this experience, as we heard a couple of weeks ago. So—what are we doing when we play in such a way that this sublime experience is possible?

D: And you think?

I: First off, I know that a technically inferior performance is distracting. Distracting and annoying. If ensemble is sloppy, if intonation is bad, if balance is off, it's difficult to be fully absorbed in the performance, regardless of how passionate or committed it is.

D: From which you conclude?

I: From which I conclude first that we have to play in tune. If I hear a performance and a note is out of tune, it divides my consciousness. I am no longer free to lose myself because the sounds no longer come to me as one.

D: One . . .

I: But this brings up a question: one what? They're different pitches, so how could they be one? And I began by thinking about the floor here in your studio.

D: The floor? You mean that loose tile?

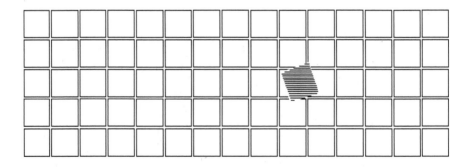

I: Exactly. I was thinking about how that tile is always crooked. And I realized that it's not crooked at all. If you pick it up it's quite square, just like the others. The only thing crooked about it is its placement. Same with a note that's out of tune. The note, considered separately, isn't in tune or out of tune. It's just out of tune compared with how the others join.

D: But joined how?

I: Joined with the other tones in my consciousness, in a single system of intonation. If a note is sharp, it is sharp to me because it belongs to a different system of intonation. I then must judge the tones as belonging to different intonation systems, and no loss-of-self experience is possible.

D: Good work! However, our challenge is not to play in tune.

I: Huh?

D: Our job is not to play in tune; our job is to not play out of tune. Look at these tiles again. If you measure them with precision instruments I'm sure you'll find that none is exactly parallel to any other. But they are sufficiently parallel that they don't seem out of place, all except that one. There are degrees of inaccuracy which we are able to accommodate as acceptable, but there is a limit. There is some kind of latitude of acceptable placement beyond which the tile appears crooked.

I: You're saying for intonation too?

D: Just so for intonation. There is a degree of variance which we accept as in tune, but beyond a certain point a tone strikes us as out of tune.

I: Well I have noticed that intonation is a very slippery thing. It doesn't want to be pinned down. For example, here's something I've been struggling with. (*Taking out his violin*) I'm going to play G, A, and B very slowly so each tone sounds perfectly in tune, like this (ex. 4.1◀»):

Icarus plays slowly.

I: Now the B sounds in tune. But if I hold that exact B and play a G underneath it, the B sounds sharp (ex. 4.2◀»).

This was quite confusing to me. Finally I realized that we must be constantly adjusting, and fudging, and this must be okay. In other words it must be possible to play each of those major seconds—G to A and A to B—slightly smaller than what would be linearly perfectly in tune to end up with a B that is not sharp to a G underneath.

D: Yes, that's right. Mathematically, if the interval of an octave is 1200 cents, the pure major second has 204 cents and the pure major third has 386 cents. So when you played the linear progression G to A and A to B perfectly in tune you played two pure major seconds, each of 204 cents. You ended up with a B that was 408 cents from the G, much higher than the harmonically perfectly in-tune pure B which has only 386 cents.

I: 386 to 408. Quite a difference.

D: And I'm sure you find playing with a piano even more slippery, because the equal-tempered minor seconds all contain 100 cents, the major seconds 200 cents, and the major thirds 400 cents.

I: Ouch. So if I'm in tune with a piano . . .

D: You're just within the latitude of not being out of tune.

I: But if I would play that by myself, or with non-equal-tempered instruments, the B would be out of tune.

D: But even within the constrictions of playing with another instrument, there's a latitude—perhaps a few cents either way depending on the intervals— within which you can put your pitch and still not be out of tune.

I: Hmm. The next obvious question is ensemble . . . playing together. Is there a latitude with ensemble as well?

D: To some degree. An entrance, or chord, or any simultaneous event that sounds not together also eliminates the possibility of a loss-of-self sublime experience by forcing me to judge that event. And yes, like intonation there is also a latitude. Tones that come to us as speaking together will—by a precise physical measurement—likely prove to begin at different times.

I: Like the floor tiles that strike us as parallel.

D: Yes. We can safely assume a measurable physical variation in both the spacing of the floor tiles and the temporal beginning of sounds that are unperceived by us. Let's be clear, though, that the perception of sounds as speaking together is sufficient, because music exists within our perception.

I: But perhaps less latitude for ensemble than for intonation?

D: Perhaps. But interestingly, we are more likely to perceive a simultaneity when the high, small-wave sounds reach our ears first than we are when the lower, longer-waved sounds reach our ears first. So there's a greater latitude for hearing a simultaneity when the high sounds actually speak before the low ones.

I: The moral of the story being that if somebody's got to be late it better not be the violins. Speaking of which, I've got a rehearsal . . . *right now*! Yikes. Can we continue after?

D: As you wish.

* * *

D: Come in. How was rehearsal?

I: "Follow the ink. Play what's on the page." That's all we heard from our esteemed conductor. "Play what the composer wrote."

D: The literal approach, eh? Well that sounds eminently reasonable.

I: Sure, if we're doing something that contradicts the page, then I suppose it's a suggestion that can get us closer. . . . Aw, wait a minute, you're just goading me. You know better than I do that our music making with her is so pedestrian, and so uninspiring. She thinks our responsibility ends when we play what's on the page, and of course that's not enough. I can play that C♯ that the composer wrote and it can be assuredly a C♯, and it can just as assuredly be out of tune, and thus wrong. Balance too. She says, "Play the written dynamics." And of course then we get blasted out by the brass, or covered by the cellos. It ends up sounding okay I guess. But it's never truly—magical.

D: So what's needed?

I: Well I've found that to truly blend things, lower tones have to actually be softer than higher tones.

D: Go on.

I: There's something I learned in my Physics of Sound course.

D: See there is value to school!

I: (*ignoring the comment*) Whatever. Anyway, I heard an incredible experiment. We had two sound-producing instruments at different pitches. With the volume of the upper tone steady, we increased the volume of the lower tone until it completely obliterated the upper tone. Then we reversed the process. We kept the volume of the lower tone steady, and no matter how loud we made the upper tone we still could not drown out the lower one. We even decreased the volume of the lower tone until we could barely hear it, and yet we still could not drown it out with the upper tone, no matter how loud we made it.

D: Wonderful. And from that you learned?

I: It has to do with how we process sounds. We also learned that we could hear low bass sounds quite clearly from tiny headphones, which are too small to produce those fundamental bass frequencies. But we do hear the low tones because we hear the succession of overtones that would sound above that fundamental bass. Although we don't hear the bass tone itself, we put together the overtones that we do hear and assume that the fundamental is sounding. We assume it to such a degree that we hear it, it enters our consciousness.

D: So from all this?

I: From all this it's become clear that we assign greater weight to lower sounds than to upper ones. I'm guessing that it has to do with overtones—that because a tone consists of its overtones, a higher tone is subsumed into the overtones of a lower tone, and thus not only exists as a tone in its own right, but adds weight to the lower one. If four tones of a chord are played at precisely the same decibel level, the lowest tone will dominate, followed by the next lowest, and so on. To be genuinely balanced, lower tones must actually sound softer than louder ones. Listen. If I play this chord so that each member has the same volume, the lowest tone dominates (ex. 4.3◀⦆).

Icarus plays a four-note chord so that each tone has precisely the same volume.

But now, if I play the tones in succession, so that each successive tone does not interfere with the tones already sounding but joins it, I find that I have to play each one successively softer than the previous one (ex. 4.4◄»)).

To play the chord simultaneously in a beautiful balance, so that all members blend into one magical combined sound, in fact I am playing the highest note the loudest, the next highest not quite as loud, the next highest softer still, and so on. This is how I think we need to structure the sounds in our quartet: from top down to bottom. Our cellist is very resistant. She insists on sitting inside so her F holes point out. As it is she's louder than any of us.

D: Yes, well then your group will fit right in. In nine out of every ten quartets the cellists play too loud. Even the famous ones. Of course they sound blended, but it's the old story of the boy and his dog. The boy and the dog have a close relationship. The boy feeds the dog, and the dog helps him hunt. The two depend on each other for their survival, and through that relationship they are unified into a single unit resulting from the equal participation of two individuals. If the boy gets hungry and decides to eat the dog, however, the two are also unified, but in such a way that the dog has become the boy.

I: Or if the dog eats the boy.

D: Twisted youth. But exactly. These cellists play too loud when they have their own sound as the focus of their attentive consciousness. Each player in any group must focus on the totality of the sound. Each member must play the entire quartet.

I: Our seating doesn't help.

D: Your seating is a problem for two reasons. The first is—as you've discovered—that it exacerbates the problem of the cello being fundamentally too loud for the rest of the instruments. For God's sake, for this very reason we even out the playing field in an orchestra: the lower the instrument the fewer we put on stage. In other words, we make them softer. But the second reason is even more important. The second reason is listening. If, as is most frequently the case, the responsibility of the cello is to play under the viola, whose responsibility is to play under the second violin, whose responsibility is to play under the first violin, then the logical and necessary seating is like this:

Daedalus draws on the blackboard.

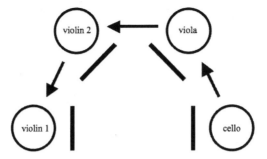

But with your cello in the middle, look how much more difficult it becomes for the entire quartet to listen in function.

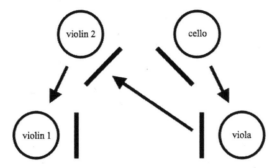

I: But now just to play devil's advocate, didn't you say that every musician has to listen to the whole. So if that's true, it wouldn't really matter who you sit next to, no?

D: Your ultimate responsibility is to the whole. Your immediate responsibility is to the person next higher in function: cello to viola, viola to second violin, and so on.

I: But what about orchestras? Some put the second violins on the outside, some have violas on the outside, cellos facing out, basses in left field.

D: It's the same issue. Conductors who seat the orchestra that way are making seatings on the basis of how each individual section sounds the best. Although for the life of me I can't figure out why anyone would think violas or second violins sound better with their F holes facing in, so their sound projects into the orchestra, rather than facing out, so their sound projects out into the room, as do all the other instruments.

I: Aren't they looking for the stereophonic effect? Especially in classical-era pieces? And wasn't the now-traditional seating of left-to-right first violins, second violins, violas, cellos, with basses behind the cellos—wasn't that a twentieth-century convention to make orchestras sound better on recordings?

D: Perhaps, but it comes down to the goal. If the goal is historical accuracy, then to discover how the violins sat at the premiere is indeed valuable. If the goal is the best possible experience, that comes when the musicians can hear best, and blend best.

I: "Come to one" best.

D: Yes. But there's another issue of balance that's critical, too: not only the blend of tones of different pitches, but the blend of tones of the same pitch. How can they combine so that our consciousness includes not the two different instruments but a third, combination sound. For instance—a unison flute and oboe blending magically to produce not the sound of a flute and an oboe playing together, but a combination of the two—a "floboe" if you will.

I: Do they need to play at exactly the same volume then?

D: Actually not. The flute has a "flatter," more neutral sound than the oboe, which has a very intense, rich sound. This is a function of the overtones: the oboe sound has a much greater participation of the overtones than the flute. If two different sounds need to blend in unison, you are well advised to start with the less rich sound and blend the most overtone-rich instrument right up into it until you reach that third combination sound. Similar to blending paint. In blending a pale color with a richer color, the richer one will dominate easily. You will get the best blend if you start with the pale color and add in the rich one bit by bit until it joins with the pale one to the desirable degree.

I: How do you know which is the richer tone color and which is the paler one?

Daedalus glowers at him.

Okay, okay. You listen.

D: Which is richer, the horn or the cello?

I: The cello.

D: The bassoon or the clarinet?

I: The bassoon. So to blend either of these two sets of instruments in unison the cello would blend up into the horn sound? And the bassoon up into the clarinet sound?

D: Right.

I: But if the two tones are not in unison, then we blend the lower pitched tone up into the higher one, regardless of sound quality?

D: Yes, assuming that the primary melodic material is in the higher register, as it usually is.

I: How do we know what's the primary mel . . . I know, I know, don't hit me. We listen. But that's not something we often get to do in the school orchestra. Our conductor is constantly saying "Watch me," or "Put eyeglasses in the part there." It's such a mechanical, nonmusical process for her.

D: Doesn't she ask nicely at least?

I: She's not asking, she's just telling us what to do.

D: Hmm. Actually, you need someone to tell you what not to do.

I: What not to do?

D: Musicians rehearse like a sculptor sculpts, not like a painter paints. The painter starts with a blank canvas and adds material until he arrives at the truth. The sculptor eliminates the unwanted conditions in stone or wood until the truth is revealed. Just so, in rehearsal we eliminate conditions that prevent the ultimate experience: too loud, too sharp, too late, too long, too this, too that, too . . . something . . . to allow the magical, spiritual aesthetic experience to result. No, no, no, no, no . . . aaaah. Yes.

I: So rehearsing is a negative process.

D: Not negative in tone, just in substance. Not only does the conductor not need to be abusive, or dictatorial, but in fact the conductor, to be effective, cannot be dictatorial.

I: Because you catch more flies with honey than with vinegar?

D: No, because of the very essential function of the conductor. What's the purpose of the conductor? Why is there a need for a conductor at all?

I: Probably because it's more difficult to hear with so many people on one stage.

D: It certainly can be more difficult to hear, but generally that's not a debilitating problem. More often than not, orchestras can be arranged on stage so that the members can hear each other. So hearing isn't the major problem; it's seeing that's the problem.

I: But . . . making music is about hearing. Why do we have to worry about seeing?

D: Music *is* hearing. We make music only by hearing. You are right.

I: We had a guest conductor recently with the most extensive collection of colored pencils; his score was marked up like a Christmas tree. And the parts . . . I could barely see the notes for all the markings.

D: A score marked up like that is a red flag. It suggests that the conductor makes music with his eyes, not his ears. And if that's the case, then the process for him involves the musicians doing the same. And if the musicians make music with their eyes and not their ears, then we listeners have no hope of achieving any kind of aesthetic transcendence via open listening.

I: But sometimes we do have to make some markings, no?

D: Oh absolutely, as long as the markings are only hints—just like the composer's dynamic, tempo, and articulation markings are hints. But the determinant of any musical inflection, anything that might be marked, is the quality of the experience that it yields. If the musicians are sensitive to the conditions in sound under which beauty may come about, they are infinitely more likely to create those conditions than if they are responding to a visual stimulus.

I: What's the difference whether a conductor is telling us to watch their gestures or to follow the written instructions? It's the same problem: they're letting the visual element supersede the aural. So why do you say we need a conductor so that we can see?

D: In your string quartet, you play together in every way because you hear together, assuming it is a sublime performance, that is. But you have the added security that comes from being able to see your partners. You see them breathe, you see their bows. Your hearing is the sole determinant of everything about the way you join them. Your vision confirms the information you receive by hearing.

I: So the conductor's job is only to confirm?

D: In part. A conductor becomes necessary when the ensemble is too big for all the players to have visual contact with every other player. But whether it's an orchestra, a string quartet, a chorus, whatever—music is made on the basis of hearing; our vision only confirms what we hear.

I: What about the beginning of a piece. Of course we need the visual cue there.

D: Yes, but it's an issue of confirming the musicians' energy, not creating it. In fact, the purpose of the conductor's preparatory beat is not essentially to dictate the temporal point at which to begin.

I: Wha . . .

D: At the start of the piece, all the musicians are ready to come together. The silence before the beginning allows a process of communal uniting-of-consciousness on the part of the musicians. The visual signal—whether it is from the quartet's first violinist, or the orchestra's conductor, or the pianist in a sonata performance—does not dictate when to start. Rather it is a coalescing agent that allows the musicians to lock in their consciousnesses synchronously from the very first sound.

I: That's nuts. Of course it dictates when to start.

D: Why do you think the great orchestras begin together in the face of incomprehensible preparatory beats from conductors, preparatory beats that would bring about mayhem in lesser orchestras?

I: I don't know—maybe some equally mystical powers from these great conductors.

D: Pah! The orchestra members are so experienced, and such good musicians, and such great instrumentalists, that they are open to the process of coming together in the context of the given composition to be performed, and it doesn't take much for them to lock in together.

I: What about tempo? Doesn't the conductor's preparation indicate how fast to play?

D: The conductor's preparation doesn't dictate that any more than the first violinist's signal in a string quartet dictates it. In the quartet all four are ready for the experience, all four have a very similar idea of the tempo, so that when the first violinist gives a signal, all of the ensemble members' consciousnesses lock in to a single, collective consciousness. Try this with your quartet. With your eyes closed—or better yet sitting back-to-back—get ready to begin a performance. No visual cues, no audible cues, nothing. There will come a momentary silence in the room—an intense concentration—and you will each individually sense the moment that it is time to play. It will be a matter of a second or two of silence, and then you'll sense the right time to play. You will be shocked to discover how close you are. I've seen this myself with orchestras—all eyes closed, so there are no visual cues whatsoever—and people begin astonishingly close together. The visual cue from the conductor or concertmaster or first violinist doesn't dictate a temporal location from a blank slate; it merely coalesces, synchronizes, locks in similarly attuned consciousnesses.

I: And an entrance that's not together?

D: When an ensemble doesn't enter together it is because the consciousnesses of the musicians are not joined—some or all do not have a similar idea of the tempo; some or all have not entered the world of the performance about to begin. This may of course be because the signal was sufficiently poor that the musicians were unable to join into a collective consciousness. Or there may have been some other reason, such as that the tempo was not part of their consciousnesses.

I: Okay, but you're not saying this is the conductor's only function—confirming stuff and getting out of the way.

D: No, the conductor joins the musicians.

I: Joins? Wait a minute. The conductor's job is to control the performance . . . to shape it, to create it, to give it life.

D: Yes and no. The conductor is in one sense the least important person on stage by far, because—ideally—she makes no sounds. But in a critical way the conductor is also the most influential, because she's the only person with visual contact with all the players. And so the conductor takes on a global responsibility, and a global influence.

I: But not by showing us her wishes?

D: By joining. Let's consider your quartet. If the first violin has a melody and the viola and cello have an accompanying figure, the violin will influence their sound, intonation, volume, and so on, assuming of course that the consciousnesses are locked in together. Similarly, the viola and cello sounds in turn will influence the violin. Now if the conductor's gestures are synchronous with the sounds, locked in with the sounds, she has a similar kind of influence, not in terms of intonation, but certainly in terms of volume, duration, and temporal placement, and possibly timbre. So she joins, connects, influences.

I: But the bottom line is that she has to lead.

D: As a famous conductor said, "I don't want to lead, because I don't want to follow." The bottom line is that in an ideal situation the conductor participates with the musicians. She walks a fine line between on one hand dictating to musicians who perform to her demands, and on the other ceding responsibility to musicians. Ideally the conductor comes to the process with a good idea of how the tones can come to life to result in the most magical experience. And ideally, the musicians come to the process open to the exalting possibilities of the sounds, open to the experience that results from playing with superb ensemble, or phrasing inflections, or tempo inflections, or articulation, or, or, or, or, or—as demanded by the sounds. On the contrary, if they come with a consciousness focused on the conductor's demands, or the visual cues, or the ink on the page . . .

I: . . . it cannot be focused on the sounds, and therefore it cannot respond to the sounds, and therefore the sounds cannot come as an indivisible object, and therefore . . .

D: . . . no magical, aesthetic experience could possibly result.

I: It sounds like the conductor is more of a guru than a musician.

D: Yes. Yes, exactly. Ideally the conductor is a guru, the musicians are gurus, we are all gurus. When we are doing our job to the highest extent possible, we are gurus, for the sounds we make are spiritual guides, guides to enlightenment, to self-knowledge, to exaltation.

I: I'm a little concerned—you're starting to make sense to me.

D: You should be more concerned—you're starting to make sense to me.

April 16

I: We talked about technical considerations yesterday, and I think I have a pretty good grip on the responsibilities of a performer there. But I'm still struggling with musical considerations—how we play musically, you know, questions of interpretation.

D: Let me just finish sweeping up these cobwebs. (*descending from a stepstool*) So. You feel as though you understand the logical necessity behind why you have to play well technically. Let's see, we discussed intonation, and balance, and ensemble. But you find another, different element of performing, which you define as the "musical" element, having to do with interpretation. Is that about it?

I: Yes, in a nutshell.

D: Good. Unfortunately, there is no such thing.

I: Uh-oh. Here we go again. What do you mean, no such thing—no such thing as what?

D: Sit down. Make yourself at home. Now . . . let's start with this question. What do you mean by interpretation?

I: You know, phrasing inflections, pacing, character, articulations, quality of sound.

D: And you think these are at the discretion of the performer—therefore they become elements of his individual interpretation?

I: That's what I've been assuming, yes.

D: And it is also at the discretion of the performer to play in tune, with good ensemble, and so on.

I: (*pensively*) You're . . . you're saying that it's the same question? You're saying that a performer has as much discretion about interpretative issues as about intonation?

D: Precisely. Let's take phrasing inflections.

I: Okay, but we already heard that the composer gave us the shape of the phrase, by virtue of the melodic shape, the harmony, the dynamic inflections, and rhythm, and like that. It's given to us.

D: It is and it isn't. The composer suggests a tone, B♭, let's say. What are the original attributes of the tone?

I: Pitch, duration, volume, and timbre, and temporal placement.

D: Which of these are specific, fixed, inviolable, and which are at the discretion of the performer.

I: Pitch is . . . no, duration . . . no—when you think about it all of them are at the discretion of the performer, more or less.

D: How so?

I: Well, the pitch is given, B♭, say. But, as we know, there is a latitude of frequencies within which we would accept a tone as a B♭.

D: And on what basis does the performer decide exactly which frequency to choose?

I: On the basis of the requirement to play in tune.

D: There is no requirement to play in tune.

I: Yeah, yeah; on the basis of the requirement to not play out of tune.

D: No. There is no requirement that anyone play in tune, or not play out of tune. It's not required.

I: But . . . of course you have to play in tune. What do you mean? If you want to have a sublime experience, you must play in tune.

D: Of course. There is no obligation to play in tune. There is no obligation to have a sublime experience from music. But to have one, you must not play out of tune. And temporal placement? Where you begin the tone?

I: Well I guess it's up to the performer to place the tone where it belongs so that it will be together with the other tones . . .

D: . . . among other things. But go on . . .

I: And he chooses where to place the tone so that the ensemble will be good, and he doesn't particularly have to do that either, unless he wants to provide a good musical experience, because if the tones do not sound together, the object comes as multiple, and it is up to the subject to judge the tones, and no loss-of-self experience, et cetera.

D: Right. And where is the discretion of the performer?

I: In this case, you wouldn't think in terms of discretion. You would imagine that the performer has an obligation to play in tune, and with good ensemble.

D: So it's not part of the performer's interpretation whether or not he plays in tune, or with good ensemble? Only that he must do so for the sounds to provide the kind of object that will allow a great experience?

I: Yes.

D: Now, consider a chord that comes to you as joined magically in tune. Is it possible that someone else will have a better experience if the chord is tuned differently?

I: No.

D: You're sure?

I: Yes. I think that once I have that incredible, magical sensation of the chord coming absolutely in tune, if it were tuned differently it would be out of tune, and it wouldn't provide a great experience.

D: What about the volume of that B♭?

I: Volume affects a few things. Like balance, as we heard.

D: Is it the performer's obligation to play in balance?

I: Yes, I think so. The performer must be obligated to play within a structure of balance that can yield a magical experience, for the same reason that he is obligated to play in tune with good ensemble.

D: So the volume of the B♭ might be determined by the requirement to play in sublime balance, which has to happen for the object to be indivisible, which has to happen for the performance to allow a magical, sublime experience. And if we are not concerned with a magical, sublime experience, then it does not matter whether or not the object comes to us as indivisible, and then it does not matter if we structure the volume in terms of balance. Where then is our interpretation? Could different people have a different idea—a different interpretation—of good balance?

I: My intuition is that chords beautifully in balance will provide a similar high experience to anyone who comes fully open to them. And that chords not in balance will likewise provide a lesser experience to anyone.

D: It's either in tune or not, it's either in balance or not?

I: Yes.

D: So is balance for us to interpret, or is it given by the requirement of providing a magical, sublime experience?

I: I can see how you would say it's given.

D: What do you say?

I: Okay, it's given.

D: What other aspect of music besides balance is determined by volume.

I: Phrasing inflections?

D: Yes. In some cases it's the same thing.

I: I'm not sure I understand.

D: Let's take a major triad. Write an E♭-major triad on the blackboard there (ex. 4.5◀》).

Icarus writes.

How must we structure those tones so they come to us as an indivisible unit?

I: Down from the B♭, like this.

Icarus plays the three tones on the piano simultaneously, balanced beautifully down from the B♭.

D: To present those tones in sound in such a way that they can join into one indivisible consciousness of them you structure the volume so that the G supports the B♭, and the E♭ supports the G?

I: Yes.

D: Now, what would the difference be between the relation of the three tones sounded simultaneously, as you wrote it, and the relation of the three tones sounded in succession, like this (ex. 4.6◀))?

I: Hmm. I guess . . . well . . . just in terms of temporal placement.

D: Outside of temporal placement, what's the difference?

I: Ummm . . . I can't think of any.

D: "*Ummm*" Of course you can't think of any. There is no difference!

I: Right. There's no difference.

D: So what? So what does that mean?

I: I imagine it means that if we structure the sounds up to the top B♭ when the tones sound simultaneously, then we would structure them up to the top B♭ when they sound in succession.

D: Why? To what end? Why would we structure them up to the B♭ when sounding simultaneously?

I: Calm down. I got it. So they come to us all together, as an indivisible object. So that's the reason for structuring the tones up to the B♭ when they sound in succession?

D: Yes. Bravo. So try it. Play the triad simultaneously, so that it comes to you as a single, indivisible object. Then unfold the triad in succession, also so that it comes to you as a single, indivisible object (ex. 4.7◀)).

Icarus plays the two triads.

I: It's the same. It is the same. The same structure of volume, growing up to the top.

D: Let's examine some music in which this occurs. How about the opening Allegro from the "Harp" Quartet? After the first chord, how can you structure those next three chords so they come to you as an indivisible object?

I: First, each chord must be balanced, each chord must be structured so that it comes as its own indivisible object.

D: Yes, and . . .

I: And second, over the course of the three chords, it's structured by the unfolding of the three triads, up to the top-line B♭.

D: Absolutely. Try it (ex. 4.8◄))).

Icarus plays the first three chords, growing up to the third.

I: Yes. There's a crescendo up to the final chord.

D: I wouldn't use the term "crescendo," because that implies a substantial increase in volume, but certainly the volume does grow all within a *forte* dynamic. What about the opening of Beethoven's Piano Concerto No. 3. How does the performer structure the sound (ex. 4.9◄))?

Icarus plays the passage several times, structuring the volume differently each time.

I: It makes the most sense to me if it follows the line this time—if the height comes with the G, and if we structure the volume down from there. So it would match the structure of the balanced C-minor chord.

D: Really? Try letting the volume grow to the first quarter note C (ex. 4.10◄)).

Icarus tries again.

I: (*frustrated*) It just doesn't feel right. It doesn't sound . . . logical. Any hints?

D: Patterns of energy.

I: Patterns of energy?

D: Patterns of energy—dynamic structure. Not in the sense of dynamics, remember, but in the sense of energy. Impulse and resolution. Let's listen to these fragments in terms of the dynamic structure.

I: Well in the case of the "Harp" Quartet fragment, there is only impulse.

D: There is? What would you say then had Beethoven composed this (ex. 4.11 ◀))?

I: Well it's squeezed. There's no time for it to breathe.

D: In terms of dynamic structure?

I: The eighth-note passage is growing—building energy.

D: Yes. But the first *piano* eighth note represents a drop in impulse from the last chord. The impulse is growing through those eighth notes. So the eighth notes participate in their own grouping, different from the chords. But we want to know about the grouping that includes the chords, and not that of the ensuing eighth notes. Play the passage as Beethoven gave it to us, with the silence after the downbeat (ex. 4.12 ◀)).

Icarus plays.

I: It's in the rest! The resolution is in the rest! The grouping begins with impulse that grows until the final chord, and then is resolved within the rest. That's why it feels squeezed if you leave out the rest.

D: Perhaps not only in the rest. But the rest plays a big part in the resolution. Now perform the passage with a structure of volume that falls from the first of the three chords (ex. 4.13 ◀)).

Icarus plays.

I: Not enough impulse. The energy dies. So we have to make the impulse happen. The performer is responsible for the dynamic structure. *We* have to do it. But I thought back in February when we discussed phrases it seemed as though the composer gave us the dynamic structure.

D: The composer gives us a landscape, a succession of tones that combine into a variety of factors affecting dynamic structure. A possibility. Of course we can structure them in an infinite variety of ways, just like there is an infinite number of positions for B♭ that satisfies the composer's requirement. The composer writes an ascending melodic line, and yes, an ascending line may suggest impulse. It may provide some. Yes, a harmonic expansion may suggest impulse, and provide some. A metric conflict may suggest impulse, and so on. But the impulse is not in the written sounds. The impulse is in our experience of the sounds. And we experience only performed sounds. The performer brings those sounds into existence in order to bring us to a higher plane. A guru. The performer plays in tune because playing out of tune prevents us from transcending. And the performer plays with a structure of energy for the same reason. There is no difference between so-called technical issues and so-called interpretive issues. So, on the local level of phrases, volume is our most powerful tool in putting forth the dynamic structure. When we say it is the obligation of the performer to make the music, it follows that it is up to the performer to structure the volume in a way that creates a pattern of impulse and resolution . . . for what end?

I: Well the end has to be the musical experience. So it is up to the performer to present the sounds within a structure of impulse and resolution that allows the object to be absorbed as indivisible.

D: Yes. *Yes!* The ascending line creates impulse, but how much? The harmonic expansion creates impulse, but how much? The ritard, the diminuendo, resolve impulse, but how much? That is the performer's responsibility, and it is pretty well given: enough impulse to accommodate the ensuing resolution; enough resolution to play out the impulse created.

I: This sounds quite fascistic, though—like you think everyone should play exactly the way you want.

D: Not at all. I am not suggesting that anyone play the way I want them to. I am suggesting that everyone should play the way they want, in the way that is necessary for them to have the most magical experience. What is true is that while you can have ultimate, maximally exalting performances that may and must differ in tempo, volume, color, et cetera, et cetera, they will all—they must all—unfold the same structure of energy, as required by the landscape given by the composition.

I: The composer guides us. So he's *our* guru.

D: The composer is our guru, and we are the audience's, through the medium of the tones we produce. The composer and the performer are partners in the process, this business of providing sounds that can allow the most high, sublime, spiritual musical experience.

I: So my conductor's philosophy of "play what's on the page and let the composer speak for himself" is flawed because the loss-of-self experience couldn't happen if we didn't structure the sounds . . . for example if we just played all the notes the same volume because the composer just wrote *piano?*

D: (*barely audible*) How loud am I speaking now?

I: Softly. (*to himself*) For once!

D: And in speaking softly, is there inflection in my voice over the course of a sentence? Or does every syllable come at exactly the same volume?

I: Inflections, of course.

D: But still overall I'm speaking softly?

I: Thank goodness, yes. So in music it's the same!

D: *Absolutely the same!* Play the opening of the Beethoven concerto with every tone at precisely the same volume, and tell me what you think (ex. 4.14◀》).

Icarus plays the passage with every note at the same volume.

I: No, it's lifeless. Quite unmusical.

D: Unmusical. Yes, I think so too. Is the composer "speaking for himself?" But conductors have to say something authoritative, and rather than use their ears, the easiest thing is simply to look at the score and see a *piano* written and say most authoritatively, "Don't make any crescendo, because none is written." That's like plowing into a traffic jam at 40 miles an hour because you read the "Minimum speed: 40 mph" sign. Of course a minimum speed limit does not mean that you drive at that speed at all times, and of course a single dynamic mark applicable to a multitude of tones does not mean that all the tones are to come with precisely the same volume.

I: So then can we say that in order to unfold a line so that it can be absorbed as indivisible, the tones must be structured in such a way that if they sounded simultaneously they would be in balance? How do we know that?

D: How do we know anything about music?

I: By listening.

D: Of course. By listening. If it grabs you, if it absorbs you in a magical, sublime way, then your phrasing is apt—it will lead to a great experience. You know it will, because you had one. If it isn't structured in the most musical way, it will bother you, either immediately, or in time, as you continue to listen openly. I have found occasionally that I have structured things in less than the most musical way, in a way that might seem logical at first, but little by little as I continue to hear the passage it becomes increasingly bothersome. I actually feel a physical discomfort right at the back of my neck.

I: It's hard for me to believe.

D: That I could feel pain from it?

I: No, that you might have structured things in less than the most musical way.

D: (*laughing*) *Hah!*

* * *

I: Let me go over this. The composer gives us some tones, some relationships, that suggest maybe a certain structure of impulse and resolution. And when we make those tones in sound, we can bring about that structure of impulse and resolution within the landscape given to us by the composer. And in order to unfold the tones so that they yield the highest experience, we bring that landscape to life so that the impulse created is played out by the resolution.

D: We create energy, and resolve it—no more and no less. We create patterns of energy such that the energy we create is resolved fully. Yes, that's it, essentially. So what does "interpretation" mean?

I: (*pensive*) If . . . your . . . goal . . . is . . . this . . . highest . . . potential . . . of . . . music, then the sounds demand their unfolding, and then there isn't room for our participation in the interpretation.

D: *No . . . wrong!* We make the sounds, we bring them to life, we create the relationships. There are no relationships without us to do them. It is absolutely our human sensitivity to what is required of the sounds for the most magical experience that allows us to unfold them in the most sublime way. So of course we participate in the process. We *are* the process; how the sounds unfold is entirely up to us.

I: But not our discretion?

D: Of course, it is entirely at our discretion.

I: Okay. You win. I'm totally confused.

D: Let's think first about what the goal is, and then perhaps we can think about how you understand the notions of interpretation or discretion. Let us state right off that our goal is the most sublime experience of music. If your understanding of interpretation includes bringing the sounds into existence in a way that allows a sublime experience, yes we do that. If it includes the performer's requirement to be sensitive to the demands of the sounds and to unfold the sounds to satisfy those demands, then yes we absolutely do that. If it includes the latitude to do those things in different ways, faster, slower, louder, softer, to greater or lesser degrees, absolutely we have the complete liberty and discretion to do that. If, however, our goal is not the most sublime experience, then there is much greater liberty. Consider the high-wire performer. If the goal is to remain on the wire, the performer must maintain equilibrium. He has all the freedom—the interpretive discretion, if you will—that he wants, so long as he maintains equilibrium. Without the necessity of staying on the wire he has a much greater freedom of movement. Just so in music. To stay in this loss-of-self, transcendent state, we must structure the flow of energy, constantly in touch with our equilibrium: the balance of impulse and resolution. If we have a different goal, there is unlimited room for interpretation. Unfortunately, though, the robotic high-wire artist and the mechanical performer who act without accommodating variables—a gust of wind, a particularly resonant room, an unexpected surge of energy—will both find an unhappy end. Unlike the high-wire performer, the musician who chooses a goal other than maintaining equilibrium will not put himself or anyone else in any physical danger—he will only jeopardize the possibility of a most sublime experience. But any musician may at any time forsake the goal of the most sublime experience. Any musician may be a so-called servant of the composer and bring about a mechanical, literal unfolding of the tones. And any musician may be an interpretive "artiste," who might decide at his discretion to accentuate here, slow down there, and so on. For example: that bad-pianist habit of playing the height of an ascending line softer, in order to make it "special," thereby decapitating the climax of the phrase. But there is nothing wrong with that; we must concede the performer's right to interpret the tones in any way he desires.

I: This is a very a difficult task, though, isn't it? That every note, every phrase, every passage must be just precisely so, or you lose the highest possibility.

D: Yes. No doubt. Nobody said doing music as well as it can be done would be easy. Nobody said doing anything as well as it can be done would be easy. But the advantage of music is that all you have to do is listen. And as you listen more and more, and absorb more and more, the process becomes easier. And after a while you'll come to realize something quite fascinating, that will prove helpful.

I: (*eagerly*) Yes . . .

D: You will find that you can strip the surface ornamentation down to its underlying progression.

I: So?

D: So if the ornamental tone on the musical surface really does represent the underlying "structural" tone, then it represents it in all its attributes. The fact that the surface tone represents the structural tone in its linear and harmonic attributes allows the representational relationship: the surface tone must carry with it elements of the linear and harmonic attributes of the structural tone in order to represent it. Let's consider this progression (ex. 4.15◀》).

To be experienced as a whole unit, the dynamic structure of this phrase must build impulse to the third chord with A in the soprano, and resolve it from there to the end. Now, imagine if we add a chord—say a IV^6 with B♭ in the soprano (ex. 4.16◀》).

The B♭ ornaments the A, it prolongs it, and in so doing it represents the A, in all of its attributes, including linear and harmonic. As a representative of the structural A, the ornamental B♭ carries with it the linear attribute of the structural tone and the harmonic attribute of the structural tone as well.

I: Okay, no problem. But what's the big deal. Didn't Schenker and others already show us that?

D: Yes, but here is a remarkable thing. The ornamental tone represents the structural tone in all its attributes, including that of dynamic function. Thus if the structural tone contributes to the impulse within the structural progression, the ornamental tone carries that attribute as well, it contributes on some level to the impulse.

I: Okay, I can hear that. The climax of the structural progression in the soprano line is A; when the B♭ is added, it—the B♭—becomes the climax. As a representative of the A, it also carries the dynamic function of the A, which is climactic.

D: And this is critical because it is this hierarchy of dynamic function that allows for an extended work or movement to be apprehended as a single unit. Let's review. For a work to be apprehended in an indivisible act of consciousness, the entire work must come as a single articulation, with a single, large-scale impulse and a single, large-scale resolution. Both the extended impulse and extended resolution divide into a hierarchy of smaller and smaller articulations: sections, and periods, and phrases, and motives, and so on. In order for any smaller, nested articulation to further the gathering or release of energy on a higher level in the hierarchy, the tones that make up the nested articulation must carry with them that attribute of higher-level impulse or resolution. So a tone may participate in impulse within its motive, which participates in the resolution within its phrase, which participates in impulse within its section, which participates in resolution on the highest level of the whole piece. As you suggested, Schenker demonstrated to us clearly that the linear and harmonic functions are hierarchical, but if the dynamic function were not also hierarchical, there would be no possibility of unitary apprehension; each successive articulation would stand on its own, separated from the others by its structure of impulse and resolution. Obviously that isn't the case. Obviously units, defined by a structure of impulse and resolution, are nested within larger impulses or resolutions, which participate in units (also defined by impulse and resolution) which participate in a yet larger impulse or resolution, and so on.

I: So by extension, even the climax of the entire piece on its surface will represent the harmonic event that serves as the climax of the background controlling progression.

D: Yes, absolutely.

I: This large-scale grouping, on the level of the whole piece—it must also be up to us performers again to bring it about.

D: Yes. It won't happen on its own.

I: So again we do it with volume?

D: In fact, no. Volume will not directly assist our large-scale unitary unfolding of a work, although it may assist it in an indirect way. What is our tool? What other attributes of the tones become our domain in creating the large-scale articulation?

I: It's certainly not pitch, we know it's not the volume, timbre seems to be too subtle for such a broad purpose, duration seems too subtle as well. That leaves temporal placement.

D: And how would temporal placement affect the creation of large-scale dynamic structure?

I: Tempo, is my guess. Pacing.

D: Yes. But let's use a more meaningful term than pacing—let's say tempo orientation. But first, let's examine what we mean by tempo. Tempo is similar to, but different from, physical speed. Tempo belongs to the consciousness, speed belongs to physical reality. Tempo does not exist in physical reality, in the same way that a melody does not exist in physical reality, but only in our consciousness of the tones. The tempo depends in large measure on the speed, but other factors enter into it as well. Listen to this melody, and pay careful attention to the quality of motion—the nature of the motion (ex. 4.17◀♪)).

I: It's . . . flowing.

D: Now listen to this. Pay attention not to the physical speed, but focus your consciousness only on the quality of the motion (ex. 4.18◀♪)).

I: The quality of the motion was a bit hurried . . . somewhat faster.

D: Faster, but what happened to the physical speed? It stayed absolutely the same. In the course of a musical experience, where is your consciousness of speed?

I: Ummm . . .

D: Nonexistent. Physical speed is not part of your consciousness during a transcendent musical experience, any more than decibel level is, or frequency is.

I: Doesn't speed enter into in a big way, though? Like decibel level and frequency. If the decibel level goes up, the volume goes up, the impulse increases. If the frequency goes up the pitch goes up.

D: Yes, but consider frequency for a moment. The frequency of an A is irrelevant. If you are in Berlin it might be 450, Boston, 446, Cleveland, 442. The frequency of an A in bar 2 might be 435, in bar 20 it might be 440, and 445 in bar 200, either because the pitch of the orchestra is going up, as it tends to do, or because the A in different harmonic or melodic contexts must have different frequencies to be in tune. Is the frequency relevant? Only in that it must be sufficiently high or low to be in tune, to join with the other tones in a singular object. What about decibel level. The same tone could have a decibel level of 40.1 in one sublime performance, 39.9 in another; is the decibel level relevant? In itself, not at all. It is only relevant to the extent that the tone is present at a sufficient volume to join with the other tones in a celestial balance or a magically unfolded phrase. Phrasing inflection is a condition of the sounds within your consciousness that results from the physical element of volume; under the proper circumstances, phrasing inflection may allow for an indivisible experience of the sounds. In a very similar way, tempo is a condition of the sounds within your consciousness that results largely, but not exclusively, from the physical speed; under the proper circumstances, tempo may allow for an indivisible experience of the sounds.

I: What would those circumstances be?

D: Do you remember when we were at the museum back in December? We walked away from and toward the painting in order to find an ideal point from which to view it.

I: Of course. When we were too close we were unable to include the entire painting within our focused field of vision. And when we were too far away we couldn't limit our field of vision only to the painting. Of course I remember. Every time I look at a painting, the first thing I do is find the ideal viewing point.

D: Good. Now there is another aspect of the distance from the painting that we can consider. When we are too close to the painting the details become overly prominent, and unconnected to the entire visual image offered by the painting. And when we were too far away the details become somewhat blurred or indistinguishable from each other; the painting loses the relationship of its component percepts. In neither case can we have a magical aesthetic experience. In music, tempo is the condition within which we can absorb the sounds as a singular, indivisible object. If the tempo is too slow, it is analogous to being too close to the painting; the details—the individual tones and smaller groupings—become overly prominent and lose their connection to the whole. And if the tempo is too fast, then the details become blurred against each other and lose their distinction.

I: But ideally the tones are not distinct; ideally the tones come as indivisible, no?

D: Yes, but remember it is the unfolding of the individual tones within the hierarchy of groupings that results in the indivisible performance. Remember the boy and his dog? The two must be distinct to have a relationship. Tones must contribute on an individual basis so that there can be a blend. If the tones do not contribute on an individual basis there is nothing to be blended—no *thing* to be blended—whether that lack of being—lack of thing-ness in the consciousness—results from being swallowed by lower tones that are too loud, or jumbled in a tempo that is too fast.

I: How do we find the tempo then? Obviously if the composer gives us a metronome mark it's helpful, but otherwise?

D: Metronome? *Metronome?* The day I learn something about music from a metronome is the day I will study with one.

I: But . . .

D: But what? Are you not listening? Is your mind not open? Metronomes are about physical reality. Tempo is the quality of motion. Which is faster, careening downhill on a bicycle at 40 miles per hour, or driving your luxury car with the windows closed on a deserted highway at 80 miles per hour?

I: I had to sell my luxury car, remember. But I don't think it ever could go 80 miles per hour.

D: Which is faster?

I: Driving the car is faster, twice as fast—80 as compared to 40.

D: Which feels faster. In which experience is the sensation of speed greatest?

I: On the bicycle.

D: Even though in physical reality it is only half as fast?

I: Yes.

D: You say the bicycle definitely feels faster even though you know that in reality the car is faster?

I: Yes.

D: In music there is no such thing as reality outside of our experience. Our experience *is* the reality. The only fact of musical tempo is the sensation of motion.

I: But I can measure the tempo. This one is "quarter note equals 60," this one is "quarter equals 72."

D: And where is your consciousness when you make those measurements?

I: Ummm . . .

D: Not on the sounds. Not absorbed in the musical object exclusively. Your consciousness is focused on the relation between the sounds and some measuring machine. Transcendent musical experience? Loss of self?

I: No.

D: So what brings about a tempo? What brings about a perception of motion? What accounts for the perception of the bicycle trip as faster than the car trip, or the perception that the lower, louder version of Twinkle, Twinkle is faster than the higher, softer version?

I: Darned if I know.

D: Which is faster, a trombone playing Twinkle, Twinkle in a practice room or in the football stadium.

I: Faster? My guess is that it would seem faster in the practice room.

D: Mine too. Why so?

I: In the stadium the sound would disappear, it would be weak.

D: And in the practice room?

I: It would be very present.

D: What is happening to the sound waves in the practice room that is not happening in the stadium?

I: In the practice room they are bouncing back and forth from wall to wall. In the stadium they just keep on going.

D: And if you are in the practice room listening . . .

I: . . . the sound waves strike your ears more often.

D: There is your answer. More information. Tempo is a condition that results from the amount of information you are given to process. The more information you process, the faster your perception of motion. Why did the bicycle ride seem faster than the car ride?

I: More information maybe—from wind resistance? You don't feel the wind resistance in the car.

D: And why was the lower, louder Twinkle, Twinkle faster than the higher, softer version?

I: More information. Because it was louder, the amplitude of the sound waves was bigger, and so there was more information to process. But lower?

D: More overtones within our field of hearing.

I: So physical speed doesn't have anything to do with it.

D: Now wait a minute. That's not true. Physical speed has a great deal to do with it. The faster you play something, the more information you are providing. Physical speed influences tempo more than any other factor. But when you experience tempo you are experiencing something other than physical speed.

I: I understand this. But if the composer gives a metronome mark don't you have to pay attention to it? And even if the answer is no, doesn't it help?

D: Luckily we have recordings of composers conducting their own music. Who was wrong, Stravinsky the composer or Stravinsky the conductor, when his performances varied by 40 or more points from his markings? Who was wrong,

Copland the conductor or Copland the composer? When these men were conducting, they were using their ears and responding to the sounds made by live musicians in specific rooms for a musical end. Not just speculating with a pen. How important to us are Tchaikovsky's metronome marks? Or the metronome marks of that crazy man Beethoven—marks that he made when he was virtually completely deaf for pieces he wrote years before—how much like gospel do we treat those? About as much as Brahms's metronome marks.

I: But Brahms didn't write metronome marks.

D: Exactly! Brahms understood that if you can't find the tempo, a metronome isn't going to help you. And if you can find the tempo then of what use is the metronome? Yes, that's precisely it.

I: Well how about at least to help us know the pulse. If a composer writes a metronome mark of half note equals something, as opposed to quarter note, wouldn't that tell us the pulse?

D: Conceivably, but then you have conductors beating the first movement of Eroica in one, one beat to the bar, because Beethoven put a metronome mark of dotted half equals 60. Of course that's obscenely fast, but that's beside the point. His metronome only went up to 150, so had he wanted to write "quarter note equals 180" he couldn't have.

I: How do you know that's obscenely fast? How do you find the tempo?

D: Just like you find the frequency of a pitch that must be in tune. Trial and error to begin with, but the determinant is that you find the quality of motion that allows for the absorption of all the sounds in the indivisible act of consciousness. And remember there is a latitude in tempo as well. So we're not aiming for it to be in the right tempo, we're aiming for it not to be in the wrong tempo . . . not too fast and not too slow.

I: But you said that we use tempo orientation to structure the dynamic forces on the broadest level. How so?

D: By orienting the tempo forward or backward. It's quite simple. Allow the tempo to move forward toward the climactic point of greatest expansion, the height of the impulse. And allow it to settle back through the course of the playing out of that impulse.

I: You mean speed up and slow down?

D: I mean allow the tempo to go forward, by providing a greater rate of information. That might mean adjusting the speed, and it might mean other factors as well, such as playing louder, or with a greater degree of volume inflections.

I: But doesn't the composition do that for you? Isn't the large-scale impulse the job of the composer?

D: Remember that Beethoven symphony performance a couple of weeks ago? Among the problems with that performance was the large-scale structure of the first movement. Immediately after the climax the conductor dropped the tempo, and let it move forward all the way into the recapitulation. Instead of releasing energy back home to the recapitulation, as that music screamed for from any remotely sensate human being. But this deaf conductor . . . if it had been a house it would have fallen down.

I: But it was a piece of music, so no one noticed.

D: (*looking at his watch*) Speaking of physical time, it's getting quite late.

I: I know you have to go soon. But just a couple more questions? What if the performer plays at one steady tempo all the way throughout, wouldn't that allow the large-scale structure to come through, as a result of the harmonic motion and fragmentation?

D: What if the performer plays a phrase at one steady volume throughout, wouldn't that allow the phrasing inflections to come through?

I: No it wouldn't. Okay, okay. But what about tempo inflections written by the composer? He wants you to relax the tempo. He writes ritardando. But how much do I ritard?

D: Six.

I: Huh?

D: Six, precisely.

I: (*quizzically*) Huh? Oh, okay, I get the point. You relax the tempo as much as is needed to release the energy. But what about pieces that end loud? Or like the end of the last movement of the "Harp" Quartet, which ends with a crescendo and an accelerando?

D: Volume has little if anything to do with large-scale impulse. So in a piece with a loud ending, what is effecting the resolution is the harmonic settling on the home key. The accelerando at the end of the Beethoven movement is unusual, but again it's the harmonic settling on the home tonic E♭ major that is releasing energy. And what would you speculate is the reason for the accelerando?

I: Otherwise there would be too much resolution?

D: Of course. Now I'm afraid I must rush out too.

I: (*thinking*) All right, all right, all right, okay, okay. But there are some more questions that keep popping up. Like everyone is always talking about style. Stylistically appropriate performance. Is that important? Or emotions—we sort of left that issue hanging . . .

Daedalus opens the door for Icarus.

Okay, I'm leaving. How about tomorrow?

D: Tomorrow, or whenever *you* are ready to tell *me* about emotions, and style. Come find me when you're ready to explain it to me.

I: You got it!

May 15

D: Where have you been? I haven't seen you in a while.

I: Holed up. Trying to work this stuff out for myself. Like you told me to.

D: Not practicing?

I: You wanted me to practice, too? Why didn't you tell me? Of *course* I've been practicing . . . and rehearsing . . . and thinking. We've been asked to perform the "Harp" Quartet at the graduation ceremony.

D: Congratulations. How is it going?

I: It's going all right, I guess. I'm still up in the air over a number of things. Like the repeat in the first movement. Do we or don't we take it. They say take it, because Beethoven wrote it, and if we screw anything up the first time, then we have a second chance at it.

D: And you say?

I: Unsure. That argument is logical, but when I try to hear the entire piece, it doesn't seem to make sense. We got where we got by the end of the exposition; why just go back where we started? But . . . on the other hand . . .

D: On the other hand?

I: On the other hand we do take the repeats in the third and fourth movements, and it doesn't seem to bother me.

D: Excellent. You're in good shape, you understand the issues. In fact, if you take the repeat of a sonata-form exposition you ruin all hope of unitary apprehension of the movement.

I: But why is that so?

D: It's very simple, really. What is the function of the exposition of a sonata-form movement?

I: Creates contrast, A material to B material. It sets something up and then creates energy by presenting something contrasting.

D: Yes, and what happens to the contrast if you·hear it again? What is the effect on the contrast made by the B material if you hear the exposition a second time then?

I: I'm not sure. It's reduced?

D: Criminal defense lawyers with shocking visual evidence against their client sometimes show it over and over to a jury because seeing it repeatedly reduces the horror factor. Yes, the contrast is reduced. And what is the purpose of the contrast?

I: To create impulse.

D: Then what happens to the impulse if you play the exposition again?

I: Lessened.

D: So what happens to your structure of impulse and resolution? Kaput.

I: That explains a lot. But why is it that when we take the repeat in the first movement of the "Harp" Quartet it feels so out of place, like we've been there already, like we're starting over again. But it doesn't feel that way when we take the repeats in the third and fourth movements. Why could that be?

D: The first movement of that quartet has what form?

I: Sonata-form.

D: And the third and fourth movements?

I: Well the first part of the third movement is a binary dance form. And the fourth is a series of binary dance forms that are variations on a theme.

D: Yes. And the first movement, a sonata-form, depends on substantial contrast. Imagine that you go to a play. The curtain rises and out comes the king: "I am king of all my lands, and all my castles and all my people. I am so happy here, with my lovely wife, the queen, and my little dog." The dog runs in, followed by the queen, who says, "Hello honey. Why, I'll have to have your shirts washed better, there's a stain. A stain? Wait a minute, that's lipstick." KING: "No, no it isn't!" QUEEN: "It is!" "You—you had an affair with the baroness. You lied to me! I want a divorce." And the curtain comes down. Act II. The curtain rises and out comes the king: "I am king of all my lands, and all my castles and all my people. I am so happy here, with my lovely wife, the queen, and my little dog." The dog runs in, followed by the queen: "Hello honey . . ."

I: That's a cute story.

D: Let's think of it another way. You travel from New York to Los Angeles. In Saint Louis you decide you've gone far enough, you want to rest. You find a great spot, set up your tent, dig out a rain trough, chop some firewood. On your way to Los Angeles, remember. What's your next move? Pick up all your things and return to New York? So you can go back to Saint Louis again?

I: No, of course not. So you're saying that this is why you can't take the repeat in sonata-form movements—because you've gone to an intermediary point on the way to somewhere else, and there's no point in simply returning to where you started? But what is the difference in the binary dance form movements? Why is it okay to take the repeats in dance form movements?

D: Because we didn't actually go anywhere firmly. We didn't go as far and we didn't set up camp, we just scouted around. We took one step, and came back. We can take the same step more firmly again, and it will propel us forward on to where we are going. "Why that's lipstick on your shirt." "No, no it isn't" and again "Why that's *lipstick on your shirt!*" "no, *no, No It Isn't!*"

I: But that leads to the obvious question, why did Beethoven, and Mozart, and Mendelssohn, and Brahms, and so on, why did they all write exposition repeats, and even compose out second endings, if they didn't intend for them to be played?

D: Why do the people of Great Britain retain the monarchy if it has no effect?

I: You're saying because it's a tradition that is comforting?

D: And sonata-form repeats are a tradition, from the dance forms. Plus, repeats lengthened the movement. We don't need longer concerts. As time went on, composers began to drop the exposition repeat just as they dropped the development-recapitulation repeat. Brahms dropped it, Bruckner dropped it, Tchaikovsky dropped it, Shostakovich dropped it.

I: Okay, but there is always this issue of balance that everyone brings up—that we need to repeat the exposition to balance the development and resolution.

D: Hmmm. Balance. Wouldn't it be wonderful if there were such a thing as balance on the basis of numbers of bars. There would be an entire library of books explaining composition on the basis of numerical balance, just like there is already half a library of books explaining Bartók's music on the basis of numerical relationships.

I: It's not true about Bartók?

D: Of course it's true, to some extent, but it's irrelevant. Bartók's music succeeds on a different basis entirely than its golden ratio.

I: What basis is that?

D: What basis is that? You tell me.

I: It allows for its apprehension as an indivisible object, in part by allowing for the playing out of the impulse created.

D: *Bongiorno!* The balance within a sonata-form movement, or any composition derives not from any equivalence of bars, or temporal symmetry, but from the dynamic structure. There is a kind of a balance: the impulse must be played out consequently, it must be balanced by a resolution that is appropriate. If repeating the exposition were necessary to balance a piece, and that balance was some kind of requirement for a great piece, then a piece without an exposition repeat could not be a great piece, because it would not be balanced. Is the Ninth Symphony first movement unbalanced? Is Brahms's fourth? Bruckner's seventh?

I: No, of course not.

D: And if in your sonata-form movement you reduce the impulse by repeating the contrast from the exposition, or you interrupt your experience by returning to the beginning after firmly establishing a midpoint, then what happens to your indivisible object? What happens to your magical, sublime experience?

I: But wouldn't it be possible to have an extremely good experience if a great sonata-form movement is performed spectacularly well but the repeat is taken?

D: Extremely good? Yes. Isn't it possible to run fast with a fifty-pound weight on your back? Of course. But without the pack?

I: All right. But just one last question about it: wouldn't the repeated exposition in concerto movements be proof that the exposition should be repeated? In a concerto movement composers had a reason to write out the repeat, because the material would be introduced first in the orchestra and then would be given to the soloist. So couldn't you make a good argument that when they had a reason to write it out they did, and when the repeat would just be verbatim, without a soloist added, they saved themselves the trouble and wrote a repeat sign.

D: On the contrary, the restated exposition in the concerto movement provides clear and unassailable proof that the exposition repeats must be ignored. In a concerto, what key is the second theme in?

I: Usually the dominant.

D: Yes, in the repetition, during the solo entrance. But the first time, in the orchestral introduction?

I: Hmmm. The first time it's in the tonic.

D: Always?

I: I'm guessing most of the time.

D: Ah. And, so?

I: So . . . you didn't really go anywhere, so returning to the tonic for the soloists entrance is perfectly okay.

D: So when composers knew the repeat would be taken what did they do to the second theme? What did they have to do? Leave it in the tonic. If composers expected these repeats to be taken, and expected them to lead to a musical result including a move to the dominant each time, then they would have been perfectly content to do it that way when they wrote out the repeat, as in the concerto movements.

I: Another question—what about the relation of the movements to the whole? When we perform an individual movement do we need to take into account the way that it joins the whole? In other words, is there a climax of the entire multimovement piece within one of the movements, and is there a global structure of energy encompassing all the movements that might affect the way we perform the individual movements?

D: Can a Chinese man and a black man be friends?

I: Sure.

D: Can the Chinese man be free?

I: Yes.

D: Can the black man be free?

I: Yes.

D: And what does it do to their relationship if one or the other is not free?

I: Another enigma. I see. So you're saying just play each movement so that it creates a whole in and of itself. And then the performance will be the most rewarding? Gotcha. I understand. But I've also been troubled by this question of stylistic accuracy. Our violist has been pushing us all to go to an authentic performance seminar next week, so we can play with stylistic accuracy. But I don't know what that means. Does it mean to play the way the composer might have heard it at the first performance? If so, does that mean we have to play with gut strings? Does a stylistically accurate orchestra performance have to include raucous and out of tune woodwind instruments, or natural horns that produce quite different sounds between stopped and open notes? Seems ridiculous.

D: It's not ridiculous . . . not if the performers have as their goal an experience of history. And if people find it interesting and want to pay good money for that then it's perfectly harmless. Better than them hanging on street corners. But seriously, these concerts can even be interesting and fertile in terms of giving historical information.

I: But if their goal is stylistic accuracy, the goal couldn't also be sublime music making, and it doesn't seem likely that sublime music making would result. Not only that, but we can't know how the first performance of a Mozart symphony might have sounded. We know for sure that it would have sounded quite different from city to city, even cities fairly close to each other, because the instruments, instrumental styles and forces, and the intonation systems were often altogether different.

D: What might be meant then by a stylistically appropriate performance? How might we measure it?

I: Some people might say we could measure it by the prevailing standards of performance. For example, some musicologists think tempos were faster in the Baroque era. But I think that's ridiculous too. How would they possibly know? What we know is that tempo is a condition under which we can absorb the sounds. For us to absorb the sounds at a different rate means that there would have to have been a fundamental change in the human acoustic process. Maybe some such evolution could take place over a few hundred thousand years, but certainly not over the last two centuries. What an absurd notion.

D: But there are some broad aspects of performance typical to Baroque times, no? If you study Baroque instruments you'll find that in general, with perhaps the sole exception of the double reed instruments, they produce less volume than modern instruments. Gut strings at lower tensions, harpsichords compared to pianos, much smaller trombones, serpents instead of tubas, smaller timpani, and so on.

I: Are you saying that this affected tempo?

D: With less information the physical speed would have to be faster to achieve the same quality of motion.

I: Here you go, confusing me again. You're saying it's true that Baroque tempos were faster than what we're accustomed to?

D: Actually what I'm saying is that it's irrelevant. We can only experience what we experience; we can only absorb the information that we receive, and we can only find a tempo that—given that information—is not for us too fast or too slow.

I: Isn't there such a thing as changing tastes in performance styles, for instance from late nineteenth-century exuberantly romantic to late twentieth-century more austere? What about grossly inappropriate styles of performance, like the full Berlin Philharmonic string section performing Brandenburg concertos, which are nothing like what Bach would have imagined?

D: Irrelevant, and irrelevant. To us, that is. If your focus is the history of performance styles, then it is certainly of interest. For us seekers of the highest musical experience, there is no consideration such as style independent of the requirement to unfold the tones as an indivisible object. We know that there is a latitude for pitch, for temporal placement, and for physical speed, within which it is possible to achieve the highest experience, and beyond which it is not. Let's consider a couple of elements of that full-string-section Brandenburg concerto performance that you found so distasteful. To accommodate so many players, in such a resonant space, the physical speed had to be?

I: Slow.

D: Slower than with a smaller group. And there is a point slower than which the physical speed is too slow to accommodate all the material in one act of consciousness.

I: It doesn't hold together.

D: Right. Now another contributing element to this stylistic disjunction you sense is the length of the notes.

I: Yes, the note lengths are generous and luxurious in the romanticized, full-orchestra version, which is anathema to the Baroque purists.

D: That may well be, but again it's irrelevant. Because it is again a question of the capacity of those tones to be absorbed fully, in one act of consciousness, as a simultaneity.

I: And because longer notes require a slower physical speed . . .

D: Yes, absolutely, a too-slow physical speed. Let's look at another example. Your orchestra is performing Schubert's "Unfinished" Symphony. Listen to these two bars (ex. 4.19◀》).

(Allegro moderato)

In the rehearsal I heard, the orchestra was sustaining the quarter notes, and your conductor suggested that it was stylistically incorrect to do that, because in Schubert's time the quarter notes would have been short.

I: She's right, isn't she?

D: She's right that the quarter notes must be short, but the reason is not that they were short in Schubert's day. Of course how would she know? But again even if she were certain, it would be irrelevant. Again it goes to indivisibility of the object. Here. Listen to the entire passage, which begins in bar 9. It is characterized by this continuing rhythmic figure of three eighth notes and one quarter note, first in the violas and cellos pizzicato (ex. 4.20◀》).

The growth of energy through the passage comes about through an increase in volume, and by the addition of instruments, and maybe with the transition to arco in bar 26. The gradual growth culminates with bars 36–38, in which the original rhythmic figure is abbreviated from three eighth notes and a quarter note to one eighth note and a quarter note (ex. 4.21◀》).

If we extend the quarter notes of bars 36–38 to their full notated value, they would be significantly longer than the quarter notes of the earlier statements of the figure (ex. 4.22◄)).

This results in a multiplicity that requires us to provide the connection. And it prevents an indivisible experience of the passage. The experience may not be unpleasant; it may be exciting, it may be beautifully in tune, and together, and in balance, and it may stir the emotions. But essentially important is this: such a lengthening of quarter notes may be considered stylistically inappropriate, but that's not the reason it is not preferred. The reason it is not preferred is that it yields a lesser experience.

I: But playing in the Baroque era had to admit of legato performance, no?

D: Playing in what Baroque era? What city, as you point out? In Rome? In Berlin? In London?

I: Oh . . .

D: Regardless, the fact is that legato was a problem in the eighteenth century. For example, the keyboard instrument of choice, the harpsichord, has an almost immediate decay. Stringed instruments playing with convex bows were not able to produce sustained legato. So trills and other ornamentations, which have generated bookshelves of theories and recommendations, had the primary purpose of compensating for the decay and sustaining the tone.

I: Might that change how people think about performing ornaments?

D: Ideally, again, not. Ideally modern performers can approach eighteenth-century music as they would any music, and understand that the highest goal is the quality of the experience. Understanding that Baroque bows produced lighter, shorter sounds than modern bows, or that ornamentation was a Baroque-era musician's best hope of sustaining a line, may well lead a modern performer to a better performance . . . to a performance that can provide a better experience. But if we understand that Baroque oboes tended to be raucous and out-of-tune, it wouldn't serve us or our audiences to play in a particularly raucous or out-of-tune manner.

I: I guess that would be like eating food with dirt in it to reproduce the dining experience of earliest man.

D: Of historical interest, surely, but not very tasty. Some progress actually is positive, and it would be foolish to ignore it. Toward the end of his life Bach tried some early piano prototypes, which he dismissed. He loved the clavichord, which could play at differing volumes but was almost inaudible. And he was not enthusiastic about the piano, not because he wasn't interested in a variable-intensity keyboard instrument that was actually audible, but because the early piano didn't do it well enough. Brahms steered clear of valve horns, not because he didn't want the evenness of sound available from the modern valve horn, but because the valve horns of his time created a greater difference in sound between open and valved notes than was created between open and stopped notes on the natural horn. We are left to speculate that in every likelihood Bach and Brahms would have been delighted with later developments. Are we serving Brahms by playing on natural horns? Do we define that as stylistically appropriate? And if we do, is it good? If the highest musical experience is your goal, your obligation to stylistic appropriateness is secondary to your obligation to create the conditions for an optimal experience.

I: What about someone who insists that I would play a piece better if I understood the details leading to its composition?

D: For example?

I: (*sheepishly*) Well, I got in an argument once with a teacher.

D: Another one?

I: Yeah. Anyway, I disagreed with her. I mentioned the program behind Berg's *Lyric Suite*, which had recently come to light with the discovery of Berg's annotated score. And I suggested that a quartet who performed the final movement sublimely could not play it any better after they learned that it was intended as a love song to his mistress, despite her insisting that it would. If it was a superb performance the first time it could not be a better performance now. It might in fact be a worse performance, but not a better one.

D: Personally I think you won that argument.

I: I just had another argument with a different teacher, though, and I think I lost that one. It annoys me a bit, too, because I see the world so differently from this guy. His entire musical concern is with the "grand, dramatic gesture."

D: So what was at issue?

I: The whole notion of emotions and characters, which you and I have talked about. He insisted that the most important element of a good performance was whether or not it effectively expressed the character of the music. I argued that character was irrelevant to the aesthetic experience. Later I suggested that the opening of Beethoven's Symphony No. 1 is funny (ex. 4.23◄)).

Icarus plays while narrating.

Aha - F Major! I guess not - it's C Major. Oops, deceptive cadence

Here we are, no really! Here it is - G major, yeah, yeah, That's it, G major. Yeah!

Oops again - just kidding. Fooled you. See, you were in C major all along

So I said that was a joke, and he reminded me that I had said that character was irrelevant. I had no answer for him, and I felt stupid.

D: But you have one now?

I: No, I sure don't. And how is it that the piece can begin in F major? Is it in F major? Does it begin in the wrong key? Don't you have to start in the home key?

D: Ah yes. It's simultaneous.

I: What is simultaneous? Of course, it's our experience.

D: If the home key serves as a referent, the work need not begin with the home tonic. Beethoven's first symphony begins with V^7–I in F major, establishing F as tonic. Then comes V^7–vi in C major, establishing that key as tonic. Then V^7–I in G major, establishing it. G major is no more securely established than F major, although it might seem to be because it is louder and takes longer. And when C major is finally presented, it is confirmed in the Adagio introduction and then reconfirmed repeatedly at the opening of the Allegro. The keys of F major and G major are touched on; the key of C major is confirmed. But much more important is the notion of simultaneity. We experience the entire piece as one uninterrupted continuum. We experience the F and G majors in the context of the C to come.

I: Retroactively?

D: Simultaneously. And that's why it's a joke. If the opening were not experienced in terms of the entire continuum, if it were just—here's F major, here's G major, and here's C major, then there is no joke.

I: Okay, that sort of makes sense. But what about Hugo Wolf songs that begin and end in different keys? What about the last movement of Mahler's Fourth Symphony; it begins in G major and ends in E minor.

D: Yes, that Mahler movement is problematic in terms of leading to an indivisible aesthetic object. Because G major is fully confirmed as the tonic for the entire opening segment of the movement. And then the movement establishes and confirms C major, and finally it ends in a fully confirmed E minor. So there is no way that it could ever come to the fully open listener as whole.

I: So it couldn't be a joke, like Beethoven's First Symphony is.

D: Precisely. The Mahler Fourth Symphony movement just can't make up its mind whether it's in E minor and begins halfway through, or is in G major and ends in the middle.

I: Why couldn't it simply be a whole movement that begins in G major and ends in E minor?

D: It can. But with two reference systems it can't be received as an indivisible object—it then can only come to the listener as divided, and will never provide the highest sublime aesthetic experience.

I: But that movement is absolutely stunningly beautiful.

D: Remember—beauty on all levels. Yes, in the most superb performances of it, it can be extremely beautiful. But the continuum of sound cannot come to you completely connected. A superb performance of this movement will never be as stunning as a superb performance of one that can come to you as completely connected. It will never provide an exclusive loss-of-self experience across the entire experience of sound.

I: What would happen? Theoretically in an absolutely sublime performance of this movement you would get to the end and it would simply stop. So the experience would end. How would it affect the experience you already had?

D: The experience is one of simultaneity. Remember the sounding of your name—just as the beginning of the sounding of your name is shaped by the end of the sound, the G-major section of that movement is shaped in your experience by your experience of everything that follows. If you are open to a sublime experience that is foiled by the failure of that movement to end, the experience of the G-major section is not over, untouchable, but rather it is present, simultaneous. So, given a superb performance of this movement, if you are truly open to a transcendent experience of indivisibility—if you are focused exclusively on the totality of the sounds—your experience is not one of sublime beauty ended, but one of a certain dissatisfaction, or hollowness. The ending of the piece in such a way that no one single tonal referent has been established creates a multiplicity, prevents loss of self, and changes that ongoing experience of the opening material in G major.

I: Okay. But how often does a listener come truly open to a sublime performance—how often would someone be truly focused exclusively on the totality of the sounds in a performance of this work?

D: Probably not as often as we would like. Some listeners will take in some beautiful sounds, look at the program to see why there are five movements in this symphony, take in some more beautiful sounds, see if the conductor made any recordings, take in a few more nifty sounds, check out the poem, and at the end he thinks he's heard a stupendous performance and has had a magnificent experience, especially if he found that the conductor had made a lot of recordings. Magnificent? Maybe. In fact, certainly it was magnificent, if the sounds were beautiful—if they provided him with an experience of beauty. But the absolute highest?

No. And the fact is that across time and untold multiple performances, Mahler's Fourth Symphony has not risen to the ultimate pantheon of greatest works.

I: But back to character. Even though character is not part of our focused consciousness in the highest musical experience, don't we have to express the character of the piece in our performance?

D: I take issue with the notion that music—in its highest form—expresses anything . . . in fact, in order to be in its highest form it must express nothing. And just to be clear, while we may be scientists together here, I am in no way advocating music making that is analytic. The analysis, the science . . . they end when the music making begins. In fact, in the act of making music we are the epitome of rage, we are the essence of joy—we cannot make music on the highest level without every fiber of our being involved including every raw human passion available. Emotive musical character colors the aesthetic experience like the blue river or the red boat color the visual aesthetic experience of the Renoir painting. Change the color and you throw off the interplay of the forces that lead to that most magical aesthetic experience. In the same way, change the joyful character of a Haydn symphony by elongating articulations, or change the fearsome character of a Mahler symphony by playing too slow, or ignore the joke in the opening of Beethoven's First Symphony by playing it too fast and loud, and you have eliminated the conditions that allow an aesthetic experience of the work in an indivisible act of consciousness.

I: The character-rich performance is necessitated by the higher need to transcend.

D: Precisely. When we have a transcendent experience it is not because we are stirred by the passion of the musicians or the conductor, or because we relate to the suggestion of a familiar human emotion, but because the sounds have come together in our consciousness as an indivisible object, allowing us to lose ourselves. We transcend time, we transcend space, we transcend emotions—what remains is only our consciousness of sound.

I: Okay. But in the end, aren't we still really saying that all performances should be pretty much the same?

D: Oh my goodness, no! There is a vast range—of tempi, of volume, of color, et cetera, et cetera—within which performances can reach an ideal. Orchestras with different instruments, conductors of different temperaments, halls of different acoustic properties, they can all produce sublime performances. Or even the same performers in the same room under different conditions. Let's say your quartet members each have a couple of chocolate éclairs before you play. The performance will be quicker, or more frenzied, or more intense. Or instead of éclairs, you each had a warm bath. This performance will be somewhat more relaxed. Or imagine that you played on much louder instruments. Your performance is quite different. Or you play in a different room. Or you play it twice consecutively. The second performance will be different from the first. And each of these different performances could be optimally rewarding . . .

I: . . . if they share the same dynamic structure.

D: There is hope for you after all!

I: And that means a performance with a different dynamic structure cannot be as good. There are better ways to play and worse ways, and we must assume that a better way is right, and a worse way is wrong. So we *can* pursue better performances.

D: Of course.

I: And be gurus.

D: (*smiling*) And try to be gurus.

I: So I don't have to settle for these weak excuse-makers who say, "Whatever you do is fine as long as it's convincing, or sincere, or committed," and "There's no right way." Pitiful excuses for not pursuing the best.

D: Come talk to me when you've lived in the world. Of course everyone wants to be comfortable. Give them a break. You and me too. Your comfort might come from sublime performances; others might be more comfortable not having to deal with wise guys like you.

I: Or nasty old sourpusses like you. I don't bother you, though?

D: Of course you bother me. Now go learn about dynamic analysis if you're still curious about dynamic structure.[1] In the mean time, I'll just keep trying to leave the world a little bit better place than I found it. Now where did I put that broom . . .

Chapter Five

First, Last, and Always

June 1

Daedalus: Congratulations. I wasn't sure you would make it this far, but you're graduating, let's see, tomorrow, isn't it?

Icarus: Yes it's tomorrow afternoon. And I have very mixed feelings. It's time to join the real world. But I'll miss our talks. You've taught me a lot.

D: No, I'm quite sure I haven't. In fact, no one has ever taught you anything.

I: I know, you think I'm insufferably arrogant. But the fact is that you've taught me an awful lot; things that are very important to me.

D: Of course you're insufferably arrogant. But that's not what I mean. I think I haven't taught you anything. Nor have I tried to. Nor has anyone. I've put some information and ideas out, and you've taken what you've been ready to learn when you've been ready to learn it. Some of it you've taken, and some of it you haven't yet.

I: I think I've understood it all.

D: Of course you do—people understand what they want to understand, or are ready to understand. So we usually think we've got the whole picture no matter how what percentage we're missing. I recall a seminar with a brilliant man who spoke about a world of musical thought that was largely new to me. I wrote down everything—what I understood, what I believed, what I didn't believe, what I didn't understand—I just wrote it all down. I went to the man's seminar a year later, hoping to refine my understanding on a few points, and I found him talking about an entirely new realm of issues. I couldn't fathom why he hadn't brought up these things the year before, but when I looked in my notes from the first seminar it was all there—all the "new" issues were right there with the ones I had grasped. I had heard everything, but I was absorbing only that part that I was ready for. I was only able to take in these "new" issues after I had a firm grasp of the other material. We learn what we can when we are ready. A teacher can lay out information, can establish a standard of knowledge or skill for the student to meet, and can show the student how to meet it. That's all a teacher can do. As far as learning, as far as meeting that standard, that is up to the student. So yes, you have taught yourself.

I: And I'll keep going over my records of our talks—I too have kept detailed notes, you know. I'm sure I'll find things I missed. But let me run the basics by you to make sure I've gotten the point. Would you mind?

D: Not at all.

I: First you have a composer. The composer imagines a succession of sounds that can lead to an experience of beauty. He writes a piece, which is a suggestion for sounds.

D: No. *No, No, No, No, No, No!* First you have the possibility of the human consciousness to reach a magical, transcendent, sublime state; a loss-of-self experience. First, last, and always, you have the aesthetic experience, this experience of sublime beauty. The composer? Yes, composer suggests relationships of sounds, which ideally can lead to an experience of beauty.

I: Okay. The suggested sonic relationships can move us, can stir us, can lead us to an aesthetic experience. When the composition is great, it can provide the ultimate: an uninterrupted transcendent, loss-of-self experience—a life-enhancing, life-changing experience of pure consciousness. Now the composition itself is not the aesthetic object; the aesthetic object is the sounds given by the performance. For the piece to lead to an experience of beauty, it has to allow a performance that can come to the listener as an indivisible object, experienced in a single, indivisible act of consciousness. The composition then has to allow the aesthetic object to be a singular articulation, with a single broad-scale impulse, or gathering of energy, which is resolved or played out in a single resolution.

D: Yes, go on.

I: The obligation of the performer is simply to unfold the sounds in such a way that they can lead to the highest aesthetic experience. So every note must be in tune, every simultaneity must come with a celestial, magical balance, and with good ensemble, and with a quality of sound, a structure of rhythm, a continuum of articulations, of phrasing inflections, of tempo orientations—in short of all the factors of the tones—such that the dynamic structure allows the whole to be experienced indivisibly. And ultimately they all combine to create an indivisible object, an object that can be experienced indivisibly. For that indivisible object to come about, the dynamic structure—the gathering and playing out of energy—must allow it. The entire work or movement must be articulated by a single large-scale impulse played out in a single large-scale resolution. The entire hierarchy of impulse and resolution must also unfold so that the sounds come as joined, not as a multiplicity, so that they can be experienced without judgment. Given the relationships suggested by the composer, the performer must determine what dynamic structure will allow each phrase, each period, each section, and ultimately the entire work to result in a whole, singular object. The performer uses volume to create that structure on the level of the phrases, and tempo orientation to create that structure in terms of the entire work.

D: And the listener?

I: The listener has the easiest job. He comes to the experience open, free of any preconceived notions, free of any thoughts at all. Empty. He focuses his open, empty consciousness on the sounds, on all the sounds. He allows the sounds to work on them, he absorbs them, they absorb him. If the performance allows it, the listener is stirred, moved; if the performance allows it the listener experiences moments of ecstasy . . . of beauty; and if the performance allows it, the listener's open consciousness focused exclusively on the totality of the sounds results in an indivisible, spiritual, transcendent experience, an ultimate loss-of-self experience.

D: Yes? Well you have a good grasp of what's possible. Then it's good-bye now. My very best wishes go with you . . .

I: Wait. Wait, I have some more questions.

D: Yes?

I: Ummm . . .

D: Yes, next question?

I: Yeah, yeah, yeah. Okay, well I have been wondering about a few points. If there's a latitude for intonation, and ensemble, and balance, why isn't there a latitude for energy flow—for dynamic structure?

D: Of course there is. The more energy you create, the more you have to resolve. You just can't create more energy than the composition can resolve, and the impulse you create has to be sufficient to sustain the energy through the entire piece. There's no latitude in the *structure* of energy required for the most aesthetically rewarding experience—the dimensions and shape of the nested groupings— but there is considerable latitude in the *degrees* of energy you can create.

I: All right. You said the test of finding the dynamic structure is that you have the highest experience, but then only if the piece allows it. Does that mean that a lesser composition has no dynamic structure? Or that a dynamic analysis of a lesser work is invalid?

D: Dynamic structure—the interplay of impulse and resolution—absolutely plays a critical role in the optimal performance of any work. If the work has a structure of articulated units, those units will be performed to best effect with impulses consequently resolved. The difference between a lesser work and a masterwork is wholeness: the masterwork allows it and the lesser work does not. The masterwork allows a single, overarching impulse and a single, overarching consequent resolution. Lacking that, the component articulations stand dynamically unconnected, the piece will never become an indivisible object in the consciousness, and will thus never lead to the ultimate aesthetic experience.

I: Then if the definition of a masterwork is one that allows an indivisible experience, which depends on the performance, which is rarely ultimate, then how can great pieces survive mediocre performances?

D: Let me put it another way. A transcendent experience is prevented when there are deficiencies in the aesthetic object, and those deficiencies can result from the contribution of either the performer or the composer. Further, it is only the rarest of performances that actually presents an indivisible aesthetic object, in other words that is not deficient in some way.

I: Then if most performances are deficient, why can a great piece survive weak performances? How do we know Beethoven is better than Cherubini? How does the music of Bach and Palestrina and Bartók and Bruckner and Mozart and so on and so on—how does their music survive if generally it results in a deficient object? There must be some way in which an aesthetic object that is deficient because of problems in the performance yields a better experience than when it is deficient because of problems in the composition. Why?

D: Again, wholeness. It still has to do with the wholeness of the object. In a deficient performance of a sublime piece, the object comes as a multiplicity, and I as listener must judge them to be parts of the same whole object. I make the connections. There is a duality between me, here, and the object there, a duality between me the listener and the external world. In even the most magnificent performance of a weak piece, however, there are no connections to be made. The object comes as an irredeemable multiplicity, beautiful at best only from moment to moment. That the multiple fragments come in the context of an inorganic larger whole that renders even potentially beautiful fragments illogical, uncomfortable, and—if you are focused on a maximal experience—annoying. In the deficient performance of a masterwork, the whole work is there. This performance does not provide me with the means to transcend on the highest level, but it can bring me—somewhere. It's also possible—less important but possible—that the better piece will get better performances, as performers find it more rewarding, play it more, and come to better understand its possibilities. The better the piece is, the more it's played, and the more it's played, the better the odds that people will find their way to a more complete grasp of the whole, which may actually lead to better performances.

I: Sort of like better performances make better listeners—better pieces make better performers?

D: Perhaps.

I: Now what if you had really bad ears. Could you have an ultimate experience with a slightly out of tune performance?

D: How do I know?

I: Or how about an untrained listener? Does the professional musician have more discerning ears, such that a somewhat out-of-tune performance would prevent him from having a sublime experience but the untrained listener would not be prevented?

D: If you are open, you are open; if the object is indivisible, it is. If you are only halfway open to the experience, subtle intonation problems may not stand in the way of a very enjoyable halfway experience. If you are completely open, a note out of tune is out of tune, and you are out of luck.

I: So it would be better to be blissfully ignorant! Gee thanks. It seems like you are dooming me to a life of unhappy concert going.

D: Or happy concert nongoing. As you wish. The trade-off is an occasional ultimate experience for regular very good experiences. But I'm not sure you have a choice at this point. I suspect you're in too deep.

I: Maybe I am. So this all comes down to listening, and being open. But if it's all about listening to the sounds, being fully open to the sounds, then why do we need to study music history or music theory? How could we possibly benefit from dynamic analysis; from analysis of any kind? Why think about what we do if it only gets in the way of doing it?

D: Knowledge only gets in the way of doing it in the act of making music. You can learn by studying and thinking about music like you learn from a map. If you want to get to Albuquerque you have to go there. You have to find it. You are virtually certain to find Albuquerque eventually if you get in your car and start driving. If you zigzag the country enough times, at some point you will get to Albuquerque. But if you have a map it may help you get there more quickly. The map doesn't substitute for the trip; you still have to go there in order to be there, but it can aid you greatly. If you are playing a movement in sonata-form, you have a good idea that the climax will likely come somewhere toward the end of the development, in the key farthest by consecutive fifth tonicizations from the home key. You don't know this, but you surmise it, because it is true of just about every other sonata-form movement you have encountered—it is the essence of the form. On the basis of the information you have you suspect where the climax of the movement is. You won't know that this is climax is for sure until you perform the work so that this point caps the large-scale impulse, which is resolved consequently in the remainder of the movement. If you came to the work fresh, without any prior experiences, there is no reason that you would not find the climax, but it would be more of a trial-and-error process. In the same way, a historical understanding—a familiarity with styles—might point you more readily to finding the articulations, intensity, tempo, and other conditions that are needed for a sublime performance. But let's be clear about this: ideally you come to the process open—as listener, as performer, and even as composer— and allow the sounds to guide you, without memory, without bias, naked, just your open consciousness and the sounds working on it.

I: I have a friend who doesn't believe that people could ever approach music in this "phenomenological" way, as if listening for the first time, without any biases, without focusing on any one aspect of the music, losing one's consciousness. She tells me that music is all about connecting with the world, that its meaning comes from expectation based on memory, based on prior experience with the piece and understanding of a great network of facts about it, and she didn't fully believe that the transcendent, sublime musical experience could really be attained.

D: So?

I: So how do I convince people . . .

D: *You don't convince people!* You can't convince anyone. You can describe an experience that they most likely had and you can help them understand it. If they don't want to understand it, that's not your problem. If they have never had this glorious experience, that's a shame, but again it's not your problem. You have, and you want to have it more, and that's all that's important. What's more, she may be right.

I: How could she be right?

D: I don't know for certain that there is such an experience. I certainly believe I've had the experience and it comes to me as completely real, and completely available to others, and many other people have described a similar experience. But it may be that this woman is right, that this experience does not exist, and those of us who have had this experience may all be crazy, irrational, hallucinatory. To me this is irrelevant. If I'm crazy, let me be crazy.

I: And to those who say, "What an unbelievably selfish goal it is to satisfy yourself, and not to want to serve the audience, and not to want to serve the composer . . ." or to those who say, "You take all the joy out of music, you take away all the richness, by depriving me of my artistic freedom . . ."

D: If you fly low, so that your wings are soaked by the ocean spray and cannot lift you, where is your freedom? If you soar to great heights and allow the proverbial sun to melt your wings, where is your freedom? Your freedom comes in finding the wind and joining it, molding it to your flight, molding your flight to the wind. Then, and only then, do you fly free. If you play music by slavishly following an irrelevant metronome mark, an editor-placed crescendo mark, an imprecise articulation, you may claim to serve the composer, but you provide no sublime aesthetic experience, no freedom—you serve no one well. If you play music to demonstrate your individuality, you provide no aesthetic experience, no freedom, no transcendence—again you serve no one well. But to contribute to a sublime, transcendent aesthetic experience you must be sensitive to the demands of the sounds. You must take over the sounds, you must let them take you over. To the "composer's servant" you are shamefully self-indulgent; in your urge to satisfy yourself you unfold the sounds within unwritten ebbs and flows of energy—phrasing inflections, tempo orientation. To the "unfettered artiste" you are fearfully restricted; you confine yourself to a determined dynamic structure. But you know the true freedom that comes with the experience of an indivisible object in an undivided act of consciousness. And when the conditions exist that enable you to have a maximal experience, then and only then can anyone else— performers who share the stage with you and audience members—have it too.

I: But what about people who say such performances are predictable, boring, lacking in variety?

D: Someone who suggests that sublime performances are boring is a *deaf person*!!! Why would I care? This is irrelevant to me. Lacking in variety? Variety is good. The driver of a BMW might drive a Volvo for variety. Or a Mercedes, or a Saab, or a Lexus, or even a Cadillac. Or even a Jeep. Or a Ford station wagon. But he would not drive a car that did not work. He would not try to drive a broken down Pinto, no matter how different it might be. For us, we have Bach, and Haydn, Tuesday and Wednesday, these are all different experiences.

I: But if there is only one set of relationships that can allow that highest experience, why don't we just have one perfect performance on a recording, and listen to that? Why go through all this trouble?

D: Come now. Have you ever had the most sublime experience listening to a recording?

I: No. I like recordings, though.

D: Of course you do. There is beauty on all levels. But a performance that allows the most extraordinary, sublime experience involves sonic phenomena so subtle that they will not survive the transfer process. To blend a flute and an oboe into a "floboe," to balance a chord into a celestial event, these come to us as so magical not simply because of the volume of the fundamental tones, but because through their relationship they create a new structure of overtones, a blended structure of aural phenomena too delicate to be retained across the recording process, even by the most sophisticated equipment. In addition to expunging the magical quality of sound, you have changed the tempo, so two strikes against you.

I: Changed the tempo?

D: Yes. Haven't you ever noticed that the tempo of a recording usually seems slower than when you experienced the performance live?

I: Yes. In fact I had a teacher once who used to try to convince me that we don't hear accurately. Because, obviously, if we did hear the tempo accurately it would not always seem too slow when we heard the recording.

D: Well, his was one possible conclusion. Either our hearing is defective and the recording process is accurate, or our hearing is accurate and the recording process is defective. I put my trust in myself, in my hearing. But it is more than a question of trust, it is simple acoustics. The recording process distorts the sounds by maintaining the speed but eliminating sonic information, which results in a slower tempo. Every time.

I: Couldn't you just play it faster, so that in the recording it will sound right? That was my teacher's solution.

D: Couldn't you paint wearing rose-colored glasses? Of course you can. You can do anything you want. But one of the beauties of the sublime aesthetic object is that every aspect is dependent on every other. You will never hypothetically create a sublime aesthetic object by superimposing some contrived condition of tempo that does not exist, because other conditions—the volume, the degree of contrast, the nature of the articulations, and so on and so on—depend on the tempo. But there is a third strike as well: room acoustics. Even if the electronic equipment could reproduce precisely the acoustical information in the room at the time of the recording, your speakers are producing sound in a completely different room. The microphones are picking up the reverberations from the entire recording studio or hall; the sound emanating from your speakers is further reverberating through your room. What do you get? A somewhat muddled sound.

I: How about with headphones, though. Wouldn't headphones eliminate that problem?

D: Only partly. Our ear lobes have strange ridges and loops and projections that shape and channel the sound waves in a different way than microphones receive them. Theoretically the only way that a loss-of-self transcendent experience would be possible is if the recording were made by exceptionally sensitive microphones placed inside the ears of a mock-up human head, and listened to with headphones. Even then you have some small degree of distortion and signal loss. But more problematic is the cognitive dissonance between hearing an orchestra in full bloom and sitting in your living room looking at some black electronic boxes. The heart may say, "Yes," but the brain says, "No sirree."

I: So why do you make recordings?

D: For money and fame. So I can live another day and have more opportunities to do music. And because despite all the uncompromising idealism that is necessary for the true and good and right path to the highest possible experience of music, we all ultimately have to live in the world.

I: Amen brother. Is that the same reason you do opera? Because opera is a representative art. Theoretically it can't lead to the same kind of aesthetic experience as pure music. I mean, you have drama, lighting, costumes, music . . . you're thinking about the quality of the voices, the sets, the dialogue, etc.

D: (*smiling*) And if you're lucky you'll get animals on stage. Exactly as you say: with multiple elements your consciousness is divided, and so the experience requires an act of judgment, and thus a loss-of-self, aesthetic experience is not possible. But what is possible is a superb intellectual artistic experience. At essence opera is theater. And the great appeal of opera is that the music can intensify the dramatic experience.

I: Couldn't the drama intensify the musical experience?

D: It's a musical experience only in that it's an experience that involves music. As long as the experience has a dramatic component—which requires you to connect consciously to your experience of the world—you cannot be having the highest possible aesthetic experience from sound.

I: But some opera is extraordinarily beautiful!

D: There's beauty on all levels.

I: Okay. One more question. You're suggesting that when a listener has a sublime musical experience, the performer has had the same sublime experience.

D: Must have had it.

I: But playing in orchestra I couldn't imagine having any kind of ultimate experience.

D: For the listener to have an ultimate experience the conditions in sound must be present, and that requires that the performer—in the case of an orchestra, at the very least the conductor—is open to the experience. If the performer is not sensitive to the demands of the sounds toward that experience, he will never be able to unfold them in such a way that allows it. So the performer must also have a sublime experience. If anything, though, it is more difficult for the performer, because to open himself up to the experience he must first transcend the intellectual involvement with playing the instrument.

I: You mean turning pages, putting on mutes, and so on?

D: No, I mean any intellectual activity required in actually playing the instrument. When you began driving a stick shift, you probably had to think carefully all the time—clutch in, shift into first, clutch out easy—accelerate—clutch in, shift into second, clutch out easy, and so on. The act of shifting was firmly in your focused consciousness, which was therefore unavailable to other objects. Now, though, you are comfortable with the technical demands of shifting gears. It is second nature; you don't think about it; it does not need to be part of your focused consciousness. You could focus on a ball game, on a chess match, on a poem, or whatever, all the while you accelerate from first through fifth gears. It's the same with a performer. To be open to the most sublime, magical experience you must first have transcended the embouchure, the breathing, the relaxed hands, the shifting, the contact point of the bow—any and all technical demands of playing the instrument. You can do that when you are sufficiently comfortable with those demands that fulfilling them becomes instinctive, when it no longer needs to be a part of your focused consciousness when you are playing. Now . . . (*looking at his watch*)

I: And speaking of stick shifts, I need to go pick up my new car! Can I take you for a spin in it?

D: How about tomorrow. Outside the music school.

I: Deal.

June 2

D: What a vehicle! Congratulations. So, what's on your mind on the day you become a certified musician?

I: Back to Oog and Goog—way back, I guess. Could they have the same kind of ultimate, sublime musical experience?

D: What an arrogant question. Did they not revel in the beauty of the oceans, the mountains, the sunset? Did they not paint pictures on caves, and was that not for the sake of beauty—for the sake of an aesthetic experience? Is your enlightened generation the only one able to have such an experience? Could earlier generations not have a stirring, moving, spiritual experience from sounds also? Of course they could.

I: What about different cultures—Africans, Asians, South American Indians—if they can have the most magical experience from music, are you suggesting that they would value a sublime performance of Bach or Mozart or Bartók? Or wouldn't the fact that they are unaccustomed to listening to Western classical music make it impossible for them to have this experience?

D: Regardless of cultural background or experiences, if the listener is open to the experience, and it is available, it will come to him. The difficulty is not in the listener having the experience, but rather in convincing him to be open to it.

I: Do you think this would be true if Bach came back and heard a sublime performance of a great piece by Bartók?

D: Just like we can have a moving experience from an exquisite cave painting. Of course one reason a cave painting moves us is the sheer mass of time that it has survived—this is an intellectual experience. But some cave paintings are also beautiful. That beauty is no accident—they must have been beautiful to the artist, and we share that experience millennia later. We can only hypothesize that if Bach heard a sublime performance of a great work of Bartók, or of Bruckner, or of Beethoven, he would be able to have a sublime experience. Once he made whatever adjustments might be necessary to open himself to a different style, a different kind of sound.

I: Theoretically then, why do we have different styles? Why not just one piece? If two coins in a square can provide the most magical experience, why bother painting pictures of boats in a river? If a Palestrina Mass can provide it, why did Bach, and Beethoven, and Mendelssohn, and Bruckner write music too?

D: That's a ridiculous question. Bach's church needed music, and Beethoven's Viennese society needed it, and Mendelssohn's Leipzig community needed it.

I: Schoenberg's society didn't need it. Stockhausen's society didn't need it.

D: Maybe that's what enabled Schoenberg and Stockhausen to write music that nobody wanted to hear.

I: Are you saying that atonal music can't allow an ultimate experience? aleatoric music? electronic music?

D: Aleatoric music? The highest, transcendent experience? I suppose it is possible . . . and one day that proverbial monkey with the typewriter is going to create the plays of Shakespeare. But realistically? It's quite unlikely, because indivisibility is not an issue of chance or randomness. Electronic music faces the same obstacles as electronically reproduced music—the acoustics of the listening room or hall will never duplicate those of the electronic lab. As for atonality, though, of course it is possible. There is no requirement of tonality to produce indivisibility. But it is tonality that enables the hierarchical nesting of articulations and it is nesting that enables the extended work to come to us as one.

I: If it's possible, how will that happen?

D: You may live long enough to find out how. But again, all we know for sure is that it won't happen ever if people try to do it in theory. It will happen only when the composer comes along who is sensitive to the possibilities of this experience, and accepts nothing less. It won't require composers who are electronic wizards, or master mathematicians, or jazz fusionists, or inventive score-painters, or visionary environmental artists. It simply requires composers who are aware of the highest experiential possibility of music and who know how sounds can unfold to lead to it.

I: If listeners demand it by opening their ears to the possibility of the experience and don't support compositions that are unrewarding aesthetically . . .

D: It certainly couldn't hurt the future of composition, or of performance, for that matter.

I: One last question. Do you see the fundamental human urge as a drive for oneness? Connection? As in music?

D: Nonsense. The fundamental human urge is for survival. We're talking here about the exaltation of the spirit. We come to one as artists, we come to one using sound to transcend. Of course we also come to one when we are scientists. To understand is to connect thoughts and experiences, to place them within a larger whole, to eliminate conflict.

I: Eliminate conflict?

D: Eliminate conflict and multiplicities. An inaccurate conception is incompatible with other, accurate conceptions; improving the accuracy of your understanding eliminates the conflict. Mookie's assumption of a flat earth was in conflict with his recognition of the disappearing masts. His more accurate understanding of a round earth eliminated that conflict.

I: Ultimately, then, striving for understanding is striving for peace.

D: Yes.

I: Like doing music.

D: Perhaps in a sense. Intellectual understanding eliminates conflict and multiplicities, and provides the security of knowing the self apart from the world. Each element of the world that participates in my understanding is one more point on which I am aware of the distinction between myself and that external world. Thus the more comprehensive my understanding of the world is, the more firmly I am established as a distinct being within the world but apart from it. Doing music also involves eliminating conflict and multiplicities, but results in a lack of judgment about the world; the most sublime aesthetic experience eliminates the duality between me and the external world.

I: But it enables you to connect with others—wouldn't you think that musicians in the act of doing music connect in a powerful way?

D: Doing music together is one of the most profound ways people have of connecting; it requires us to join on the level of the deepest essence of consciousness. Listeners too, if they share fully in that experience, participate in a similarly profound coming together.

I: So how is that connection between us and the world different from the connection involved in intellectual understanding?

D: When Mookie understands that the earth is round, he says, "There is an earth there, and I, Mookie, over here, understand it—know it to be round." His understanding enables him to know his physical surroundings better; it also enables him to know himself better, in the more secure distinction between him and those surroundings. When Icarus plays a sublime performance of the "Harp" Quartet this afternoon, you become the sounds, you join your consciousness with that of your colleagues, and together they each eliminate the barrier between their individual selves and the external sounds. In your conscious activity, there is no distinction between Icarus and the sounds; you become the sounds. You know yourself better and know your environment better by becoming it, by eliminating the duality between the two. And in the process you will touch your own soul, most profoundly.

I: Isn't there a paradox, though—we do music to lose our selves so that we know ourselves better?

D: We pursue music—this most high, sublime aesthetic experience—to transcend the everyday world of physical reality. We escape the pain of human suffering. We experience an existence in which an outside reality does not participate—we are free from the division between us and external world. The sum total of our conscious being is the sounds, our consciousness of them. We lose our sense of the division between our self and an external world; we have an experience of pure consciousness, of our spirit, of our essential beings. Armed with this experience of essential self, we return to the real world of everyday experiences strengthened by our own self-knowledge, trusting of our selves, secure in our acceptance of our beings. And that is why we do music. To provide for ourselves and our society this same ennobling, fortifying, liberating experience. It is our way of fulfilling man's highest purpose: to leave the world a better place than we find it.

I: To leave the world a better place than we find it . . . that's beautiful.

D: It *is* beautiful. And this afternoon you have a chance to do just that. I'm looking forward to sharing this performance with you. I wish you all good things . . .

I: But wait. Don't leave. I have so many questions.

D: Yes, you have many questions. Good. But I know that you know how to answer them. I have great faith in you—you have come a long way, and are firmly on the right path. Stay open. Keep listening. Keep questioning. Think about what you hear, and trust yourself, trust your experiences. Take the unmatchable experience that is musical beauty as your sole and unceasing guide in all your musical activities, and you cannot go wrong.

I: Our time together is over? I'm sad. Very sad. You must know how much I appreciate what you've done for me. All the time you've invested in me. But this isn't good-bye forever—I'll see you later at the performance, won't I?

D: Yes. We'll meet at the performance.

Part Two

Articles

Chapter Six

Remembrance of Things Future

On the Listener's Contribution

In *The Phenomenology of Internal Time-Consciousness*, Edmund Husserl distinguishes between the two temporal perspectives from which we experience: the present and the now.[1] The present has duration; it is the temporal perspective from which we experience the temporally extended object of a single act of consciousness. A new act of consciousness takes place in a new present; each new act of consciousness effects the end of the previous present. This is easily demonstrated. Clap twice in quick succession, and focus on the sounds. The succession of clap sounds is a temporally extended object, which we hear in a single act of consciousness. The two claps make up one succession. The second clap is heard not as a separate and unrelated event, but as part of the succession, because it comes in the context of, or in relation to, the first clap. The entirety comes to us as a present perception, in a single act of consciousness. If this single act of consciousness has a duration of one second, it takes place in a present that has a duration of one second. The passage of railroad cars at a crossing is an example of a similar kind of temporally extended object. The sounding of an incomprehensible sentence is another. If I hear an incomprehensible sentence with a single act of consciousness that lasts ten seconds, then the present has a duration of ten seconds. If I perceive a succession of railroad cars at a crossing with a single act of consciousness having a duration of half a minute, then the present likewise has a duration of half a minute.

Every experience, however, takes place from the specific perspective of the now-point. The now-point is the almost durationless border between future and past. Any temporally extended present is made up of a continual flow of almost durationless now-points. With the coming of each new now-point, the previous now-point becomes past. If the continuum of almost durationless now-points participates in a single temporally extended present, then a difficulty arises. How could a now-point become past, and yet remain part of the present?

By way of explanation, Husserl offers the concept of *retention*. At any now-point we have in consciousness the corresponding now-phase of the object. As a now-point is replaced by a new now-point, the experience of the earlier now-phase passes. Although the experience is unquestionably past, our consciousness of it is not as past. We are conscious of the previous now-phase as "just-having-been." We

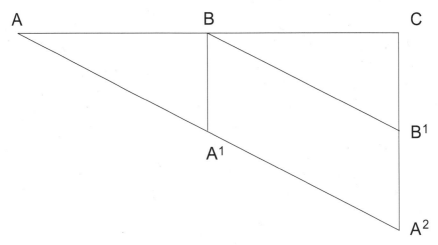

Figure 6.1. The temporal structure of our experience of a succession. After a diagram by Husserl in *The Phenomenology of Internal Time-Consciousness*, 49.

experience the new now-phase of the object simultaneously with the retained experience of the previous now-phase. The "just-having-been" experience is still present for us because we are conscious of both it and the actual now-phase simultaneously.

This is illustrated by the diagram in figure 6.1. Line A–C is the time line; it represents the continuum of now-points. At each now-point our experience includes two components: the actual now-phase of the object (represented by a point on the horizontal line A–C); and the continuum of "just-having-been" now-point experiences in retention (represented by a vertical line extending below it). Point A represents the now-point at the first experience of the object; we are conscious of only the first now-phase of the object, and have nothing in retention. Point B represents a now-point in the middle of the object; we are conscious of the now-phase, along with the retention of our experience at point A and of the continuity of now-points in between (line B–A^1). Point C represents the now-point at the last experience of the object; we are conscious of the entire object: the final now-phase along with our retention of the continuity of previous now-phase experiences (line C–A^2). The diagram illustrates the two ways in which we experience the continuity of now-phases: (1) as a succession of actual now-point experiences (line A–C), and (2) as a simultaneous retention of previous now-point experiences (line C–A^2).

If the diagram represents our experience of the succession of railroad cars in a single, undivided act of consciousness, then point A represents our first experience of the first car. Because there is nothing in that conscious act that preceded the first experience of the first car, there is nothing in retention. Let us say that point B represents our experience of the tenth car. Our experience at now-point B includes more than the experience of the tenth car. It also includes the retention of our experience of the railroad cars at each of the now-points in the entire continuum from now-point A up to now-point B. Our experience at now-point A, and at every now-point in between, is included in our experience of the cars at now-point B. We have therefore a *simultaneous* experience of the first ten railroad cars. *Certainly we do not see or hear all the cars in the same now-point, but in each new now-point we experience a new actuality* simultaneously *with the retention of the continuity of "just-having-been" now-point experiences.* At now-point B we experience in actuality only the tenth railroad car, but we experience it *simultaneously* with our retained experiences of the first nine. This is an example of simultaneity that grows with the perception of the object. Each now-point is added on to the simultaneity as it (the now-point) is replaced by the next now-point. Any temporally extended object is experienced as this kind of cumulative simultaneity.

The temporally extended objects described above are experienced as partite—divisible into individual parts that stand alone. The experience of the succession of clap sounds is divisible into individual claps; the experience of the succession of railroad cars is divisible into individual railroad cars. One or more of the parts experienced separately from the succession remains largely the same as the part experienced within the succession. For example, if we hear a single clap sound, it is still constituted for us in very much the same way as it would be if it were part of a succession of several. Likewise, if we experience one railroad car, it is constituted for us in largely the same way as it would be if it were part of a succession of several.[2]

Another type of temporally extended simultaneity is experienced as indivisible—the sounding of my name, for instance. If I hear the sounding of the name *Markand*, I perceive it as a single event. I perceive it as one thing, indivisible, even though it has two syllables, and seven component sounds (m, a, r, k, a, n, and d).

When I perceive the r sound I have in retention the experience of the m and a sounds. I perceive the r sound simultaneously with the m and a sounds. When I perceive the final d sound, I have in retention my experience of all the previous sounds. I perceive the d sound simultaneously with all those previous sounds. By itself, the experience of a d sound does not constitute my name. It does, however, when the d sound is actual for me simultaneously with the previous experience of all the sounds of the name *Markand*. Likewise, the experience of the m sound does not constitute the name *Markand*. It does, however, when it is actual for me as simultaneous with the experience of all the sounds of the name *Markand* yet to come. In a present experience of the entire name *Markand*, with the sounding of the d I am conscious of that d sound in the now-phase simultaneously with a retention of the continuum of my experience of the rest of the name, which has passed into the "just-having-been."

I can hear the d sound simultaneously with the rest of the name because the rest of the name is in retention when the d sound is actual. But how is it that

I hear the *m* sound simultaneously with the rest of the name, when the rest of the name has not yet been sounded? Husserl refers to the defined future part of a conscious act as *protention*.[3] In any experience of an indivisible (in other words, not a partite) temporally extended object, our focused consciousness at any now-point includes the corresponding now-phase, the retention of "just-having-been" now-point experiences, *and* the protention of "as-yet-to-come" now-point experiences.

The sounding of my name is a temporally extended object experienced as indivisible; the parts do not stand on their own. The two syllables *mar* and *kand* take much of their essence from their specific context; standing alone or in a different context they are experienced as essentially different. The difference between partite and indivisible simultaneities is protention. We experience a succession of individual parts as an entity because the continuity of now-phases is retained, with each new now-phase, as a "just-having-been." Protention is not part of the experience because the "as-yet-to-come" is superfluous to the now; the current perception will be unchanged regardless of the future. But we experience my name as indivisible because of protention. At any now-point, the "as-yet-to-come" is as essential to the experience as is the current now-phase and the retained "just-having-been."

The diagram in figure 6.2 (adapted from figure 6.1 above) illustrates this kind of indivisible simultaneity. At each now-point our experience includes three components: the actual now-phase of the object (represented again by the horizontal line A–C); the continuum of "just-having-been" now-point experiences in retention (represented by the solid vertical lines); and the continuum of "as-yet-to-come" now-point experiences in protention (represented by the dotted vertical lines). Point A represents the now-point at the first experience of the object; we have in consciousness the first now-phase of the object, with nothing in retention, but the "as-yet-to-come" experiences of virtually the entire rest of the object in protention (dotted vertical line A–cc). Point B represents a now-point in the middle of the object; we have in consciousness the now-phase; the retention of our "just-having-been" now-point experiences (vertical solid line B–A^1), and the protention of our "as-yet-to-come" now-point experiences (vertical dotted line B–c). Point C represents the now-point at the final experience of the object. We have in consciousness the final now-phase along with our retention of the continuity of previous now-phase experiences (vertical solid line C–A^2); and nothing is protended.

*   *   *

But an essential dimension has been omitted from the two graphs above. At a given now-point we have in consciousness the corresponding now-phase simultaneously with the retention (and/or protention) of "just-having been" (and/or

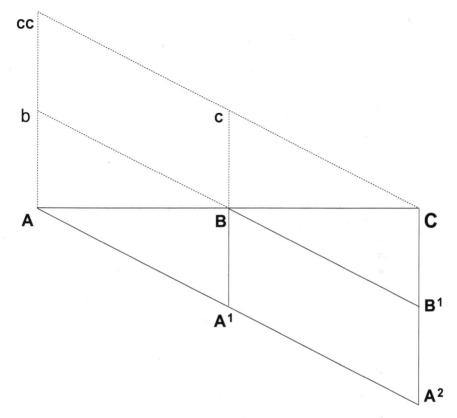

Figure 6.2. The temporal structure of our experience of an indivisible temporally extended object

"as-yet-to-come") now-point experiences. What is retained or protended is not now-phases, but now-point *experiences*. A now-point experience is composed of not only the corresponding now-phase, but also includes retentions and/or pro-tentions. When a now-point experience is itself in retention, it is retained in its entirety—with all its components. In other words, at point B in the experience of a succession, the retention of a previous now-point experience includes the now-phase *with* retentions of experiences previous to *it*. Similarly, at point B in the experience of an indivisible object, the retention of a previous now-point experience includes the now-phase *with* retentions of experiences previous to it *and* protentions of experiences to be. These experiences are multidimensional.

Figure 6.3 gives three cross-section views of the experience of a succes-sion: at now-points A, B, and C. The black background represents the

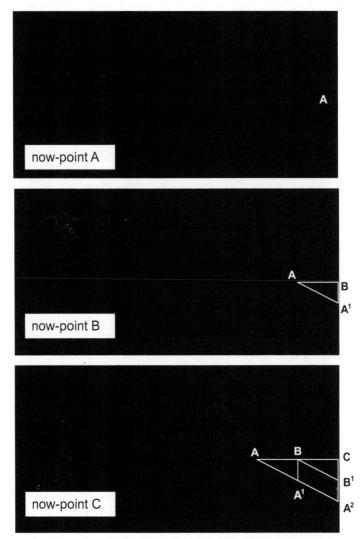

Figure 6.3. The structure of our experience of a succession at three different now-points

"just-having-been"; anything showing in the black background is in retention. The border between black and white backgrounds represents the almost durationless now-point. As it recedes in time, a given point appears farther and farther to the left in the three successive cross-section views.

The first cross-section view represents now-point A—the initial now-point in the experience of the object. At now-point A we experience only the corresponding now-phase (point A). We have nothing in retention. The second cross-section view represents now-point B—a point in the middle of the experience of the object. At now-point B we experience the corresponding now-phase of the object (point B), simultaneously with the continuity of previous now-point experiences in retention: now-phases (line B–A),[4] and all of the retentions at each of the previous now-points (the black triangular area extending down from line B–A). The third cross-section view represents now-point C— the final now-point of the experience of the object. At now-point C we have a simultaneous experience of the entire object. We experience the corresponding now-phase of the object (point C), simultaneously with the continuity of all previous now-point experiences in retention: now-phases (line C–A), and all of the retentions at each of the previous now-points (for instance; point B occurs in retention along with its retentions, represented by vertical line B–A[1]).

In a similar way, the experience of an indivisible temporally extended object is multidimensional. At any now-point we experience simultaneously (a) the corresponding now-phase, with (b) the retention of the "just-having-been" now-point experiences with their now-phases, retentions, and protentions, and (c) the protentions of "as-yet-to-come" now-point experiences with their now-phases, retentions, and protentions.

The diagram in figure 6.4 gives three cross-section views of this type of experience. Again the black portion of the diagram represents the "just-having-been," the white portion represents the "as-yet-to-come," and the border between black and white represents the now-point. The first cross-section view represents now-point A—our first experience of the object. At now-point A we experience the corresponding now-phase, point A, simultaneously with the protention of the continuity of now-point experiences (represented by the horizontal solid line A–C).[5] We have in protention not just the now-phases to come, but the total experience at each of those now-points. For example, the protended now-point B experience includes the corresponding now-phase (point B), and the simultaneous experience of the attendant retentions that will occur at that point (vertical solid line B–A[1]), and the attendant protentions that will occur at that point (vertical dotted line B–c).

The second cross-section view represents now-point B—a point in the middle of our experience of the object. At now-point B we experience the corresponding now-phase (point B), simultaneously with the retention and protention of the entire continuity of now-point experiences (represented by the horizontal solid line A–C, half in retention and half in protention). We have in retention and/or protention not only the "just-having-been" and "as-yet-to-come" now-phases, but the total experience at each of those now-points. For example, the simultaneous experience of the entire object at now-point A has receded into the "just-having-been"; it includes the now-phase (point A) and its attendant protentions (dotted vertical line A–cc).

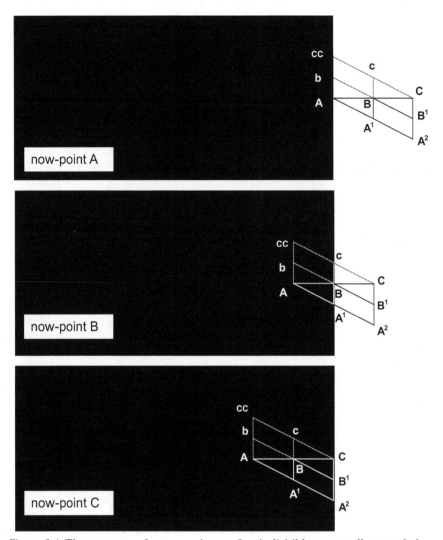

Figure 6.4. The structure of our experience of an indivisible temporally extended object at three different now-points

The third cross-section view represents now-point C—our final experience of the object. At now-point C we experience the corresponding now-phase (point C), simultaneously with the retention of the entire continuity of now-point experiences (represented by the horizontal solid line A–C, which is now almost entirely in retention). We have in retention not only the "just-having-been" now-phases, but the total experience at each of those now-points—each now-point in retention including the corresponding now-phase and any attendant retentions and protentions.

In summary, we intuit that a temporally extended object moves in time from the future through the present and into the past. While this is may be an accurate description in physical terms, it does not accurately describe our conscious experience. We perceive a temporally extended object only as in the present. Within the present experience of a partite succession, the "past" is not constituted as past, but as a kind of "just-having-been," that is retained in the experience of the now-phase. Throughout its entire duration, the experience of the partite succession is constituted as present. And within the present experience of an indivisible object, neither is the "future" constituted as future, but as a kind of "as-yet-to-come," that is protended in the experience of the now-phase. Throughout its entire duration, the experience of the indivisible object is constituted as present. It is the simultaneous experience of the entire continuity in retention and/or protention that allows us to experience it as a single entity in the present.

*   *   *

A musical experience is the experience of a temporally extended object. Musical experiences provide—on the most basic level—organization and order to our conscious activity. Music organizes the temporal aspect of the listener's conscious experience (an aspect of our experience that ordinarily comes to us as random or chaotic). In a direct way, the musical pulse organizes our experience within a metrical reference system: musical sounds come to us in the context of a meter. In a somewhat more complicated way, a musical object organizes our experience in that the component tones unfold in a specific order, such that changing the order changes the object essentially. But our conscious activity during a musical experience may have one of a variety of different structures. The nature of our conscious activity during a musical experience is determined by three factors: the possibilities allowed by the composition, the specific combinations of sounds produced by the performer, and the attitude of the listener (the degree of our openness to the sounds).

One common attitude is *associative listening*: focusing on the musical object and something else. At a performance of Beethoven's String Quartet, Op. 74, "The Harp," someone listening associatively may use the sounds as a springboard for a network of thoughts about Napoleon, or early nineteenth-century Vienna, or other works by Beethoven, or by his contemporaries. Or he might think about aspects of the performance in comparison with other performances or recordings of the same work. Such a listener might find himself reliving emotional experiences, as sparked by the character of the music. He might relive a proud moment in the first movement, a sad one in the second, or a playful one in the third.[6]

Another common attitude is *selective listening*: focusing on less than the total-ity of the sounds. Someone listening selectively to an orchestra might focus on the chord progression, on the structural melodic progress, or on the formal con-siderations. Or he might focus on the bow strokes, on the conductor's gestures, on the synchronized page turning, or on the sound of the clarinets, or the per-cussion, or the brass intonation.

Any act of consciousness has a structure of subject–mode of consciousness–object. For example, consider the structure of my experience when I remember my first car. I am the subject, as I am in all my conscious acts. The object is the car. The mode of consciousness is remembering. Or I could imagine the car I want to buy next. I am the subject again; the object is the car in the future. The mode of consciousness is imagining. I might be looking at the table: I (the subject) am conscious of the table (the object) by looking at it (the mode of consciousness).

The structures of associative and selective listening also involve a subject, a mode of consciousness, and an object. If, at a performance, my focused atten-tion is taken up with a comparison of the tempo to that of some other perfor-mance, I am listening associatively. I am focusing my attentive consciousness on more than the sounds; I am associating the sounds with some other object. In this case I am the subject, the object includes the current tempo and the other tempo to which I am comparing it, which I am conscious of by remembering and comparing. The experience takes place in an extended present that lasts as long as I am focused on the object; the extended present has the nature of a cumulative simultaneity. If my focused attention is taken up with the sound of the tuba, I am listening selectively. I focus my attentive consciousness on less than the totality of the sounds; I am selecting an object from the totality of the sounds. In this case I am the subject, the object is that part of the sounds pro-duced by the tuba, which I am conscious of by listening. This experience too takes place in an extended present that lasts as long as I am focused on the object; the extended present also has the nature of a cumulative simultaneity.[7]

Music can be the stimulus for another experience, different from that avail-able through associative or selective listening. This is a transporting experience; an experience in which we lose ourselves; in which we lose our *selves*; in which we are moved, seized by the sounds, taken over by the sounds; an experience in which we become the sounds, and in becoming the sounds are relieved of mundane concerns and human suffering. This is an aesthetic experience: that highest, most sublime experience of beauty.

If the musical object allows an aesthetic experience, whether or not it occurs depends on the attitude of the listener. The subject must come to the experi-ence open, free of all extramusical or intramusical thoughts. The object of the focused attention must be nothing more and nothing less than the totality of the sounds. And the mode of consciousness must simply be open listening; not thinking, or remembering, or imagining, or anything other than simply listening—being open to the sounds.

The structure of our experience of musical beauty is similar to that of an indivisible temporally extended object. Every component of the object has a contextually determined essence. Thus the experience of the entire continuity of the object (as retention, now-phase, and protention) is included simultaneously with every now-point experience.

There is a difference between the two experiences, though. The experience of the indivisible, temporally extended object—the sounding of my name, for example—involves a three-part process: I–listening–name. But the experience of musical beauty is characterized by a loss of self. Through the complete absorption into the totality of the sounds (assuming that the musical object allows it), the subject disappears as a subject from the experienced conscious act, and the object disappears as an object from the experienced conscious act. The experience for us includes no subject, and no object. Although physically there is clearly a subject (the listener) and an object (the musical sounds), they are not constituted in our experience. Our experience of musical beauty then is pure consciousness.

A loss-of-self experience can happen only when the act of consciousness does not involve *judgment*. My awareness of an object involves the act of judgment. Judgment in this sense means the consideration of something *as* something. I can perceive something as a thing—any thing—only through an act of judgment. If my dog comes into my room I perceive it as my dog. I evaluate the way it looks, sounds, and smells, and judge it to be my dog. I might not judge it as my dog, but only as a dog. I am still judging: I see, hear, and smell a thing, and judge that it is a dog that I am seeing, hearing, and smelling. If I do not judge it as a dog—if I have no idea what this thing is—I am still judging. I am judging this thing to be a thing, different from all else that is not this thing.

I am defined by my relation to the physical world. I understand myself only insofar as I am differentiated from the other things that I experience. I judge the objects, and—to the extent that I am not one of them—the objects define me. If I am no longer judging objects, then I am no longer defined. There is no longer anything for me to *not* be. *When I do not experience sounds as objects, I lose my sense of self.*

We might think of the structure of such an experience as a sphere, as represented in figure 6.5. Its beginning is its end; its end its beginning. There are no identifiable parts, and any now-point is barely distinguishable from any other.

The experience of musical beauty exists in a present; it passes through the now-point in a familiar way, as illustrated in figure 6.6. At point A, the initial now-point, almost all of the continuity is "as-yet-to-come," in protention. At point B, in the middle, some of the continuity has passed into the "just-having-been," in retention; some is still "as-yet-to-come," in protention. At point C, the final

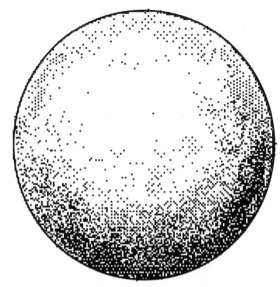

Figure 6.5. The temporal structure of the experience of musical beauty

now-point of the experience, almost all of the continuity has passed into the "just-having-been" in retention.[8]

So far we have considered the object of consciousness only from the standpoint of the listener's focus. But the structure of the object itself affects the nature of the experience. If the object of my consciousness is a plurality, I must experience it with an act of judgment. To discern more than one part takes an act of judgment, an act that defines the judg-er. For example, the set of chopsticks is in reality two sticks; they become a set only in my simultaneous consciousness of them—in my judgment of the two as belonging together. Thus any experience in which the object of consciousness is a plurality must include a subject, and cannot be a loss-of-self experience.

This is true also of temporally extended objects. I cannot experience a partite succession without judging: I judge the parts to belong to a whole, and yet to be distinct from each other, thus also distinct from myself. When my focused consciousness is taken up with the totality of the succession of clap sounds, for example, I cannot but judge them as discrete events, separate from each other and separate from myself. In defining the clap sounds I am defining myself—my conscious act necessarily involves a subject. These random clap sounds cannot provide an experience of musical beauty. Nor can I experience without judging the indivisible object we examined previously: the sounding of my name. The sounding of my name represents me—the name *Markand* represents my person. Although the sound is experienced to an extent as indivisible, the act of consciousness still requires the subject making the connection between the

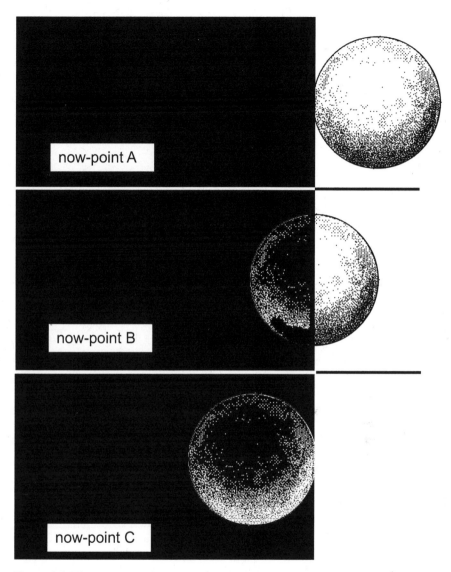

Figure 6.6. The structure of our experience of musical beauty at three different now-points

name and the represented object. In fact, any act of consciousness whose object signifies or represents something else involves such a duality, and must involve judgment. I cannot have an experience of musical beauty when the perception of the sound represents or signifies something else.[9]

Most commonly, the musical sounds in a performance serve as a background for a chain of conscious acts. Consider the nature of our conscious experience while biking down a country lane. We might focus our attention on the smells or on the sky, we might catch a bird call, remember a family reunion, imagine winning the lottery—and all of this across the continuum of being conscious on a background level of the winding lane and nearby bikers. If we were not conscious of the lane we would ride off of it; but we can stay on it and at the same time have a concentrated consciousness of other objects.

In listening to a musical performance, our conscious experience is likely to have a similar content: a chain of separate conscious acts, all connected by the background continuum of the sounds. We might think about the tempo, the trombone player's hairdo, the woodwind intonation, the baby-sitter. Occasionally we might experience a moment of sublime beauty, perhaps an extended moment, perhaps several. Typically such moments will not envelope the entire work, but will take their place in the succession of distinct conscious acts, followed by a thought about our neighbor's dress, our tax returns, the clarinet melody, and so on. Each member of such a chain of conscious acts takes place in an extended present; the nature of the chain is determined by the succession of objects. The first conscious act in the chain has as its object the tempo in comparison with other performances of the work. This conscious act lasts as long as the object remains the same. When the object changes, say to the question of tempo itself, or to a given section dragging the tempo, or to any other object, the extended present of the initial conscious act comes to an end. The first conscious act becomes past, and assumes its place in the chain of conscious acts; and a new conscious act takes place in a new extended present. The same is true when the conscious act is one of musical beauty; the object is the totality of sounds absorbed in an indivisible experience. It ends when the consciousness shifts to a new object; it takes its place in the chain of past conscious acts experienced across the continuum of the performance.

A typical musical experience, one that involves a pleasurable organization of time serving as a background for a chain of conscious acts, may be enjoyable and rewarding. It is not, however, as enjoyable as the unique, transcendent, spiritual experience of sublime beauty. When such an experience occurs in listening to a performance as a member of a chain of conscious acts, its end is annoying, irksome, and frustrating. The more extended such an act is within the chain of conscious acts, the more valuable the overall experience.

Ideally, the entire work comes to the listener in a single, indivisible conscious act characterized by loss of self. For this to happen, though, not only must the listener focus exclusively on the totality of the sounds, but the sounds must be present in such a way as to allow their indivisible experience. Sounds prevent such a continued loss-of-self experience when they come to the listener as a plurality, which can only be perceived with an act of judgment. Within any performance each component tone has attributes: of pitch, of volume, of duration, of timbre, and of temporal location. Sounded in conjunction with all the other tones, each tone takes on a complex network of other attributes: the attribute of linear function (the relation of a tone to the other members of a line); the attribute of harmonic function (its relation to the other members of a harmonic event); the attribute of scale degree (its relation to the other component tones of the scale); the attribute of intonation; of rhythmic function; of articulation; of metric function—the list is long.

A plurality exists when some of the attributes stand in conflict. For example, a plurality exists if a tone of the clarinet is experienced as out of tune. The tone itself is not out of tune; rather it is functioning within a system of intonation that stands in conflict with that of the other tones. System of intonation is an attribute of the tones; the plurality of intonation systems is a plurality of attributes. In terms of their attribute of intonation system, the tones stand apart, distinct—they do not combine to form an indivisible unity. A performance that unfolds multiplicities of any kind can be experienced only with an act of judgment. The experience must involve a subject and an object, and thus it cannot be characterized as loss-of-self. It may be a stirring experience, a valuable and rewarding experience, but it cannot be one of sublime musical beauty.

Assuming an open attitude of the listener, an aesthetic experience depends on the nature of the aesthetic object: the sounds. In other words, it requires contributions of both composer and performer.

The performer has front-line responsibility for the experience of musical beauty. He creates the object of the experience—the sounds. It is the responsibility of the performer to create sounds whose attributes do not conflict. In the case of the out-of-tune clarinet tone, it is the responsibility of the performer to reduce the plurality of intonation systems to a single entity. He does this by adjusting the pitch of the "offending" tone so that it joins the intonation system of the other tones. In a similar manner, the performer takes into consideration each attribute in the vast and complex network. This is not as difficult as it sounds, if the performer keeps as the primary goal the *experience*, and not the means to achieve it. By way of analogy, the thought process necessary to drive a car on a hilly, curvy road involves a frightfully complex network of judgments and minute calculations: the speed of the car, its weight, the traction, the degree of curvature of the road, the severity of the gradient, the wind, and so on. To drive the road successfully by focusing consciously on these calculations is unimaginable. If, on the other hand, the consciousness is focused simply on keeping the car on the road, it is a fairly simple matter. Likewise, although the act of playing beautifully involves a network of attributes of mind-boggling complexity, the musician in technical command of his instrument *can* play beautifully, not by focusing on the network of attributes, but by focusing on the experience of beauty.

The composer is like the structural engineer; he builds the road that makes it possible for the driver to drive successfully. If there is a fissure in the road, the finest driver will not be able to maintain the continuity of his drive. On the other hand, even if he has built the finest imaginable road, the poor driver can easily drive off it. It is the contribution of the composer to create a work that allows for such an indivisible presentation. (Note that the work created by the composer is not the object of the experience, but instead is only a design for that object, which is the sounds.) He does this by suggesting a combination of tones whose attributes may exist in sound as a fully indivisible entity.

Consider again that performance of Beethoven's "Harp" Quartet. The composer left us with a masterwork. Each movement has the potential—given a sublime, faultless performance—to be experienced not in a succession of connected but separate acts of consciousness, and not in small "bubbles" of sublime beauty, but as one complete, all-encompassing, simultaneous moment of beauty. This is, in fact, what defines a masterwork: its capacity to be presented in sound so that every attribute of every tone combines with every other into a single, perfectly indivisible unity of experience. In experiencing such a unified object, no subject is needed to make connections among tones, because all the connections, all the relationships come "ready-made" with the sounds. As open listeners to a faultless performance, the sounds grab us, absorb us, take us in, take us over, across the entire movement. This experience is an ultimate beauty, a beauty that begins with the first sound and ends with the last. This is an incomparable and celestial experience; this is the highest experience available through music; an elevating, ennobling, self-defining experience that glorifies human existence.

Chapter Seven

Patterns of Energy

On the Composer's Contribution

Musical Forms

Musical works have long been classified into standardized forms on the basis of the nature of the material (i.e., A theme, B theme, development, coda, episode) and the key relationships. But form is not like the design of a walkway that might be made as easily of brick, or stone, or concrete, or logs. Nor is it an arbitrary shaping applied to the musical material, like a hairdo to hair or a clipping to a hedge. Rather, the material determines its unfolding; the structure determines its material.

The fundamental purpose of music is to lead to that transcendent experience we know as beauty. So the overriding consideration for the composer in those mutually dependent determinations of material and structure is the potential of the performance of the composition to enable the highest experience of beauty. Since this highest experience comes about only when the tones are absorbed in a single, undivided act of consciousness, and since they can be absorbed as such only when they come to the listener as singular, the overriding consideration for the composer is creating a work whose performance can come to the listener as singular.

The possibility of experiencing the multiplicity of tones of a musical composition as singular depends largely on its structure of energy. Any musical unit is defined by a singular creation of energy and the resolution of that energy: a single note, a motive, a phrase, or an entire movement. The single note obviously has a singular impulse (injection of energy) and a singular resolution of that impulse. A motive begins with an impulse, which is followed by the resolution of that impulse. The resolution is ended by the beginning of a new impulse; the complete motive is defined by its complete impulse and complete resolution. The same is true of a phrase: it is defined by its impulse and the resolution of that impulse. A succession of tones unfolding less than a single apprehensible impulse and resolution cannot be perceived as a unit: thus a succession of tones that gathers impulse continuously without releasing it is heard as incomplete; it is perceived as part of a continuing unit and not as a complete unit in and of itself. In other words, what makes such a succession of individual tones singular is its singular, overarching impulse followed by the singular, overarching resolution of that impulse.

A resolution is *consequent* to its impulse when it plays out or releases all the energy created, not more and not less. It is the consequent playing out of the singular overarching impulse by the singular overarching resolution that unites—binds together—the individual elements of an entire work or movement into a singular unit, and leads to the ultimate experience of beauty.

But musical compositions unfold units on many levels. On the highest level is that of the whole work (or self-contained movement). The greatest masterworks can be apprehended unitarily: they can be performed so that the entire work articulates a single, comprehensive impulse that is resolved completely.[1] An entire work, articulated by a comprehensive, broad-scale impulse and resolution, divides into smaller units, each articulated by an energy-gathering impulse that is released. Smaller groupings may be built of still smaller groupings, each defined by its own impulse and resolution. Nesting of articulated groupings exists on multiple levels, all the way to the musical surface.[2]

Because groupings are nested, a given tone may participate in different dynamic forces on different levels. A tone may participate in a motive, which is part of a phrase, which is part of a larger section, which is part of the entire work; the tone may participate in impulse within the motive, which may participate in the resolution within its phrase, which may participate in the impulse of its section, which may participate in the resolution of the entire work.

Impulse is generated by the composer by numerous factors. On a local level—the level of motives or phrases—more influential factors are harmonic tension and melodic direction. Other factors include rhythmic activity and instrumentation. On a global level—the level of the entire work—the most influential factor in the creation of impulse is harmonic: the structure of key relationships. Other factors that can lead to the creation of energy on the global level are broad-scale rhythmic densification and the opposition of contrasting material.

Broadly stated, then, form is the way in which the work divides. That divisibility is effected not only by the two commonly accepted considerations of the nature of the material and the key relationships, but more importantly by the controlling forces of impulse and resolution. In fact, the necessity of creating and resolving impulse on all levels of the hierarchy determines the nature of the material as it unfolds, and it determines the structure of those key relationships.

Tonicization

Broad-scale impulse is a function of key relationships: it results from moving away from the home key by tonicizing other keys. But a new tonality can affect the broad-scale dynamic structure only if it is fully tonicized.

Generally, three conditions must obtain for a new tonality to be tonicized.[3] First, the operative pitch field must be that of the new key; second, a tonic harmony or tonic substitute must sound within that operative pitch field; and third, a dominant harmony that includes the 4:7 tritone must also sound within the operative pitch field. The latter two conditions are relatively simple. The passage must include—in any inversion—a tonic harmony or a submediant harmony (which functions as a tonic for the purposes of establishing tonality). It must also include a dominant seventh chord, also in any inversion.

The first condition is somewhat more complex. The term *pitch field* denotes those pitches that participate in a given tonality. The pitch field of the major mode consists of the tonic, its upper and lower harmonic neighbors (scale degrees 5 and 4), its upper and lower linear neighbors (scale degrees 2 and 7), and two tones that characterize the mode (scale degrees 3 and 6). The pitch field of the minor mode consists of the tonic, its upper and lower harmonic neighbors (scale degrees 5 and 4), its upper and lower linear neighbors (scale degrees 2 and 7), and two tones that characterize the mode (scale degrees 3 and 6). Linear direction is a determining factor in the orientation of the 6th and 7th scale degrees. The 7th scale degree is in its lowered position, one whole step below the tonic, when it participates in a linear (stepwise) descent from the tonic to the 5th scale degree. The 7th scale degree is in its raised position, one half step below the tonic, when it participates in a linear ascent from the 5th scale degree to the tonic. Ordinarily the 6th scale degree in the minor mode stands one half step above the 5th scale degree, but to participate in a linear ascent to the tonic through scale degree 7 it is raised by a half step.

The linear functions of the 6th and 7th scale degrees in the minor mode are illustrated by the opening theme of Beethoven's String Quartet, Op. 95 (ex. 7.1◀))). A line consists of half and whole steps; motion by an interval larger than a whole step is perceived as harmonic, not linear. The linear descent from the tonic F to the 5th scale degree C includes the 6th scale degree D♭. To avoid a nonlinear augmented second between the 6th and 7th scale degrees, the 7th scale degree must be in its lowered position, E♭. Similarly, to assist the ascent back to the tonic, the 7th scale degree E♮ is in its raised position. To avoid a nonlinear augmented second between the 6th and 7th scale degrees, the 6th scale degree is raised to D♮.

Example 7.1. Beethoven, String Quartet in F Minor, Op. 95, 1st mvt., Allegro con brio, bars 1–2

The *operative pitch field* is that pitch field in effect at any given point in a musical work. A tone is operative until it is cancelled by chromatic inflection. For example, an E sounding once remains in the operative pitch field until—perhaps bars later—it is canceled by the sounding of an E♭ or an E♯. The pitch field consists of seven diatonic tones, one for each letter name. Operative tones of E, F♯, G♯, A, B, C♯, and D♯ result in an operative pitch field of E major. Operative tones of G, A, B♭, C, D, E♭, and F♯ result in an operative pitch field of G minor. If the operative pitch field is that of C major (C, D, E, F, G, A, and B) and a B♭ is sounded, the operative pitch field becomes that of F major (F, G, A, B♭, C, D, and E). Chromatic inflection may result in a pitch field that is not associated with any major or minor key. If the operative pitch field is that of C major (C, D, E, F, G, A, and B) and a D♯ is sounded, the operative pitch field becomes C, D♯, E, F, G, A, and B, which is has elements of E minor and C major but does not belong to any one key.

To reiterate, to effect a full tonicization, the operative pitch field must be that of the new key, and it must include both a tonic or tonic substitute harmony and a 4:7 dominant harmony. The absence of any of those conditions results in a tonicization that is only partial. A passage from the end of the second movement into the beginning of the third movement of Beethoven's Piano Concerto No. 4, given in example 7.2 (◀)), illustrates partial tonicizations in which the operative pitch field of the new key is present but the 4:7 dominant harmony is lacking.

The example begins at bar 64 of the second movement, on a fully tonicized E minor. In bar 68, a full tonicization of A minor is effected by sounding of the G♯ diminished seventh chord, while the operative pitch field (A, B, C, D, E, F, and G♯) is that of A minor. In bar 69, F♯ and D♯ sounding on the final eighth note suggests E minor, but the operative pitch field belongs to no key (A, B, C, D♯, E, F♯, and G♯). The G♮ of bar 71 creates an operative pitch field of E minor (E, F♯, G, A, B, C, and D♯); however without the sounding of a 4:7 dominant harmony (one that includes A and D♯), the key of E minor is never fully tonicized.

The beginning of the third movement is characterized by a nebulous tonal footing. The previous movement ends in a weakened, partially tonicized E minor. The opening root-position C-major chord in an affirmative character sounds something like a tonic chord, but the D♯ and F♯ are still part of the operative pitch field. The sounding of the D-major chord in bar 6 cancels the previously operative D♯, creates a pitch field of G major, and thus effects a partial tonicization of that key (although only partial, as nowhere in the first ten bars does Beethoven give us a 4:7 dominant harmony in G major). The pitch field of C major is established with the F♮ of bar 11, effecting a partial tonicization of C major. The pitch field of G major is reestablished by the F♯ in bar 16, which replaces F♮ in the operative pitch field. And G major is finally fully tonicized in bar 18 with the G-major chord, after the sounding of the C♮ in the upper line (17) over a D-major chord that results in a dominant seventh chord.

Example 7.2. Beethoven, Piano Concerto No. 4 in G Major, Op. 58, end of 2nd mvt. and beginning of 3rd mvt.

Conversely, the passage from the final movement of Brahms's Sonata for Clarinet (or Viola) and Piano in E♭ given in example 7.3 (◀)) illustrates a partial tonicization in which a 4:7 dominant of a new key is present, but the operative pitch field is not. The passage begins in the home key, E♭ major. A dominant seventh chord sounds on the third eighth note of bar 4, the successive resolution to a B♭-major harmony functions in the key of B♭. However, the operative pitch field (B♭, C, D, E♭, F, G♭, and A) is not that of B♭ major. The G♭ sounded earlier in the bar in the bass suggests the key of B♭ minor, but B♭ minor could

Example 7.3. Brahms, Sonata for Clarinet (or Viola) and Piano in E♭ Major, Op. 120, No. 2, 3rd mvt., Andante con moto, bars 2–4

not exist without the lowered third, D♭, which is not part of the operative pitch field. As a result there is no full tonicization.

A full tonicization cannot be effected without the sounding of a tonic or a tonic substitute (a chord built on scale degree 6). Example 7.4 (◀)) illustrates a passage in which both the operative pitch field of the new key and a dominant seventh of that new key are present but no full tonicization is effected due to the absence of a tonic or tonic substitute. In this passage from the final movement of the "Harp" Quartet, a full tonicization of C minor occurs in bar 7. With the first beat of bar 9, the operative pitch field is that of F major, and the harmony is a dominant seventh of that key, but without the sounding of an F major or D minor harmony, no full tonicization of F minor occurs. Similarly, with the second beat of bar 9 the operative pitch field is that of B♭ major, and the harmony

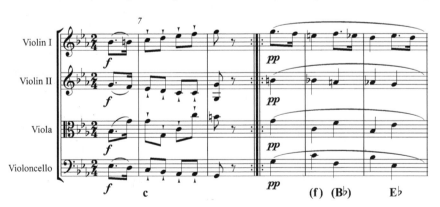

Example 7.4. Beethoven, String Quartet in E♭ major, Op. 74, "The Harp," 4th mvt., Allegretto con Variazioni, bars 6–10

is a dominant seventh of that key, but without the sounding of a B♭-major or G-minor harmony no full tonicization of B♭ major occurs.

To tonicize a minor key, the 6th scale degree must be present in its descending or lowered position, one half-step above scale degree 5, and the 7th scale degree must be present in its ascending or raised position, one half-step below scale degree 1.[4] Example 7.5 (◀)), from the Poco Allegretto of Brahms's Third Symphony, illustrates a tonicization of F minor that is rendered partial because of the absence of a 6th scale degree in the lowered position (D♭ would be required, instead of the D♮ that is present).

Example 7.5. Brahms, Symphony No. 3 in F Major, Op. 90, 3rd mvt., Poco Allegretto, bars 4–12

To summarize, the pitch field of a minor tonality shares the 1st, 2nd, 4th, and 5th scale degrees with the major mode; and its 3rd scale degree is always lowered. The position of the 6th and 7th scale degrees may vary. The 6th scale degree must be in the lowered position to establish the tonality, but may be in the raised position in linear ascents. The 7th scale degree is in the raised position in linear ascents and to establish the tonality, and may be in the lowered position in linear descents.

Finally, and of critical importance, the presence of a pedal tone renders an otherwise full tonicization partial. Even if all three necessary conditions are present—a new operative pitch field along with a tonic and a 4:7 dominant harmony in the new key— will not effect full tonicization of the new key if they occur in conjunction with a pedal tone.[5]

Structural Harmonic Motion

Over the course of an entire work, broad-scale harmonic motion is the overriding factor in creating the structure of energy. The farther a new key lies from the home key, the greater the impulse it engenders. To create significant impulse, the new tonality must be perceived as distant from the home key, not simply different, and tonalities other than the home key must be perceived as having varying degrees of distance from the home key.

Activity occurs on different levels. A baby lying on her back can be extremely active, throwing her arms and kicking her legs wildly. Yet on another level the baby has not moved; she has remained stationary on the bed.[6] Similarly, linear activity also occurs on levels, as determined by stepwise motion. Example 7.6 (◀)) offers a most basic illustration.

Example 7.6. An illustration of the hierarchic nature of linear activity

The A is a harmonic aspect of the C; there is a sense in which the melodic activity is suspended until the B is sounded. The resultant perception is of a structural stepwise descent D–C–B. During the sounding of the A, the melody has moved on a local level, but not on a structural level.

As the unit of structural linear motion is the step, the unit of structural harmonic motion is the fifth. Just as in example 7.6 the C holds a structural linear priority over the A until a tone one step from the C is sounded, a given tonality holds a structural harmonic priority over any new tonicized tonality until a tonality a fifth away is tonicized. For example, if a passage is in C major, structural harmonic motion will result from the tonicization of F major (one fifth down) or G major (one fifth up). The tonicization of a key other than one a fifth away is perceived as motion on a local level only. If a passage is in C major, the tonicization of E major or B major or A♭ major or F♯ major or any key other than F major or G major constitutes no motion whatsoever on a higher structural level. The tonicization of F major or G major results in the perception of a single step of harmonic motion on a structural level, even if it is preceded by the tonicization of another key; just as in example 7.6, the sounding of the B results in the perception of a single step of linear motion on a structural level, even though it is preceded by the C–A leap.

Motion on a higher level requires contrast, not just difference. There is no contrast without commonality. Considering the height of a person at the ages of three and thirty does not yield the perception of progress, because there is insufficient commonality for meaningful contrast. Considering the height of a person at the ages of three and four, however, yields the perception of progress, because there is commonality, and thus basis for contrast. Structural harmonic progress is measured in steps of fifth tonicizations because keys whose tonics lie one fifth away have the most in common, and therefore the greatest contrast.

Between tonalities, commonality leading to contrast is a function of the pitch fields. The keys with the most pitches in common stand a fifth apart. For example, the key of E♭ major has a pitch field of E♭, F, G, A♭, B♭, C and D. It shares six pitches with B♭ major, which has a pitch field of B♭, C, D, E♭, F, G, and A. There is maximum contrast between these two tonalities, because six out of seven members of the pitch field change their function (F changes from scale degree 2 to the dominant; G changes from scale degree 3 to scale degree 6, and so on). The key of E♭ major is fairly remote from G major, with which it shares only three pitches, G, C, and D. And it is quite far removed from B major, with which it has no pitches in common. There is relatively little contrast between E♭ major and G major, and virtually none between E♭ major and B major.

A second consideration is the stability of tones within a pitch field: their inclination to motion. Scale degree 1 is the most stable; it is the least inclined to motion. Scale degrees 4 and 5, lying a stable perfect fifth below and above the tonic, are relatively stable, and anchor the pitch field. Scale degrees 3 and 6 provide color by defining the mode; scale degrees 2 and 7 stand in stepwise relation to the tonic and are relatively unstable.

Another critical factor generating contrast between pitch fields is the transformation of the tonic (scale degree 1) to an anchor (scale degree 4 or 5), and an anchor to a tonic. Such a tonicization creates a powerful contrast, more powerful than if that tonic becomes one of the weaker, less stable scale degrees. This tonic-anchor transformation occurs in the tonicization of a key one fifth away. When the new tonic lies a fifth above the old tonic, such as D major to A major, the original tonic (D) becomes scale degree 4, and the original scale degree 5 (A) becomes the tonic. When the new tonic lies a fifth below the original tonic, such as D major to G major, the original tonic (D) becomes the 5th scale degree, and the original 4th scale degree (G) becomes the tonic.

Tonicizations of a minor-mode key work in the same way. The structural form of the relative minor includes the 7th scale degree in its lowered position.[7] Although this "natural" form of the minor mode and its relative major have all seven pitches in common, they do not have any tonic-anchor commonality. The tonicization of a relative major (or relative minor) does not result in a tonic-anchor transformation, and thus does not create much contrast. The pitch field of A minor includes A, B, C, D, E, F, and G. All seven pitches participate in the pitch field of C major. In the tonicization of C major from A minor, the tonic A of A minor becomes a fairly unstable scale degree 6 in C major; the 5th scale degree E of A minor becomes a relatively unstable scale degree 3 in C major; and the 4th scale degree D in A minor becomes an unstable scale degree 2 in C major.

Because the greatest contrast occurs between tonalities whose tonics lie one fifth apart, the fifth is the unit of structural harmonic motion. Distance from the home key can be measured in terms of the number of successive fifth tonicizations in a given direction. The impulse of a work climaxes at the point of greatest energy—the point farthest from silence. The climax of the work then comes at the point of greatest energy within the key area farthest by successive fifth tonicizations from the tonic (within that key, or in the motion toward or away from that key). Thus, in a work in which the structural harmonic expansion by ascending fifth is greater than that by descending fifth, the climax occurs with the key of the farthest ascending fifth, and vice versa. In a work in which the structural harmonic expansion occurs by the same number of fifths in each direction, the climax comes with the farthest descending fifth.[8]

Note four additional characteristics of structural motion by successive fifth tonicizations. First, the succession of fifths need not be successive. For example, if tonicizations of the first, second, and then third fifths are followed by a return to the home key, a subsequent tonicization of the fourth fifth would continue the impulse generated through the earlier motion to the third fifth. A harmonic step of a fifth may be established though retroactive connection: if a tonicization of the fourth fifth is followed by, say, tonicizations of the first and second fifths, a subsequent tonicization of the third fifth would connect up with the earlier fourth fifth, rendering it part of the succession and thus impulse generating.

Second, the return from the climactic key to the home key need not occur by steps of fifth tonicizations. Once the farthest fifth has been connected up by steps of fifth tonicizations, the successful return to the home key can skip any number of intervening fifths. Third, in returning from the climactic key to the home tonic, compositions often swing at least one fifth in the opposite direction.

Finally, for the tonicization by fifth to create broad-scale impulse, the 3rd scale degree of the tonicized key must be in the pitch field of the home key. In a work in C major, the first ascending fifth is G. The 3rd scale degree of a key in which G is the tonic is some kind of B. The B that participates in the pitch field of the home key of C major is B♮, which is the 3rd scale degree of G major, not G minor. Thus in the energy-producing succession of ascending fifths from a home key of C major, the mode of the tonicized G is major. Likewise the second fifth is D minor, whose third, F♮, participates in the pitch field of C major; the next fifth is A minor, then E minor, B minor, F♯ minor, C♯ minor, and G♯ minor. The chain of descending fifths from C minor would include B♭ major, F major, E♭ major, A♭ major, and D♭ major, all of whose 3rd scale degrees participate in the pitch field of the home key.

In works in which successive fifth tonicizations extend further, the new key takes its mode from the pitch field of the next fifth from the home key. In other words, continuing the ascending succession, G♯ minor would be followed by D♯ minor, which takes its third, F♯, from the pitch field of G major, the first fifth above the home tonic. Next would come A♯ minor, which takes its third, C♯, from the pitch field of D minor, the next fifth above the tonic, and so on. Continuing the descending succession, D♭ major would be followed by G♭ major, which takes its third B♭ from the pitch field of F major, the first descending fifth below the home tonic, and so on.

While a minor-mode key requires the 7th scale degree in the ascending position to be established on a local level, on a structural level the 7th scale degree functions in its descending position. If the home key is A minor, broad-scale impulse by ascending fifth will result from the tonicization of E minor, whose third is G, the lowered 7th of the home key. It will not result from a tonicization of E major, whose third is G♯, the raised 7th scale degree of the home key.

Continuing the succession of structural ascending fifth tonicizations, E minor is followed by B minor, F♯ minor, C♯ minor. From the home key of A minor, broad-scale impulse by descending fifth will result from the tonicization of D minor, G major, C major, F major, and so on.

Dance Form

A typical binary form such as a dance form (minuet, gavotte, etc.)[9] creates energy through some kind of opposition in the first strain, then expands that energy before resolving it in the second strain. Generally that opposition is between the tonic key and the subsequently tonicized dominant; generally the opposition is expanded in the second strain by additional tonicizations by successive ascending fifths. The energy is resolved in the second strain with a return to the home key.

Many dance-form movements are constructed of two similar dances, the second sandwiched between two soundings of the first. The climax of such a movement generally comes in the second strain of the middle dance. Either the middle dance extends the chain of impulse-giving fifth tonicizations farther than the first dance, or the motion of the second dance is quicker, and thus creates more impulse.

Theme and Variations

A theme-and-variations movement[10] is in a sense the simplest musical form, because it creates its broad-scale structure of impulse and resolution primarily through varying densities of rhythmic activity.

On a local level, increasing rhythmic density creates energy, and decreasing rhythmic density releases it. Listen to example 7.7 (◀)), in which the rhythmic density increases and then decreases.[11] The height of the impulse comes with the first beat of bar 4. From that point on, the release of the gathered energy is brought about by the decreasing rhythmic density.

In theme-and-variations movements, rhythmic density is the primary generator of energy on a structural level. Generally the theme is characterized by limited harmonic activity. Successive variations maintain harmonic and melodic characteristics of the theme, but create broad-scale impulse primarily by increasing the density of rhythmic activity from variation to variation. To some extent, impulse may also be created by increasing the contrast between the theme and successive variations; in other words, energy is created as successive variations

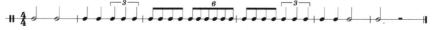

Example 7.7. An illustration of impulse built by increasing density

have increasingly fewer attributes in common with the theme. Impulse created by these means is relatively subtle; often the climax is supplemented or reinforced by a short-lived tonicization of an opposing key, or succession of such tonicizations. Resolution may be effected in part through a similar broad-scale decrease in rhythmic density. It may also be effected with an expansive passage that dwells on the tonic. Such a passage plays out the energy by extending the sounds without additional activity that would create impulse.

Sonata-form

A sonata-form movement[12] is divisible in three parts: exposition, in which an opposition is introduced; development, in which the opposition is expanded to a climax; and recapitulation, in which the opposition is resolved.

The notion of opposition resulting from contrasting A and B material seems to stand in stark contrast to the archetypal Baroque single-character movements. In fact, sonata-form is very much a logical outgrowth of binary Baroque dance forms, an outgrowth resulting from the need to create longer movements.[13] The length of a movement is directly related to the amount of energy created. The more energy created, the longer the work, because it takes longer to build more energy and it takes longer to release it. Conversely, the longer the work, the more energy needed to sustain it.

The first strain of a Baroque dance form introduces the initial opposition of tonic to—frequently—dominant. Increasing the opposition cannot be accomplished by substituting a different tonality for the B material; there is no higher harmonic opposition than between two tonalities whose tonics lie one fifth away. The harmonic opposition can be increased, however, by strengthening the polarization. This is accomplished in part by preceding the B material in the dominant with tonicizations of different keys, generally that of the dominant of the new dominant. This neutralizes the home key (the tonic of the A material) by eliminating its immediacy. More importantly, leaping a harmonic step to the second fifth before confirming the first fifth allows the B material dominant to be settled, entrenched, not as a tenuous first step forward, but as the stable return, solid in its own right.

Unlike Baroque dance-form movements, which have a single character throughout, in sonata-form movements the opposition within the exposition between A material and B material is heightened by their opposing characters. The nature of the opposition between A and B material may involve melodic direction (one essentially descending, and the other essentially ascending), or texture, or note values, or volume; it invariably involves the orientation of the tempo, one urging forward and one holding back.

The sonata-form development section presents a further expansion of the harmonic expansion that occurs at the beginning of the second strain of a binary dance form. The term development has two meanings: it refers both to a procedure and to a section within a work in which this procedure is prominent. The procedure involves elaboration, alteration, and fragmentation of musical material. The development section of a sonata-form movement is characterized by a fragmented presentation of the material, often in a contrapuntal texture, and by the frequency and remoteness of tonicizations.

In part, intensification occurs as a result of the nature of the material itself. The very elaboration and fragmentation that characterizes the material of the development section brings about intensification. That elaboration increases energy may be clear from listening to example 7.8 (◀》), a passage from the fourth movement of Mozart's "Haffner" Symphony, and example 7.9 (◀》), from the last movement of Beethoven's Symphony No. 2. In example 7.8, the second 2-bar figure is an elaboration of the first, and increases the energy. Conversely in example 7.9 the second four bars is a simplification of the first, and it releases energy; the rhythmic expansion of the last four bars further releases energy. Fragmentation also creates impulse, as can be heard in example 7.10 (◀》), from the first movement of Beethoven's Symphony No. 8. The 2-bar fragmentation of the opening 8-bar theme creates energy; the further fragmentation into 1-bar statements increases the energy. Development, then, suggests not only alteration or reshaping, but intensification—growth in energy.

Example 7.8. Mozart, Symphony No. 35 in D Major, K. 385, "Haffner," 4th mvt., Presto, bars 1–4

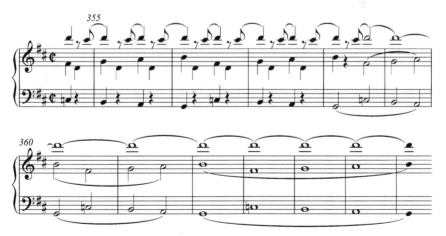

Example 7.9. Beethoven, Symphony No. 2 in D Major, Op. 36, 4th mvt., Allegro molto, bars 354–66

Example 7.10. Beethoven, Symphony No. 8 in F Major, Op. 93, 1st mvt., Allegro vivace e con brio, bars 143–51

Primarily, though, broad-scale impulse is generated by structural harmonic motion by fifth tonicization. Initial opposition between the tonic and the first fifth is expanded in the development section with additional harmonic steps, which stretch the tension from the home key and generate impulse. The harmonic motion of a development section is not random, but moves specifically by harmonic steps of the fifth. Harmonic activity other than by fifth does not bring about a stretching of the tension—an intensification of the opposition created in the exposition—but is heard as coloration without fundamental motion.[14]

Intensification continues up to the climax, which occurs within the key farthest by successive fifth tonicizations from the home key, or within the motion toward or away from that key. From that point, the development releases energy, both harmonically and by the nature of the material. Ultimately it regains the home key in preparation for the recapitulation of the exposition material.

The recapitulation carries out the broad-scale release of energy that begins after the climax; it resolves the conflict of the exposition primarily by unfolding both A and B material in the tonic. Almost always, the conflict between the two groups of material is reduced in other ways as well, ways that—combined with the harmonic agreement—bring about a lessening of the conflict of tempo orientation.

Restating both the A and B material from the exposition in the home key often would result in too much resolution for the broad-scale impulse created—the energy would be played out before the music ended. To counteract that, some sonata-form movements typically do one or more of the following: (1) shorten one of the sections of the recapitulation, usually the A material, (2) embellish one of the sections of the recapitulation, usually the A material, or (3) tonicize the subdominant to create additional impulse.

Some sonata-form movements include a coda, which takes place only after a structural final cadence ($\hat{2}$–$\hat{1}$ over V–I). The coda is necessary if energy remains after that structural final cadence; in other words if there has not been enough music to resolve the degree of impulse created. The coda typically completes something left incomplete, usually involving the harmonic return to the tonic from the climax.

Fugue

A fugue[15] is a work that treats a subject or subjects contrapuntally in a specified number of voices. As with any tonal work, the global structure of energy in a fugue is created primarily through successive fifth tonicizations away from the home key. But many fugues have a fascinating feature. The notion that the germ of an entire work is contained in the opening material is a popular and romantic one, and one that holds true to a remarkable degree for a great many of the fugues of the masters. A fugue subject, like any articulation, unfolds an impulse and resolution; the climax signals the end of the impulse and the beginning of the resolution. In a significant number of fugues the tonic scale degree of the key farthest by fifth tonicization from the home key is the same as the pitch that climaxes the fugue subject. For example, in a fugue whose subject climaxes on a B, the key farthest by successive fifth tonicizations would be B (major or minor).

To be sure, this is not true of every fugue. In many fugues, especially those in which the impulse of the subject climaxes with the tonic or the dominant scale degree, the climactic tonality is generated by the height of a secondary impulse within the subject. In some cases, the climactic tonality is completely unrelated to the dynamic shape of the subject. But the correspondence between the dynamic structure of the subject and that of the entire work occurs with such frequency, and is such a logical component of an organic composition, that it seems impossible to dismiss.

Chapter Eight

Dynamic Analysis

On the Performer's Contribution

Since the advent of music theory as a dedicated profession in the mid-nineteenth century, theorists have intuited that analysis would be at least beneficial, and perhaps even essential, to performers. Recently, "Performance and Analysis" has emerged as a distinct area of study within the field. Despite an abundance of serious Performance and Analysis studies by eminent music theorists, no universal principles have emerged, and little if any interest has been generated among performers.

The failure of efforts to date to tie performance to analysis is not due to bad writing on Performance and Analysis; rather, it points up the limitations of analysis as it has been practiced. To allow the possibility of offering assistance to performers, analysis must result in a more comprehensive understanding of a composition than has been sought, but such an analysis requires a fundamentally different process by the analyst. In an attempt to overcome the limitations of analysis for performers, this chapter presents a path toward gaining new insight into the essential nature of a composition.

A Brief Overview of Performance and Analysis

The latter part of the twentieth century saw a flurry of attempts to demonstrate the value of analysis for performance,[1] e.g., Cone (1968), Meyer (1973), Burkhart (1983), Schmalfeldt (1985), Narmour (1988), Berry (1989), Dunsby (1989), and Schachter (1991). These writings hew to a common formula: a description of some element of the structure of a composition, followed by instructions for dynamic and temporal inflections with which to effect its proper or preferred realization in performance. Some are built on the intuitive assumption that a preferred performance would "bring out" the element in question. But because this necessarily leads to pedantic or especially peculiar performances, authors recommend that in some cases the structural element should not be emphasized, and that in some cases it should be produced counterintuitively; some authors suggest that a structurally important element could be performed acceptably in opposing ways. The justifications for the performance recommendations range from assumed to poetic to tortured; none would withstand a test of rigorous questioning.[2]

Ensuing criticism—Howell (1992), Rosenwald (1993), Lester (1995), Rothstein (1995), and Cook ("Analysing Performance and Performing Analysis,"1999)—held these studies to be too one-sided: the analyst visiting requirements on the mute performer. Perhaps in response, two different and equally unfruitful types of studies followed. Some gave weight to the performer's contribution by presenting statistical analyses of multiple recorded performances of a given work: Clarke (2004), Ramirez et al. (2006), and Sapp (2008). Such studies can at best reveal tendencies in performance, but of course they do not yield any causal connection between a compositional component and the necessity of its performance. Others—Schmalfeldt (2003) and Rothstein (2005)—offered the familiar formula in reverse. Instead of beginning with an analysis which they applied to a performance, they began by describing an element of a performance, which they then tied back to a structural element gleaned by analysis.

All of these writings are grounded on the assumption that some conscious awareness by a performer of a structural element would necessarily improve the performance. To be sure, every one of these studies is thought-provoking as to the performance of a given piece. They all, however, fall short of offering—or do not claim to offer—definitive justification for that performance. And thus they all fall well short of offering useful guidance to the performer more generally.

In fact, no effort to date has produced anything approaching a set of clear, universal principles for understanding the structure of a piece in a way that aids performers. Predictably, performers have shown no significant interest. And, unfortunately for the theorist hoping to be helpful to the performer, a bigger obstacle than a lack of cogent results so far is the fact that musicians have always been able to give profoundly superb performances, largely absent comprehensive theoretical analysis. Nonetheless, it may be possible for an analytic method to be of some service to performers, and, in the practice of such a method, for theorists to themselves engage in a more comprehensive and rewarding way of considering a composition.

Underpinnings of Dynamic Analysis

Like any theory, Dynamic Analysis depends for its validity not on foregoing theories, but on its effectiveness in explaining the information at hand. Of course anyone theorizing now stands on the proverbial shoulders of giants: none more giant than Jean-Philipe Rameau and Heinrich Schenker. As do so many other efforts, this one depends substantially on their contributions to our understanding of harmony and hierarchical voice leading. Additionally, Dynamic Analysis involves several concepts well articulated by others over the past century.

One such concept is the necessity of understanding the composition as an autonomous entity, divorced from extramusical considerations such as text, program, social context, or listener bias. This is essential for our purposes, because an approach that seeks meaning from outside the composition limits the possible benefit of analysis for the performer. In the musical experience in which the sound generates an extramusical thought, the focused consciousness is absorbed with that extramusical thought, or on the connection between the sound and the thought. The quality of the experience depends then not on the quality of the performance (our concern), but on the quality of that thought, or on the ability of the listener to make those connections. So the quality of the performance is to a significant degree irrelevant to the essence of that kind of experience.

Similarly, approaching music with an eye toward the cultural biases of the listener—even considering its absorption by the familiar "experienced listener"—is limiting for our purposes. While undoubtedly there exist differences among individual listeners on the basis of experience and cultural biases, we are seeking the essential commonality beyond the differences.

A second essential concept is an understanding of the forces of energy that stand at the core of the musical experience. The tones (and percussive sounds) do not exist in and of themselves; they stand in relation to each other in our consciousness, all in the service of the creation and resolution of energy. These two notions—autonomy and energy—are found in the writings of several theorists, but are combined perhaps most directly in those of August Halm.[3]

Not only is it essential to consider a work as autonomous, but the work must be taken as a singular entity, as a whole. What is especially critical for us about Schenker's notion of hierarchical levels is that it allows for the conception of an extended movement as a singular entity.

Another essential concept is grouping: sounds in a musical context coalesce into groupings in our experience, and those groupings are hierarchic. In other words, the essential hierarchy is not simply one in which tones lower on the hierarchy prolong tones higher on the hierarchy. Rather, music comes to us on the surface level within articulated groupings, which are nested within larger groupings, which are nested within still larger groups. For Leonard Meyer, "Analysis is something which happens whenever one attends intelligently to the world."[4] And when Professor Meyer—along with sometime collaborator Grosvenor Cooper—attended intelligently to the world of music he found grouping patterns, in which groupings are nested within other groupings in a hierarchic structure.

Yet another important element is the linking of the notion of energy with that of groupings. Groupings are not articulated primarily by the interaction of rhythm and meter, as was held by Cooper and Meyer, but rather by a structure of energy.[5] Like Meyer, Fred Lerdahl and Ray Jackendoff held that music unfolds in groupings at a surface level, and that the groupings are nested in hierarchical relationships, which they represent graphically with a tree notation.[6] The groupings of Lerdahl and Jackendoff also have an added component of what they termed "tension and relaxation": essentially the creation and playing out of energy.

In summary, theorists have long understood—or have had access to the understanding—that a work is a self-contained, unitary entity; that the creation and release of energy plays a critical role; that tones prolong other tones in a nested structure; that this nested structure consists of groupings; and that those groupings involve the interplay of energy. What is missing?

Beauty—Dynamic Function—Consequence

British musicologist John Rink "wonders whether a more propitious transfer of procedural and evaluative criteria from one of these musical activities [analysis and performance] to the other might be accomplished in the opposite direction, that is, from performance to analysis, whereby the fundamental aims and approaches implicit in performing a piece were established as part of one's analytical premise in studying that work."[7] It just may be so.

The fundamental aim of the performer—as it is of the composer and the listener—is beauty: that extraordinary, transcendent, loss-of-self aesthetic experience. To reach more deeply into the essence of the composition, then, and as an added bonus to be able to offer assistance to the performer, the theorist must begin with this question: how can a conscious understanding of the structure of a composition help in bringing it to life in such a way as to enable the highest experience of beauty? Or, in other words: how can studying the construction of a piece help to play it most beautifully?

For the most transcendent experience of beauty to occur, all the individual tones of a composition must join together into the singular aesthetic object. An individual tone joins into a larger grouping when it derives meaning from its relation to the other tones in the grouping. The tones of an entire work (or self-contained movement) join together when each tone derives meaning from its relation to all the other tones.

The nature of that meaning lies in the attributes of the tones.[8] An attribute of a tone is an essential defining characteristic, so that changing the attribute changes the essence of the tone. Each tone has the attributes of pitch, duration, intensity, timbre, and temporal placement. These attributes define the tone outside any musical context, and are original attributes. In a musical context, a tone that participates in a line has the attribute of linear function; one that participates in a mode has the attribute of scale degree; one that is active simultaneously with other tones has the attribute of harmonic function; one that occurs within a meter has the attribute of metric placement, one that occurs within a rhythmic system has a rhythmic function. These and any other attributes that derive from the relation of the tone to other tones are relational attributes.

In the experience of a musical performance, each tone also participates in a dynamic structure: the gathering and release of energy. Thus each tone has the attribute of dynamic function. This is a multilayered attribute: a tone may participate in a release of energy within a motive, which participates in a larger phrase that gathers energy; that phrase may be part of a section which is playing out energy, within a global gathering of energy. To the extent that we experience the entire work in a single act of consciousness, our experience of a given tone carries within it all the levels of dynamic function in which the tone participates.[9]

Dynamic function is a kind of "super attribute," in that it results from the synthesis of all the other attributes. The attribute of volume; the attributes of pitch in terms of linear function, harmonic function, and scale degree; the attributes of temporal placement and duration in terms of the rhythm; the attribute of duration in terms of articulations; the attribute of meter (in that an emphasized weak-beat event creates more energy than an emphasized strong-beat event); the attribute of temporal placement in terms of the large-scale tempo orientation; and even to some degree the attribute of timbre—all come together to create the dynamic function: the multileveled increase and/or playing out of energy effected by a tone.

The hierarchy of dynamic structure is immutably connected to the voice-leading hierarchy (as it is to every aspect of the work). Within a voice-leading hierarchy, a passage that prolongs a single chord is controlled by that chord; it represents the chord. On a broader level of the hierarchy, that chord may participate in a progression of similarly prolonged chords; this progression may itself prolong a single chord, in which case it is controlled by that single chord—it represents that chord. On the broadest level of the hierarchy—the background level—a movement or work is controlled by a single progression. Events on any level represent or stand in for the events on the next broadest level. Representation results because the attributes of the representative events include the attributes of the controlling events. A voice-leading hierarchy exists to the extent that the attributes of linear function, harmonic function, and scale degree of each controlling component are imbued in its representatives. Representation occurs between all levels of the hierarchy, thus the attributes of linear function, harmonic function, and scale degree of the background component are imparted to the events on the musical surface. But these are not the only attributes of the background component imbued in the attributes of the events on the musical surface. Of critical importance is that the attribute of dynamic structure, as created by the other attributes, is imparted as well.

The background progression has a dynamic structure, given by the attributes of linear function, harmonic function, and scale degree, within which it must be unfolded to be indivisible (so that the impulse is played out completely by a consequent resolution). The dynamic structure of the background is in fact the overall dynamic structure of the work. The climax of the work comes within the prolongation of the tone that climaxes the background progression. The

dynamic function of any tone within the hierarchy reflects the dynamic structure of the broader grouping that controls it, and is in turn reflected in the
tones that it controls. In that the dynamic structure exists on multiple levels and
extends to a single grouping on the very broadest level, given an indivisible performance of a masterwork, there is a very real sense in which the entire piece is
contained within each tone.

Specifically, ascending pitches tend to produce energy, as do increasing intervals between the highest and lowest concurrently sounding pitches. Escalating
rhythmic density tends to produce energy; similarly an accelerating tempo tends
to produce energy. Modulation by fifth away from the tonic key has a strong
tendency to produce energy. Ascending motion by leap tends to produce energy
more than does stepwise motion. Loud tends to generate more energy than soft.
Scale degree 7 tends to produce more energy than scale degree 1. A client tone
tends to produce more energy than its agent.[10] Dissonance tends to produce
more energy than consonance. Motion from a tonic harmony to a dominant
tends to produce energy; motion to a subdominant tends to produce more
energy. Crisper articulations tend to produce more energy than gentler ones,
and so on. In most cases the converse is true: descending pitches, de-escalating
rhythmic density, decreasing volume, harmonic motion to the tonic, and so on,
tend to play out or release energy.

The composer has complete responsibility for the attributes of pitch, rhythmic function, linear function, scale degree, harmonic function, and metric
placement. The tones of all performances will have equivalent attributes of
pitch, rhythmic function, linear function, scale degree, harmonic function,
and metric placement.[11] For example, consider a particular tone in the second
movement of the "Harp" Quartet. In every performance, the first tone in bar 4
of the first violin will be scale degree 4; it will be followed by a linear descent of
a minor 2nd; it will participate in a subdominant harmony; it will be a D♭; it will
be shorter than the tone after it and longer than the tones below it; and it will
be on a downbeat.

With regard to the attributes of timbre, duration as it concerns articulation,
and the broadest considerations of volume (intensity) and duration as it concerns tempo, the composer and performer have a shared responsibility. The
tones in any number of performances will have similar—but not the same—attributes of timbre, articulation, volume, and tempo. That high D♭ of the "Harp"
Quartet second movement, bar 4, will be sounded by a violin, softly, and within
a slow tempo. But the quality of that violin sound, the specific level of softness,
and the specific degree of slowness will vary from performance to performance.
Similarly, the chords of bar 1 will have separation, but how much separation will
vary from performance to performance.[12]

The performer has complete responsibility for the attribute of volume on
the level of local phrases. Stated differently, the use of volume inflections in the
making of phrases is the responsibility of the performer. Phrasing inflections are

indicated by the composer only rarely, and where directives for volume inflections exist—e.g., sforzando, crescendo—they are essentially vague. How much sforzando, how much crescendo, which tone carries the height of the energy—these are the sole responsibility of the performer.

Similarly, tempo directions are the sole responsibility of the performer. While tempo itself is not an attribute, a tone that participates in a building tempo carries the dynamic attribute of increasing energy; one that participates in a receding tempo carries the dynamic attribute of releasing energy. More clearly stated: an increasing tempo builds energy; a decreasing tempo releases it. A large-scale, forward-directed tempo is a powerful generator of energy on a global level, and a large-scale backward-directed tempo is a powerful releaser of energy on a global level. Locally, tempo inflections also affect the dynamic structure in a particularly powerful way: an accelerando increases energy, a ritardando releases it. As with composer-indicated dynamic inflections, composer-indicated tempo inflections are essentially vague. How much accelerando, how much cédez—these are the sole responsibility of the performer.[13]

The performer's goal is beauty; that beauty can come about given a unitary aesthetic object, which involves energy. This brings us back to the issue of musical units. Any musical unit is defined by a singular creation of energy and the resolution of that energy: a single note, a motive, a phrase, or an entire movement. For an entire work to be absorbed as singular, the energy created must be resolved consequently, no more and no less. Stated differently, the music and the energy must end at the same time: there can be no energy left at the end of the music, and no music left at the end of the energy. Note that within groupings at lower levels of the hierarchy, the resolution may not be completely consequent: a grouping that participates in a larger impulse may need to create some greater degree of impulse than it can resolve fully, and similarly a grouping that participates in a larger resolution may need to resolve more impulse than it can create. The goal of dynamic analysis is to find the grouping structure that allows the resolution maximally consequent to the impulse. In other words, it seeks the grouping structure that allows the least possible extra energy at the end of each musical grouping, or the least possible music at the end of the energy.

The dynamic tendencies of the attributes of a tone given by the composer are rarely if ever uniform: consider a tonic tone reached by ascending step from the 7th scale degree; or a diminished seventh harmony achieved by contracting outer voices from a tonic; or a tone participating in both a rhythmic diminution and a diminuendo. The composition calls for its realization in performance in a hierarchic configuration of groupings, each of which has an optimal dynamic structure so that the energy created within it can be resolved. So from among the confusion of conflicting tendencies, the performer uses the tools of volume inflections, tempo inflections, and large-scale directed tempo to bring about the hierarchic grouping structure in which impulse created within every grouping is resolved maximally.

The division of responsibility between performer and composer is critically important to dynamic analysis. Nonetheless, equally critical is the understanding that the structure of groupings necessary for an optimally beautiful performance is inherent in the composition. Thus, despite the absence of indications for the subtle considerations of tempo and volume that fall within the responsibility of the performer, these too are largely given by the composer.

Dynamic Analysis

Like Schenkerian analysis, on which it leans heavily, dynamic analysis is a process that can be illustrated graphically. The process entails uncovering the nested patterns of energy within which a work must be performed to be perceived unitarily. With the use of triangular symbols, the illustration represents the optimal dynamic structure at successive hierarchical levels in association with a Schenkerian, reductive voice-leading analysis; it also incorporates the structural harmonic activity, a key determinant of dynamic structure.

The process begins at the surface level of the music, and involves two mutually dependent parts: a determination of the optimal grouping structure (where the grouping begins and ends), and a concurrent determination of the optimal dynamic structure within those groupings (where the height of the impulse must be in order for that impulse to be resolved maximally consequently).

That dynamic structure may be immediately obvious, or extremely elusive. It may take a great deal of time and repetition to distinguish between subtly different experiences resulting from subtly different relationships. Like most activities, it gets easier with experience. Tendencies begin to reveal themselves. As noted, some of the factors that tend to generate impulse are ascending melodic lines, increasing harmonic tension, increasing rhythmic density, and events that sound against the meter. Conversely some factors that tend to resolve that impulse are descending melodic lines, decreasing harmonic tension, decreasing rhythmic density, and so on. But there is no hard and fast rule. In fact, because every tone in every musical context has its own set of distinct attributes contributing in different ways to the optimal dynamic structure, there can be no rule of any kind that any given condition must create or resolve impulse. The one overriding determinant of dynamic structure is this: impulse generated must be resolved.

The process is repeated on successive levels of the hierarchy, as smaller, lower-level groupings are heard to join into larger, higher-level groupings. Each level involves the mutually dependent determinations of where the grouping begins and ends, and where the height of the impulse comes, all toward the goal of maximal consequence. At levels higher than the musical surface, critical to the analytic process is maintaining the integrity of the temporal relationships. In other words, it is essential to consider the component tones in an approximation of their temporal relationships at the surface level. The process continues up to a background level, which encompasses the entire work in a single grouping. It also has an optimal dynamic structure so that the impulse can be resolved. Unlike the dynamic structure of lower-level groupings, in which the resolution need not be fully consequent, the dynamic structure of the background progression includes a fully consequent resolution.

Because the dynamic structure at each hierarchical level reflects the dynamic structure of the musical surface, the harmonic event that serves as the height of a higher-level grouping will also serve as the climax of lower-level groupings; either that event itself, or one that represents it. Stated differently, more often than not, the harmonic event that serves as the height of the impulse of a larger grouping will also climax the impulse of the grouping or groupings below it on the hierarchy. Occasionally the height of the impulse of a grouping on a higher level will not coincide with the height of the smaller impulse on a lower level; in this case the event that climaxes the impulse of the lower-level grouping represents (prolongs) the climactic event of the larger grouping. This is true all the way from the background to the surface of the music. Accordingly, the dynamic structure of the background mirrors that of the entire work: the climax of the movement will come with the sounding of the event that climaxes the background progression, or—more likely—within the prolongation of that event.

The graphic representation of a dynamic analysis includes hierarchical voice-leading reductions, each with an associated row of black triangles, and a notation of the structural harmonic activity. At each level of the hierarchy, the black triangles illustrate the dynamic structure of its voice-leading reduction: where groupings begin and end, and where the height of the impulse comes within each grouping.

The voice-leading reductions illustrate levels of structural priority with noteheads and stems: tones of the lowest priority are indicated by small noteheads; tones of a higher priority are indicated by regular noteheads, and tones of a higher still priority are indicated by stemmed noteheads. Slurs between tones of different priorities indicate that the lower-priority tone is controlled by (represents) the higher-priority tone. Slurs or incomplete beams between two tones of the same pitch indicate a prolongation of the two slurred or beamed tones by the intervening tones. Slurs also indicate voice-leading connections, as do dotted lines or dotted slurs.

The black triangles indicate the hierarchical pattern of energy within which the work must be unfolded to allow a singular experience. Note that the triangles indicate the relative intensity of the smaller groupings they encompass; the smaller groupings retain their integrity within the larger groupings. So, for example, if the impulse within a larger grouping encompasses two or more smaller groupings, the growing triangle of the higher-level pattern does not indicate a steady growth of energy; rather the growing triangle indicates that the impulse of the each successive internal grouping is greater than the impulse of the previous internal grouping. Similarly, if the resolution within a larger impulse encompasses two or more smaller impulses, the receding triangle of the higher-level pattern indicates that the impulse of the each successive internal grouping is less than the impulse of the previous internal grouping.

The challenges and limitations of dynamic analysis are considerable. It is conceptually daunting, in that it requires a fundamentally different understanding of the composition than that traditionally held. Most theoretical analysis (in fact most musicology of all sorts) has been based on an understanding of the composition as the aesthetic object; the analysis is applied to that thing—that object. Dynamic analysis requires an understanding of the composition as the potential for an aesthetic object; the analysis is applied to that thing—that potential. Further, the object of analysis is determined by the analysis itself: we analyze the optimal potential dynamic structure of groupings that we determine as part of the analysis, and we determine those groupings on the basis of their potential optimal dynamic structure. In its inherent circularity it can easily lead to flawed conclusions. Finally, dynamic analysis has distinct limits as an aid to performers. It offers performers a process for achieving a conscious understanding of the patterns of energy within which tones of a work must be unfolded for an ultimately beautiful performance; it remains for the performer to hear and execute those patterns. This is what performers do unconsciously to varying degrees; dynamic analysis offers it consciously, systematically, and comprehensively—not more.

But not less, either. A particular beauty of dynamic analysis is that when the performer and the analyst each act to the full potential of their disciplines, their job begins in the very same way. The analyst establishes as his object of investigation the composition in its essence: the sonic relationships necessitated by the composition for it to allow the highest experience of beauty. To unfold a sublime performance, the performer must also come to an understanding of how those relationships can allow the highest experience, although the performer's understanding need not be conscious.[14] The analyst's job continues with an illustration of that potential in words and symbols; the performer's continues with a realization of it in sound. When both analysis and performance function at their best, the understanding of the performer is the same as that of the analyst; each activity involves fundamental aspects of the other to the extent that in a very real sense performance is analysis and analysis is performance.

Since the optimal dynamic structure is a vital component of the essence of the work, an analysis that does not incorporate it is not only of little use to the performer, it is necessarily incomplete. In fact, in that the dynamic structure is the result of all the elements of the work, there is a limited sense in which an analysis that fully and accurately incorporates the optimal dynamic structure is in itself comprehensive.[15]

A Dynamic Analysis of Schumann's
"Melody" from *Album for the Young*

Examples 8.1 (♪) and 8.2 (♪) present a dynamic analysis of Schumann's "Melody," from the *Album for the Young*. Beginning with the singular grouping that encompasses the totality of the piece, example 8.1 includes the level-D (background) reduction and its dynamic structure. It also includes the level-C voice-leading reduction with its dynamic structure. Example 8.2 includes the level-A, level-B, and level-C voice-leading reductions along with their associated dynamic structures; the composition itself; and the structural harmonic activity.

Level D in example 8.1 illustrates the background progression: $\hat{3}$–$\hat{4}$–$\hat{3}$ over I–V^7–I. The impulse climaxes with the 4th-degree soprano F (unless otherwise noted, the soprano tone represents all the concurrently functioning tones). Note that a final soprano D–C (scale degree 2–1) descent does occur, as indicated in the level-C reduction, but it is not supported by a sufficiently strong harmonic progression to function on the background level. So this brief and simple piano piece is controlled at the background level by an appropriately simple embellishing progression.

The level-C dynamic structure illustrates the division of the background into two groupings. The first prolongs the impulse of the soprano E with a stepwise descent to C and a repetition of the E before descending to the dominant G. To achieve a maximally consequent dynamic structure, the reiteration of the soprano E must give additional impulse to propel the energy through the grouping; thus the impulse must climax with that second soprano E. The second grouping, beginning in bar 5, unfolds an arpeggiation of a G dominant seventh chord in the soprano voice: from B to D to the structural F; this is followed at bar 9 by a variant of the first grouping. The impulse of this 8-bar grouping climaxes with the soprano F, and resolves through the final four bars.

In example 8.2, level B illustrates the composing-out of the level-C groupings into five smaller groupings. The first 4-bar level-C grouping divides into two 2-bar groupings at level B; in both of these the impulse is generated from the initial sound. The second level-B grouping (bars 3–4) generates impulse for the entire 4-bar grouping at level C; at level B its impulse is intensified by the embellishing descent from the soprano high G. The second level-C grouping of eight bars (bars 5–12) divides into three smaller groupings at level B. The ascent through the G dominant seventh (bars 5–8) is embellished by descending stepwise thirds. Within this 4-bar grouping the impulse climaxes with the soprano A of bar 7. The final four bars divide into two 2-bar groupings; these are similar to the two groupings of bars 1–4. But, where the impulse was intensified with a G and subsequent descent in bar 3, in bar 11 it is even further heightened with an A and subsequent descent; and where the bar-3 impulse resolves with a descent to G in G major, the bar-11 impulse resolves with a descent to a cadential C.

The Level A reduction prioritizes events from a functional, structural voice-leading standpoint at the level of the musical surface; the dynamic structure is that of the musical surface. The smallest groupings exist at Level A: one for each bar, with the exception of the 2-bar grouping of bars 3–4. Three of the 2-bar level-B groupings—bars 1–2, 9–10, and 11–12—each divide into two 1-bar groupings, the first of which climaxes with its initial event, the second of which climaxes in the middle of the bar. Bars 5–8 divide into four 1-bar groupings, the first three of which climax with the initial event, the fourth climaxes with the middle of the bar.

Working back up the hierarchy, at level B the impulse of bar 1 is resolved through the lesser impulse in bar 2. The same applies to bars 9–10 and bars 11–12. The impulses in bars 5, 6, and 7, each similar to the impulse of bar 1, are successively greater; the impulse of bar 8 is lesser than that of bar 7, and participates in the resolution of that greater impulse. At level C, where the first four bars join into a single grouping, the impulse of bars 3–4 is greater than that of bars 1–2. The second level-C grouping is interesting, in that the height of the impulse at level C does not coincide with the height of the impulse of any lower-level grouping. At level C the impulse of the larger 8-bar grouping (bars 5–12) climaxes with the F of bar 7, whereas at level B the smaller 4-bar grouping (bars 5–8) climaxes with the initial A. At level B, the A embellishes the structural F, adding the requisite impulse.

Example 8.2 also identifies the structural harmonic activity, which confirms the global dynamic structure. The height of the impulse of a work (in other words, the climax) comes within the key farthest by consecutive fifth tonicizations from the home key, or in the motion to or away from that farthest fifth. The home key of C major is established from the start by the pitch field exclusively in that key, and by the dominant seventh chord implied in the second beat of bar 1 and sounded in the second beat of bar 2. Bar 4 presents the three conditions necessary for a tonicization of the first ascending fifth G major. The F♯ creates a pitch field of G major, it participates in a dominant seventh chord in that key, and the tonic harmony is sounded on beat three. Through an alto-line pedal tone G from the last half of bar 4 through the first half of bar 8, F♮s in bars 5, 6, and 7–8 create partial tonicizations of C; finally a C♯ in the bass line creates a partial tonicization of the second fifth D minor.[16] C major returns with the V^7 chord on the downbeat of bar 9, and is in force for the final four bars. The overall structural harmonic activity then involves a single ascending fifth, to G major. The climactic soprano A in bar 7 sounds over the G pedal, before G major has been replaced by C major as the local tonic; thus that climactic A occurs in reference to G major, the last fully tonicized key. Perhaps significant is that the climactic soprano A also occurs on the way to the partial tonicization of the second ascending fifth, D minor. Like the background controlling melodic/harmonic progression, the structural harmonic activity is necessarily minimal in such a brief and simple work.

In the Schumann "Melody," the performer's responsibility for the dynamic structure is carried out primarily by volume inflections. The initial impulse created by the soprano E is resolved with the assistance of a decrease in volume, down to the A of bar 2. A small growth in volume to the C brings about the impulse in bar 2. The resolution within bar 2 is carried out with the assistance of a decrease in volume down to the soprano G. If the G has a similar but somewhat softer intensity than the initial A of bar 2, it completes the initial stepwise descent from E. If the tone is louder than the A or significantly softer, that connection does not exist. The entire grouping of bar 2 participates in resolving impulse generated in bar 1, so the bar 2 impulse is softer than that of bar 1. To encompass the first four bars in a single grouping, the high G of bar 3 is louder than the initial E; the impulse it creates is played out with a decrease in volume in bars 3–4; if excess impulse is created, the tempo must pull back at the end of bar 4 to resolve it.

The final three tones of bar 4, B–A–G, sound with decreasing volume. Each of the next three bars (5, 6, and 7) begins with a similar stepwise descent, and each is sounded with a similar decrease in volume. Each of these successive impulses is somewhat louder, so that within the 4-bar level-B grouping (bars 5–8) the impulse climaxes with the loudest level-A grouping: specifically with the A of bar 7. As the bass and soprano tones recede in the second half of bars 5 and 6, the alto line generates impulse with an increase in volume; a similar situation obtains in bar 8. The end of bar 8 will require a relaxation of the tempo to play out excess impulse before the end of the grouping. Bars 9–12 are performed with a similar structure of volume inflections as bars 1–4, resulting in a similar dynamic structure; again a subtle relaxation of the tempo will play out excess energy at the end of the piece, so the energy and the music end at the same time.

In fact the analysis in example 8.1 is slightly inaccurate, because it does not take into account the repeats. Schumann calls for the first four bars and the final eight bars to be repeated. Although this does not affect the dynamic structure within the repeated sections, it does affect the global dynamic structure in a subtle way. The repeated first four bars generate more impulse than the initial sounding, as it is on its way to the climax. The climax comes with the height of the impulse in bar 7 of the initial sounding of the final eight bars; the impulse in the repeated final eight bars is therefore softer. This is borne out by the voice leading: the low G bass note of the structural climactic V^7 comes at the end of bar 4; in the repetition of bars 5–12 that structural climactic V^7 actually sounds over a weaker V^6_5 harmony.

A Dynamic Analysis of the Adagio ma non troppo from Beethoven's String Quartet, Op. 74, "The Harp"

The dynamic analysis of the slow movement of the "Harp" Quartet[17] is given in four separate examples, incorporating five levels of voice-leading reductions and their dynamic structures. The seventeen-page example 8.3 (♪) includes the musical score, levels A and B, along with the structural harmonic activity. Example 8.4 (♪), six pages, includes level B in a much compacted form, as well as level C.[18] The one-page example 8.5 includes levels D and E; and finally, example 8.6 gives level F: the entire movement in a singular grouping.

The work is elegant in its simplicity. Based on a most elementary theme and variations form, it divides into six sections: the theme, an episode, a first variation, a second episode, a second variation, and a coda. With two small but important exceptions, the variations simply restate the theme with increasing rhythmic density, moving from the essentially eighth-note motion of the theme to the triplet sixteenth-note motion of the first variation, to the thirty-second-note motion of the second variation.

Within the theme (bars 2–24), numerous surface groupings (ex. 8.3, level A) join to form three larger ones (level B): the first from bar 2 to bar 9, climaxing in bar 8; the second from the pickup of bar 9 to bar 17, climaxing with the sforzando on the pickup to bar 14; and the third being the 7-bar codetta from bar 18 to bar 24, climaxing with the sforzando of bar 23. Harmonically the 23-bar theme moves from the home key of A♭ major to a partially tonicized F minor; then tonicizes the first ascending fifth E♭ major; returns to A♭ major; then tonicizes the first descending fifth, D♭ major; and then its relative minor, B♭ minor, the second ascending fifth. The home key of A♭ major returns, and is confirmed by the codetta. Variations 1 and 2 carry same dynamic structure as the theme, and essentially the same harmonic framework, with one significant exception: the F minor in the sixth bar of variations 1 and 2 is fully tonicized, while it is only partially tonicized in the theme.

The multiple surface groupings of episode 1 (level A) join to form four larger ones (level B): the first from bar 25 to bar 35, climaxing at the musical surface with the sforzando of bar 32;[19] the second from the pickup of bar 36 to the downbeat of bar 39, climaxing with the downbeat of bar 39; the third from the second beat of bar 39 through the second beat of bar 49, climaxing on the third beat of bar 48; and a fourth from bar 49 to bar 63, climaxing with the sforzando in bar 55. Episode 1 effects a tonicization of C♭ major; this is followed by tonicizations of D♭ minor and—briefly—A♭ minor before returning to the A♭ major of variation 1.

The surface groupings of episode 2 (level A) form five larger groupings (level B): from bar 87 to the second beat of bar 90, climaxing at the musical surface in bar 88; from bar 91 through bar 94, climaxing with the downbeat of bar 93; from bar 95 to the second beat of bar 98, climaxing in bar 96; from bar 99 through bar 102, climaxing with the downbeat of 101; and finally from bar 103e to bar

114, climaxing with the downbeat of bar 111. Episode 2 brings tonicizations of the first descending fifth, D♭ major, and its relative minor, B♭ minor, the already-achieved second ascending fifth. A tonicization of A♭ minor leads to the return of A♭ major with variation 2.

The coda unfolds five groupings at level B: from bar 139 through the second beat of bar 142, climaxing with the downbeat of that bar; from the pickup to bar 143 through to the climactic end of bar 146; similarly from bar 147 through to the climactic end of bar 149. The fourth level-B grouping encompasses bars 150 to bar 161; sufficient impulse is created for the ensuing resolution if the three statements of the G diminished seventh chord become more insistent, so that the grouping climaxes in bar 154. An 8-bar grouping—beginning in bar 162 and climaxing with the sforzando in bar 163—ends the movement. The coda begins with a suggestions of the tonic minor, and moves to the tonic A♭ major after a brief tonicization of E♭ major.

Within the theme, and within the two variations as well, the three impulses form a single grouping at level C (ex. 8.4). The climax comes in bar 8 (bar 7 of the theme) with the tonicization of F minor, the third and furthest ascending fifth, which connects with the motion from A♭ major through the first ascending fifth E♭ major, to the second ascending fifth B♭ minor. The succeeding impulses sustain the energy through the extended resolution. To bring the theme forth as a singular articulation requires sufficient impulse from the bar 8 downbeat, via a crescendo strong enough to carry energy through the remainder of the 23-bar grouping. It also requires restraint of the succeeding impulses, particularly those created by the crescendo to *forte* of bars 16–17 and the crescendo to sforzando of bars 22–23. Thus to allow enough energy to resolve, the volume in bars 16–17 cannot be too great, and the final two beats of bar 18 need a sufficiently generous tempo. Similarly, the volume in bars 22–23 cannot be too great for the two-bar resolution that follows.

The four level-B groupings of episode 1 join into two larger groupings at level C. The first climaxes with the sforzando diminished seventh harmony of bar 32, which creates sufficient impulse to carry through to the downbeat of bar 39. The second climaxes with the dominant F-major harmony sounded with a sforzando in bar 55, allowing for the 8-bar resolution that sets up variation 1.

The five level-B groupings of episode 2 join into three larger groupings at level C. The first of these encompasses bars 87 to 94, and climaxes with the downbeat of bar 93. The second larger grouping of 8 bars reprises the preceding grouping with ornamentation, and climaxes at the downbeat of bar 101. The climaxes at the musical surface of these first two level-C groupings are effected by the crescendos marked in bars 91 and 99, each of which assists in generating sufficient energy to carry through its 8-bar grouping. The third level-C grouping encompasses bars 103 to 114, and climaxes with the *fortissimo* octave Cs in bar 111.

The five level-B groupings of the coda join into one larger grouping at level C, the impulse of which climaxes at the musical surface with the downbeat of bar

142. The next four groupings combine to release the energy, climaxing with successively weaker impulses: the crescendo to bar 142 is more than that to bar 146, which is more than the crescendo to bar 149; weaker still is the climax occurring in bar 154, and the final sforzando in bar 163 provides just enough impulse to carry through to the end of the movement. The coda itself has an interesting dynamic hierarchy. Beethoven marks crescendos in bars 145 and 148, each unresolved, each ending with a subsequent *subito piano* (bars 147 and 150). In that none of the impulse within these level-B groupings is resolved at level A, they are rendered partial. The impulse created by the crescendo that grows to the end of bar 146 is less than that of bar 142; the impulse created by the crescendo that grows to the end of bar 149 is less than that of bar 146; thus they join together—with the remaining level-B groupings—into the larger level-C resolution.

Level D (ex. 8.5) illustrates the six singular large sections of the work. Within the singular grouping that comprises episode 1, the height of the impulse comes with the climactic bar 32; the remainder of the section constitutes an extended resolution. Within the singular grouping that comprises episode 2, the height of the impulse comes with bar 101, and resolves through bar 114 until the beginning of variation 2. While the volume grows substantially within that resolution—Beethoven marks a *forte* in bar 109 and a *fortissimo* in bar 110—these bars do not generate as much impulse as does the growth to bar 101. This is due in part to the drop in rhythmic density from twelve notes in a bar to three notes in a bar, and from the structural harmonic activity: the second ascending fifth B♭ minor at bar 99, moving to the less energy-producing tonic minor, A♭ minor at bar 102. The work divides into three large groupings at level E: theme and episode 1, variation 1 and episode 2, variation 2 and coda. The climax of each grouping comes with the impulse within the theme or variation.

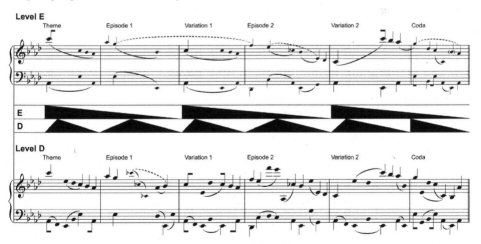

Example 8.5. Dynamic Analysis (Levels D and E) of Beethoven, String Quartet, Op. 74, "The Harp," 2nd mvt., Adagio ma non troppo

Finally example 8.6 presents level F, which illustrates the prolonged background progression of scale degree 3 (C) over I, which movies through scale
degree 2 over V to scale degree 1 over I (bars 130-31). The global impulse
climaxes at bar 121 during the prolongation of the scale degree 3, and resolves
thereafter. In that the final structural scale degree 1 over tonic occurs with
the beginning of the codetta of variation 2, functionally the coda of the movement begins with the variation 2 codetta. One deviation from the otherwise
essentially literal restatement of the pitch material by the variations occurs
at the end of variation 2. Unlike the theme and variation 1, which both end
with a cadence on the tonic, A♭ major, variation 2 ends with a dominant seventh harmony. The extra impulse necessitates an eighth bar in the codetta,
and carries energy through to begin the 31-bar coda proper. A second deviation involves octave displacement: the variations state the theme at successively
lower octaves. One result is that sounding the final structural C in variation 2
(bar 130) in the original octave helps to cement its connection with the opening structural C of the theme.

The global impulse of the movement is driven by the increasing rhythmic
density from the theme (three notes to a bar) through variation 1 (nine notes to
a bar) to variation 2 (twelve notes to a bar). But, as expected, the structural harmonic activity also plays a major role. The theme tonicizes the first and second
ascending fifths, (E♭ major and B♭ minor); variations 1 and 2 each also tonicize the third ascending fifth, F minor. The global climax comes with the tonicization of the farthest ascending fifth, F minor, within variation 2, at its most
rhythmically dense iteration. Neither the structural harmonic activity of episode
1 (C♭ major–D♭ minor–A♭ minor–A♭ major) nor that of episode 2 (D♭ major–
B♭ minor–D♭ major–B♭ minor–A♭ major–A♭ minor) affects the impulse-giving
power of the successions of fifth tonicizations.

The performers have some particular challenges in unfolding the work as
a whole. Beethoven specifies a crescendo to the climactic F minor seventh bar
within each statement of the theme and its variations; this crescendo must be

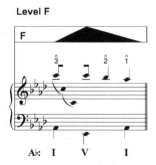

Level F

Example 8.5. Dynamic Analysis (Levels D and E) of Beethoven, String Quartet, Op.
74, "The Harp," 2nd mvt., Adagio ma non troppo

to a sufficiently loud volume as to carry impulse through the remainder of the theme. The successive impulses within the theme and its variations—sforzandos in the 12th and 13th bars, crescendo to *forte* in the 16th bar, and crescendo to sforzando in the 22nd bar—give impetus to the extended resolution. But if the volume of these successive impulses is so great as to create more impulse than the bar-7 downbeat, the 23-bar section will end with unresolved energy. On a lower lever, the crescendo to *forte* in the 16th bar comes very near the end of a small grouping beginning in the 14th bar and ending at the end of the 16th bar. To resolve the impulse from the *forte* sufficiently within its grouping requires a generosity of tempo, especially in the last two eighth notes of the 16th bar, immediately following the height of the crescendo. That grouping will not be fully consequent; the leftover energy provides impetus for the seven-bar codetta. Beethoven marks a crescendo to sforzando within the final three-bar grouping (bars 21–23 of the theme and its variations); similarly this increase in volume allows the theme statements to continue with energy to carry into the succeeding section, and similarly it must occur within the context of the overall impulse of the theme statements, which climaxes in the seventh bar.

Beethoven notates a sforzando on the pickup to bar 55, and repeats the bar exactly. The relationship of the two sforzandos is determined by the dynamic structure of the higher-level grouping in which they participate (level B). To create impulse that can be consequently resolved, the height of the impulse must come with the second sforzando, occurring on the pickup to bar 56. Thus the second sforzando must be subtly louder than the first: not so much louder that it does not sound as a reiteration of the first, but loud enough to carry the energy all the way through to the end of the level-B grouping in bar 63.

In bar 91 Beethoven marks a crescendo, with no further dynamic marking until the crescendo of bar 99; so the performer is faced with determining how much crescendo and to where. The crescendo in bar 91 begins a 4-bar grouping at level B. To unfold it as a single unit, the height of its impulse—and thus the height of the crescendo—comes with the first-violin E♭ of bar 93. To put the climax of the melody beyond this E♭ would result in too much impulse for the resolution available, but a continual diminuendo through bars 93 and 94 would result in too much resolution. Some additional impulse will result from the small growth to the downbeat of bar 94 in the first-violin melody. More importantly, though, Beethoven provides the cello ascent to G♭, which grows to the downbeat of bar 94 as it takes over melodic prominence from the receding violin melody, and injects enough impulse to carry through to the end of the grouping. Similarly, the crescendo marked in bar 99 climaxes with the downbeat of bar 101, with necessary additional impulse provided in bar 102 by the first-violin filigree. The climaxes in bars 93 and 101 serve as the height of the impulse for the level-C groupings of 8 bars. The second (bars 95–102) participates in impulse at level D; in other words it generates more energy than does the first (bars 87–94). The ensuing growth to the climactic *fortissimo* octave Cs in bar

111 creates impulse, requiring some relaxation of the tempo within the last four bars before the start of variation 2; but it cannot create more impulse than the climactic bar 101 and still resolve within the level-D grouping that encompasses episode 2.

Excess energy remains at the end of variation 2, which closes with the dominant seventh harmony hanging unresolved; the reiteration of that harmony by the second violin and viola in bars 137–38 will likely require a relaxation of the tempo to play out the energy before the beginning of the coda. (The cello statement of bar 139 leads into the next bar, and thus participates in a new grouping at level B.)

Perhaps the biggest challenge is to continue the global growth in impulse through a forward-moving tempo to the climax of the work at bar 121, resolving the energy with a backward-looking tempo from there to the end.

Appendix

Forms

Dance Form

Bach, Orchestral Suite (Ouvertüre) No. 1 in C Major, BWV 1066, Gavotte II

The second Gavotte from Bach's Orchestral Suite No. 1 in C Major, BWV 1066 is representative of dance forms. The movement opens in a C-major pitch field, and C major is confirmed as tonic by the V^6_5 chord on the first beat of bar 3. The F♯ in bar 6 brings about an operative pitch field of G major and participates in a dominant $^4_2$ chord, which contributes to fully tonicizing G major. The first strain ends with a V^7–I confirmation of G major. The C♯ and F♮ of bar 9 change the operative pitch field to that of D minor, although that key is not fully tonicized until the first-beat V^6_5 chord in bar 11. (Note that the pitch field of D minor has scale degree 6 both in its raised position—in bar 9, in the linear ascent from A to D—and in its lowered position—in bar 10, followed by the descent to A.) In bar 12, the C♮ and B♮ return the operative pitch field to C major, which is tonicized with dominant seventh harmony of bar 13. F major is partially tonicized with the B♭ of bar 15, which effects the pitch field of F major, and participates in a 4:7 dominant harmony (the tonicization of F major is only partial due to the absence of a tonic or tonic substitute harmony).[1] The B♮ in bar 16 creates an operative pitch field of C major, which is fully tonicized by the V^6_5 chord on the first beat of bar 19. The movement ends in that key.

Impulse is created in the first strain with the tonicization of the first ascending fifth, G major, and expanded in the second strain by the tonicization of the second ascending fifth, D minor. The energy climaxes with the dominant $^6_5$ chord in D minor on the first beat of bar 11, and is resolved with a return to C major.

Bach, Orchestral Suite (Ouvertüre) No. 1 in C Major, BWV 1066, Forlane

More complex is the Forlane from the same Bach suite. The 8-bar first strain opens with a tonicized C major (in the absence of a different key previously tonicized, the presence of the C-major pitch field is sufficient to render it a tonic), followed by a partial tonicization of F major with the B♭ in bar 1.[2] The B♮ in bar

2 cancels the B♭; it changes the pitch field back to that of C major, and effects a return to that key. G major, the first ascending fifth, is introduced in bar 6 and fully tonicized with the G-major harmony on the downbeat of bar 7. The first strain ends in the new key of G major. The 16-bar second strain opens in G major, tonicizes A minor in bar 11, and cadences in that key in bar 12. A partial tonicization of D minor follows in bar 14, with a full tonicization in bar 15. (All three requirements for tonicization—operative pitch field, tonic harmony, and dominant seventh harmony—have not been present without the G bass pedal functioning until the end of bar 15.) Subsequent tonicizations of C major (bar 17), F major (bar 19), and C major again (bar 20) are followed by a string of partial tonicizations: of G major (bar 20), C major and A minor (bar 21). The movement closes with a return to a fully tonicized C major with the tonic chord on the downbeat of bar 23, confirmed by a final V^7–I cadence in bars 23–24.

The initial opposition occurs with the tonicization of the first ascending fifth, G major, in the first strain. The energy thus created grows in the second strain, with the introduction of the third ascending fifth, A minor, connected to the second ascending fifth, D minor. The broad-scale impulse climaxes with the soprano-voice B in bar 10 within the motion to A minor, the key farthest by ascending fifth from the home key; the impulse is resolved through the return to the home key, C major.

The four distinctive characteristics of structural harmonic motion described in chapter 7 are illustrated in this example.[3] First, the succession of fifths is not successive. The third fifth, A minor, is connected to the second fifth, G major, retroactively through the tonicization of D minor. Second, the return from the climactic key to the home key does not occur by step of fifth tonicizations, as it omits the first fifth G major in the return from the second fifth D minor to the home key, C major. (G major is only partially tonicized in bars 20–21.) Third, the return from the climax by ascending fifth swings down to the first descending fifth, F major, before arriving at the home key of C major.

Finally, note that the keys participating in the structural harmonic activity take their mode from the pitch field of the tonic, as determined by the 3rd scale degree of the tonicized key. The 3rd scale degree of the first ascending fifth G is some kind of B; in the home key of C major the B is B♮; therefore the structural first ascending fifth includes B♮ which participates in G major, and therefore the mode of the structural, impulse-giving first ascending fifth is major. The 3rd scale degree of the second ascending fifth D is some kind of F; in the home key of C major the F is F♮; therefore the structural second ascending fifth includes F♮ which participates in D minor, and therefore the mode of the structural, impulse-giving second ascending fifth is minor. For that reason the third ascending fifth is minor (A minor), and the first descending fifth is major (F major).

Beethoven, String Quartet, Op. 74, "The Harp," Presto

The scherzo third movement of the "Harp" Quartet consists of a variant of the minuet and trio format, here characterized as Presto and Più presto quasi Prestissimo. The brief, 8-bar first strain of the Presto partially tonicizes C minor; the 69-bar second strain tonicizes D♭ major (23), the first descending fifth, F minor (31), the home key, C minor (37), and the first ascending fifth, G minor (43). C minor is partially tonicized again in bar 51. A partial tonicization of F minor (53) is followed by alternations of E♭ major (59 and 63) with C minor (61 and 65); the Presto ends in that key.

The middle section, Più presto quasi Prestissimo, opens in C major. Tonicizations of the first ascending fifth, G major (109), the second ascending fifth, D minor (126), the home key of C major (138), and the first descending fifth, F major (151), are followed by a partial tonicization of C major (153), moving toward C minor with the first-violin A♭ (165).

The movement has a somewhat unusual repeat structure. The Presto section is given three times, alternating with two statements of the Più presto quasi Prestissimo. Both strains of the initial Presto are repeated; there are no repeats in the Più presto quasi Prestissimo. In the second statement of the Presto, only the 8-bar first strain is repeated; it is again followed by the Più presto quasi Prestissimo. In the third statement of the Presto, the repeat of the 8-bar first strain is written out, with the repeated 8 bars sounding *piano*. Unlike in the first two Presto statements, the second strain is entirely soft, ending *pianississimo (ppp)*. A coda all in a soft dynamic, leads directly into the fourth movement, Allegretto con Variazioni. The coda fully tonicizes D♭ major (431), partially tonicizes E♭ minor (440) and moves toward E♭ major (447), fully tonicizing that key with the opening chord of the fourth movement.

The C-minor Presto section presents tonicizations of the first descending fifth, F minor, and the first ascending fifth, G minor. In works that move by the same distance in each direction it is the lower fifth that carries the climax. This is also true of the Presto section; it climaxes with the *fortissimo* of bar 27, on the way to the tonicized F minor. The C-major Più presto quasi Prestissimo section brings tonicizations of the first (G major) and second (D minor) ascending fifths, as well as the first descending fifth, F major. The climax of the section comes with the downbeat of bar 126, coinciding with the full tonicization of D minor.

Within the movement as a whole, the height of the global impulse is driven by the second ascending fifth, D minor, within the Più presto quasi Prestissimo. D minor would be the second ascending fifth in a work in either the major or the minor mode; thus the key of D minor is the second ascending fifth of the harmonic structure of both the Presto and the Più presto quasi Prestissimo.[4]

Theme and Variations

Mozart, Quintet for Clarinet and Strings, K. 581, Allegretto con Variazioni

The final movement of Mozart's Quintet for Clarinet and Strings, K. 581, is a fairly straightforward example of a theme-and-variations movement. The Allegretto theme has a simple binary form of 16 bars: two strains of eight bars each, and each strain repeated. The first strain includes two 4-bar phrases that essentially repeat, although the first ends on a dominant harmony and the second ends on a tonic. The second strain also includes two 4-bar phrases: one of new material, and a second that repeats bars 5–8. The entire theme, ||: A A' :||: B A' :||, does not waver from the key of A major.

Variation I is essentially a restatement of the theme, ornamented in the clarinet by a countermelody consisting largely of running eighth notes. Variation II offers a version of the melody in irregular rhythms in the first violin, accompanied by the inner strings in triplet eighth notes. Both variations I and II remain in the home key of A major. Variation III, in the minor mode, is characterized by running eighth notes punctuated with grace notes. The first strain presents a much reduced version of the melody in the two violins; the first phrase of the second strain sustains the dominant harmony under a chromatic eighth-note melisma. Variation IV restates the theme, embellished by sixteenth-note arpeggiations and scale patterns in the clarinet and first violin, again all in the home key of A major. A 4-bar extension tonicizes D major, the key of the subdominant; then E major, the key of the dominant; and ends on a V^7 in the home key, A major. Variation V is an Adagio, with clarinet and first violin alternating 4-bar statements of a vocal arioso rendering of the theme; again all in the home key of A major. A 5-bar extension ends with another tonicization of E major, the key of the dominant.

The first 8 bars of the Allegro (105–12) constitute an ornamented restatement of the initial 8-bar first strain. The following 8-bar phrase (113–20) includes a partial tonicization of B minor (117) before returning to a partially tonicized A major (118). This is followed by a restatement of the same phrase, this time including a brief partial tonicization of F♯ minor (127). The final cadence to the home key occurs in bar 128.

Broad-scale impulse is created primarily by the accelerated motion brought about by the increase in rhythmic density. Quarter-note motion of the theme gives way to eighth-note motion in Variation I and triplet eighth-note motion in Variation II. The growth of energy continues in Variation III with the color change to A minor. Returning to A major for Variation IV, the increasing rhythmic density to sixteenth-note motion continues to build the impulse. The first (and only) tonicizations of keys other than the home key are of the first descending fifth, D major (80), and the first ascending fifth, E major (81). The climax occurs with the downbeat of bar 82, in the motion away from the first descending fifth. The broad-scale impulse is resolved over the ensuing Adagio and the extended Allegro finale, which uses partial tonicizations of B minor and F♯ minor to propel the energy.

Beethoven, String Quartet, Op. 74, "The Harp," Allegretto con Variazioni

The Allegretto con Variazioni from Beethoven's Opus 74 is an interesting example: a theme with six variations and a coda. The theme is a simple dance form, with an 8-bar first strain and a 12-bar second strain. Each strain begins soft and ends loud, and the rhythmic motion is largely one-note-per-bar. The first strain begins in a tonicized E♭ major, and ends with a fully tonicized C minor. The second strain begins with partial tonicizations of F minor and B♭ major (9), a full tonicization of E♭ major (10), and a partial tonicization of G minor (11). It ends with a full tonicization of E♭ major (17), a partial tonicization of F minor (19), and a return to a tonicized E♭ major (20).

With a texture of accented *forte* eighth notes, the first variation (20–40) unfolds almost the same harmonic structure as does the theme. It begins with the tonicized E♭ major, followed by a full tonicization of C minor at the end of the first strain (27). In bar 9 of the theme, tonicizations of F minor and B♭ major were partial because there was no tonic harmony; the dominant seventh of F minor led not to an F minor chord but to a dominant seventh built on F, and that dominant seventh of B♭ major led not to a B♭-major chord to but a dominant seventh leading toward E♭ major. At the equivalent spot in the first variation (29–30), the F minor is only partially tonicized (no lowered 6th scale degree) and the B♭ major is fully tonicized. The second strain continues with a partial tonicization of D minor (31), and ends with full tonicizations of E♭ major (35) and the first descending fifth, A♭ major (37), F minor (38), and again E♭ major.

In the *piano* second variation (40–60) the theme melody is given by the viola in triplet eighth notes. C minor is only partially tonicized at the end of the first strain (48). The second strain briefly tonicizes the first ascending fifth, B♭ major (50). E♭ major is immediately tonicized, and obtains—with the exception of a partially tonicized G minor (52)—through the variation. The third variation (60–80) is characterized by *forte* sixteenth-note motion accompanied by offbeat attacks. The first strain presents a brief, partial tonicization of D minor (65), and ends in a partially tonicized C minor (68). The second strain presents in succession a partial tonicization of F minor (69), and—in the same bar—a full tonicization of the first ascending fifth, B♭ major, then a full tonicization of E♭ major (70), a partial tonicization of G minor (71), and a return to E♭ major that is fully tonicized in bar 80.

The *piano* fourth variation (80–100) presents the theme melody in the first violin in quarter notes, accompanied by eighth-note motion in the other voices, and includes a full tonicization of the fourth ascending fifth, G minor (87). The second strain opens with a partial tonicization of F minor (89), followed by full tonicizations of C minor (90) and again E♭ major (93). The fifth variation (100–120), is characterized by *forte* jagged rhythms. A partial tonicization of the third ascending fifth C minor at the end of the first strain (108) is followed by full tonicizations of the second ascending fifth F minor (109) and E♭ major (110). After a partial tonicization of G minor (111), E♭ is fully tonicized in bar 117.

The *piano* sixth variation (120–42), with the marking un poco più vivace, unfolds the theme melody in three-part chordal running eighth notes over a triplet pedal. The first strain remains in the previously tonicized E♭ major; the second strain offers a partial tonicization of D♭ (132) before returning to a fully tonicized E♭ major in bar 138. The extended coda (142–95) begins with the same *piano* character of the fifth variation, and gradually ramps up the volume and tempo to a *fortissimo*, Allegro phrase, before a final *piano* V–I cadence. The coda brings full tonicizations of F minor (155) and E♭ major (162), which remains in effect—after brief, partial tonicizations of F minor (163 and 167)—through to the end of the movement.

Broad-scale impulse in this movement is generated by the structure of rhythmic density on two tracks, as well as by succession of fifth tonicizations away from the tonic. Both strains of the theme begin with a *piano*, leisurely character of largely one harmony per bar; both culminate with a staccato, *forte* eighth-note harmonic motion. This sets up alternating *piano* and *forte* variations. The *forte* track begins with the first variation, which takes the character of those culminating eighth notes. Impulse grows on the *forte* track with the aggressive sixteenth-note character of the third variation. The fifth variation, with its combination of eighth notes and sixteenth notes, is less impulse-generating. The pattern of rhythmic density between the *piano* variations also contributes to the dynamic structure. The increased rhythmic density from the *piano* character of the theme to the second-variation triplet motion builds impulse. The fundamental motion of quarter notes of the fourth variation further builds impulse over the half-note chordal accompaniment motion of the second variation. Although the tempo of the sixth variation is faster, due to the pedal tones it is characterized by an overriding stasis, which results in less impulse than the fourth variation. The coda pulls the two strains together. The crescendo and accelerando in the final 26 bars bring about a gathering of impulse, but the degree of that impulse is limited because the entire passage repeats a tonic-confirming progression of I–IV–ii–V^7–I. On a higher level the passage serves to extend the resolution.

Harmonically the theme itself is unusual, in that it climaxes with the tonicization of C minor at the end of the first strain, instead of within the second strain as is customary. The second strain plays out that impulse. This is true of each of the variations: the impulse climaxes with the end of the first strain, and is resolved in the second. Over the course of the work, the structural harmonic activity works in concert with the structure of rhythmic density. The third ascending fifth, C minor, the second ascending fifth, F minor, and the first ascending fifth, B♭ major, are all tonicized in the first variation. The fourth ascending fifth, G minor, is partially tonicized in the second variation; the fifth ascending fifth, D minor, is partially tonicized in the third variation. The farthest fifth fully tonicized is the fourth ascending fifth, G minor, coming at the end of the first strain of the fourth variation. It is this tonicization that climaxes the global impulse of the movement. From there to the end, impulse is resolved.

Sonata-form

Mozart, Symphony No. 38, K. 504, "Prague," Adagio; Allegro

A representative sonata-form movement is the first movement of Mozart's Symphony No. 38, "Prague." An Adagio introduction opens with a D-major triad suggesting D major as a home key. Partial tonicizations of B minor (bar 4), G major (5), E minor (6), D major (7), a full tonicization of E minor (9), and a partial tonicization of D major (11), are followed by a fully tonicized B minor (12) and G major (13). A partial tonicization of D minor (16) is followed by full tonicizations of B♭ major (20) and G minor (24). After a partial tonicization of A minor (26) the introduction ends in a partially tonicized D minor, achieved in bar 28.

The Allegro body of the movement opens the forward-moving A material. After a partial tonicization of G major (39–42), the home key of D major is fully established (43). With the exception of a repeated partial tonicization of G major (47–50), D major remains solidly in force until bar 72. At that point the transition to the B material begins with a partially tonicized F♯ minor (72–74).

The transition to the B material establishes the first ascending fifth, A major (77). Partial tonicizations of D minor (89), G minor (90), and A minor (92), and a partial tonicization of F♯ minor (95) follow, before the B material begins with the pickup to bar 97. The first 8-bar phrase beings in a fully tonicized A major (96), and includes partial tonicizations of E minor, C♯ minor, A minor, and E minor again (101–3). The B material returns in A minor (105–8) followed by partial tonicizations of E minor and C minor (109–10). Apart from a brief tonicization of D major (117–18), and E major (124), a partial tonicization of D major (131–33), and a very brief tonicization of B minor (134), A major remains in effect through to the codetta (130–42) that ends the exposition.

The key of A major continues in effect at the opening of the development, which includes tonicizations of D major (151, the first-violin G of bar 150 beat 3 functioning as the 7th of a dominant seventh chord), B minor (156), and D major (159). There follows a string of successive fifth tonicizations: F♯ minor

(162), B minor (164), E minor (166), A major (168), D major (170), and G major (172). The 2-bar tonicizations continue with A minor (174) and B minor (176) before a return to D major (178), which—with the exception of a partial tonicization of D minor over a dominant pedal (191–205)—remains in force into the recapitulation.

The recapitulation A material, in the home key of D major, includes partial tonicizations of G major (218) and G minor (219) before a full tonicization of B♭ major (224). D major returns partially tonicized in bar 230, and—after partial tonicizations of C major (237) and D minor (239), and a full tonicization of B minor (242)—remains in effect through the first statement of the B material. Partial tonicizations of A minor (248) and F♯ minor (249) precede the minor-mode statement of the B material that begins with the pickup to bar 252, and ends with partial tonicizations of A minor (256) and F minor (257). D major is tonicized in bar 259, and—apart from a brief tonicization of G major (266)—remains in effect through the end of the B material. A final codetta includes partial tonicizations of G major (284 and 290) before ending in a confirmed D major.

The dynamic structure of the work is largely generated by the structural harmonic activity. The introduction suggests D major with partial tonicizations, but in terms of structural harmonic activity fully tonicizes only the first descending fifth, G major. Further tonicizations of D minor, B♭ major, and B minor do not generate impulse on a global level. Within the exposition, impulse is generated in part by the opposing characters of the forward-driving A material and the settled B material, but primarily by the B material in the key of the first ascending fifth, A major. The ever-so-brief tonicization of the third ascending fifth, B minor (134), within the B material foreshadows the establishment of that key in the development before the critical succession of fifth tonicizations. The tonicization of the fourth ascending fifth, F♯ minor, which occurs in bar 162, is followed by tonicizations of, in succession, the third ascending fifth, B minor, the second ascending fifth, E minor, the first ascending fifth, A major, and the home key of D major, itself followed by a dip down to the first descending fifth, G major. The climax of the impulse comes in bar 163, within the fourth and farthest key by successive fifth tonicizations from the home key.

The resolution of that global impulse begins in the development with the return to D major, which is largely maintained through the recapitulation. No extended coda is required to play out excess energy.

Beethoven, String Quartet, Op. 74 "The Harp," Poco adagio; Allegro

The first movement of Beethoven's Quartet, Op. 74, "The Harp" is also a sonata-form movement, but with a somewhat unusual dynamic structure. The Poco adagio introduction is quite unstable harmonically. The opening E♭-major chord establishes that key fleetingly. An immediate tonicization of A♭ major (bar 1) is followed by tonicizations of F minor (5), and the home key of E♭ major (8). The introduction continues with a partial tonicization of B♭ major and then full tonicizations of A♭ major (12) and the second ascending fifth, F minor (14), a partial tonicization of B♭ minor (16), a full tonicization of A♭ major (17), and partial tonicizations of B♭ minor (21) and F minor (23) before finally ending with a tonicization of the home key of E♭ major.

The Allegro body of the work opens in the home key of E♭ major, which obtains—after partial and full tonicizations of A♭ major (28 and 33)—throughout the A material. The transition to the B material begins with partial tonicizations of B♭ minor (43) and F minor (44), before confirming the first ascending fifth, B♭ major (48); that key returns after a partial tonicization of C minor (51). The B material, beginning in bar 52 and ending with the end of the exposition in bar 77, is in the key of the dominant, or first ascending fifth, B♭ major. Within the B material, interspersed with returns to B♭ major, are partial tonicizations of F major and B♭ minor (57) and then E♭ major (58), full tonicizations of C minor (60 and 63), partial tonicizations of F minor (64) and E♭ major (66), and a full tonicization of the third ascending fifth, C minor (68).

The development begins with a partially tonicized G major (79). Partial tonicizations of C minor (82), F minor (84), and F major (90) precede a move to C major, fully tonicized in bar 94. A brief tonicization of F major (107) is followed immediately by a return to C major (108). The development closes with a tonicization of the home-key minor, E♭ minor (116), and a partial tonicization of the dominant, B♭ major (123), before returning to a fully tonicized home key of E♭ major with the recapitulation (139).

Unlike most sonata-form movements, in which the recapitulation A material is abbreviated from its initial iteration in the exposition, in this movement the recapitulation A material is expanded. Like the exposition A material, the recapitulation A material opens in E♭ major, and follows with partial (142) and full (147) tonicizations of A♭ major. The expanded recapitulation A material includes full tonicizations of the second ascending fifth, F minor (154); brief partial tonicizations of G minor (158) and C minor (159) are followed by a full tonicization of the fourth ascending fifth, G minor (162), before ending with tonicizations of C minor (163), F minor (167), and B♭ major (169).

The transition to the B material begins with a partial tonicization of E♭ minor (169), then alternates tonicizations of E♭ major with partial tonicizations of F minor (175 and 177). E♭ major remains in effect until a brief partial tonicization of B♭ major (183), and then alternates with tonicizations of F minor (186, 190, and 194). The recapitulation ends in bar 204 with a confirmed E♭ major.

The movement ends with an unusually lengthy coda (56 bars out of a total of 262). After partial tonicizations of C minor (205) and G minor (206), a full tonicization of C minor (212) is followed by partial tonicizations of E♭ major (218), B♭ minor (221), E♭ minor (225), and a full tonicization of F minor

(233). The home key of E♭ major is tonicized in bar 240, and remains in effect for the final 25 bars.

In a typical sonata-form movement, the climax—the point of greatest expansion—comes in the development section. However, in a small handful of masterful sonata-form movements (for example the first movements of Beethoven's Symphony No. 9 and Tchaikovsky's Symphony No. 6) the climax is delayed until the recapitulation. This is such a movement. The introduction brings tonicizations of the home key of E♭ major, the first descending fifth, A♭ major, and the second ascending fifth, F minor. The exposition A material touches on the first descending fifth, A♭ major, and confirms E♭ major; the B material, within the first ascending fifth, B♭ major, also introduces the third ascending fifth, C minor. No advance of the global impulse is effected by structural harmonic activity within the development, which sits on a tonicized C major before returning to the E♭ major of the recapitulation. The expanded A material of the recapitulation is expanded precisely because it carries with it the structural harmonic expansion to the fourth and farthest ascending fifth, G minor (162). It is followed by tonicizations of the third, second, and first ascending fifths (163–68), and then the home key in the B material. The substantial coda is required to resolve the impulse, which climaxes so relatively far into the movement.

Fugue

Bach, The Well-Tempered Clavier, part I, Fugue I

Bach's Fugue I from *The Well-Tempered Clavier, part I,* is representative of a fugue in which the structural harmonic activity reflects the dynamic structure of the fugue theme. Within the subject, impulse grows through the ascent from C through the F and up to the G. Energy is released slightly through the descent to E—although not much, as the thirty-second notes propel the energy—and climaxes with the leap up to the offbeat A. The remainder of the subject plays out energy, although not all the impulse is resolved within the subject. The leap down to D releases energy; the leap up to G and the successive ascending step to A create energy, but somewhat less than the preceding leap to A. The final four descending sixteenth notes play out impulse, though again not much, as the faster sixteenth-note motion propels energy forward. In summary, the impulse grows to the climactic A, and is played out from that tone on.

The fugue opens in customary fashion, with an exposition in which statements of the subject are sounded in each of the four voices. It is somewhat atypical, in that instead of alternating statements of the subject with episodes of related material in the body of the fugue, the subject runs almost throughout in one of the four voices. The exposition opens in the home key of C major, alternating with tonicizations of the first ascending fifth, G major (bars 3 and 4), and the first descending fifth, F major (5–6), before returning to C major.

Following the exposition, canonic statements of the subject are sounded in the soprano and tenor voices (7) which bring about tonicizations of the first ascending fifth, G major, and then the second ascending fifth, D minor (8), and a return to C major (9). Another tonicization of G major (9) is followed by canonic statements in the bass and alto voices (10) beginning in a tonicized C major and moving to tonicizations of G major then the third ascending fifth, A minor (11). A statement of the subject in the tenor voice encompasses an extended segment in A minor, ending with a full cadence (12–14). In an ensuing strettolike four bars, in which statements of the subject follow one after another, a tonicization of the home key C major (14) is followed by a partial tonicization of the first fifth, G major, and a partial tonicization of the third fifth, A minor (16). After a harmonic leap down to a tonicized first descending fifth, F major, tonicizations of C major and then G major (17) are followed by a tonicization of the second ascending fifth, D minor (18). The eventual return to the home key is accomplished with statements of the subject in the tenor and alto voices (19) that move to a tonicized first ascending fifth, G major. Statements of the subject in the soprano and tenor voices (21) move through a brief tonicization of the first descending fifth, F major (22) to the final tonicization of the home key, C major (22). A 4-bar coda over a tonic pedal partially tonicizes F major (24) before closing the work with a return to C major (26).

The broad-scale impulse grows through the exposition, through the tonicizations of the first ascending fifth, G major, and through the first tonicization of the third ascending fifth, A minor. The stretto treatment of the subject increases the impulse; it grows up to the climactic soprano-voice B♭ (18). This climax occurs within the motion from the tonicized third ascending fifth, A minor, to the second ascending fifth, D minor, which connects it to the previously tonicized first ascending fifth, G major. The broad-scale resolution is carried out through the tonicized second ascending fifth, D minor, through G major, and then to the tonicized first descending fifth, F major, before the final C major. Thus the tone that climaxes the subject, A, is the tonic of A minor, the key farthest by successive fifth tonicizations from the home key; the climax of the movement comes within the motion connecting this farthest fifth to the other members of the harmonic chain.

Beethoven, String Quartet, Op. 131, Adagio ma non troppo e molto espressivo

The first-movement fugue of Beethoven's String Quartet, Op. 131, is characterized by a nebulous home key, which seems to fluctuate between F♯ minor and C♯ minor. The subject builds impulse up to the sforzando A, and releases it through the G♯ at the end of bar 4. The resolution, which begins with the G♯–

F♯ quarter notes immediately following the sforzando A, also contains within it a secondary impulse as the bar 3 descent builds energy to the low E, and releases it subsequently through the ascent to G♯. Similarly, the ensuing second-violin statement that begins on C♯ climaxes with the sforzando D; the resolution contains a secondary impulse to the low A.

The exposition unfolds statements of the subject alternating between C♯ minor and F♯ minor. The first episode begins in a tonicized B minor (17) and moves through partial tonicizations of C♯ minor (19), F♯ minor (22), B major (23), and E major with the next subject statement (25). The following canonic statement of the subject in the cello and first violin is extended to six bars. Through partial tonicizations it suggests C♯ minor (27), F♯ major, and B major (28); it moves through a full tonicization of A major (29) before cadencing in a tonicized C♯ minor (31). A 4-bar second episode begins with a tonicization of B major (32) and includes a tonicization of G♯ minor (34). The next statement of the subject is by the viola beginning in G♯ minor (35) and effecting a partial tonicization of B major (37). The ensuing 13-bar third episode effects successive partial tonicizations of G♯ minor (41), D♯ minor (45, spelled E♭ minor), G♯ major (47, spelled A♭ major), C♯ major (48, spelled D♭ major), F♯ major (50, spelled G♭ major), G♯ major (51, spelled A♭ major), and A♯ minor (52, spelled B♭ minor). In a partially tonicized B major the cello begins a statement of the subject (52) under the first violin statement in diminution; it includes a full tonicization of C♯ minor (55). The 6-bar fourth episode continues the eighth-note texture, and effects full tonicizations of E major (58) and A major (59), moving to the climactic rinforzando (61) in a partially tonicized B minor. After a 2-bar release of energy (61–62), a 4-bar subject statement in the first violin begins in A major, and effects partial tonicizations of F♯ minor (63) and C♯ minor (65) before returning clearly to A major (66).

Beginning in A major, an extended episode effects partial tonicizations of F♯ minor (69) and A major (71). Tonicizations of D major (73 and 79) sandwich a partial tonicization of B minor (76). The episode returns through a tonicized A major (81) to a tonicized C♯ minor (82). An 8-bar (83–90) passage in a quarter-note texture culminates with what seems like the structural final cadence (90) of scale degrees 3 (E) and 2 (D♯) over the dominant. The 8-bar passage takes place entirely in C♯ minor with the exception of the brief tonicization of the cadential iv, F♯ minor (89), and ends on the structural dominant; the 1 over the tonic never sounds. A 16-bar stretto follows; it consists of subject statements in the viola in C♯ minor, in the second violin in F♯ minor, and in the first violin (98) and cello (in augmentation) in F♯ minor, in C♯ minor (101), and in F♯ minor again before fully tonicizing C♯ minor (106) and then D major (107). A return to C♯ minor (108) precedes the final statement of the subject is in the cello in a partially tonicized F♯ minor (111); it is followed by a 7-bar coda.

Vagueness as to the identity of the home key as a characteristic of this fugue begins with the second statement of the subject, a real answer in the key of the first descending fifth, F♯ minor. It is in evidence in the C♯-minor/F♯-minor alternations of the stretto. It also comes into play particularly in the coda. Although it is in a fully tonicized C♯ minor, cadences to C♯-major chords within the pitch field of F♯ minor effect partial tonicizations of that key, and reduce the strength of the tonic C♯. This tonal vagueness is also evident in a remarkable way in the climax as generated by the structural harmonic activity.

Expansion by descending fifth is fundamental to this movement, and is established within the exposition. The second subject statement is in the key of the first descending fifth, F♯ minor. The last subject statement in the exposition—also in the key of F♯ minor—is extended to effect a tonicization of B minor (17), which suggests the second descending fifth, B major. The return to the home key, C♯ minor, in the first episode (18) is followed by full tonicizations of the fourth descending fifth, A major (29), the second descending fifth, B major (32), the first ascending fifth, G♯ minor (33), and the second ascending fifth, D♯ minor (45). The structural impulse of the movement is largely generated by the continuation of the descending fifth tonicizations, through the third descending fifth, E major (58), and on to the fourth descending fifth, A major (59), in which the onrushing eighth notes push to a climactic rinforzando.

But the harmonically generated impulse pushes yet further. After the embellishing F♯ partial minor tonicization (69) comes a tonicization of the fifth and farthest descending fifth, D major (73). An embellishing B-minor tonicization (76) is followed again by a tonicized D major (79) before returning, via A major (81), to C♯ minor (82). The climax of the movement comes with the crescendo to the fifth descending fifth, D major (107). The first climax (61), aided by increasing volume and rhythmic density, is in a tonicized A, which is the climactic tone of the original C♯-minor statement of the subject. The actual climax of the movement, aided by another increase in volume and tempo orientation, comes within a tonicized D (107), which is the climactic tone of the second statement of the subject in the secondary tonic of F♯ minor.

Notes

Chapter One

1. See chapter 6, "Remembrance of Things Future."

Chapter Three

1. Arnheim, *Art and Visual Perception*, 37. (*"The meaning of the work emerges from the interplay of activating and balancing forces."*)

2. After a diagram by Arnheim in *Art and Visual Perception*, 18.

3. While this passage builds energy on the musical surface, it is actually resolving energy on a higher level of the hierarchy. See the discussion of this movement in the appendix.

4. See chapter 7, "Patterns of Energy."

Chapter Four

1. See chapter 8, "Dynamic Analysis."

Chapter Six

This article is adapted from a lecture entitled "Remembrance of Things Future," written with the assistance of Paul Henry Smith and given at the First Symposium on Phenomenology and the Fine Arts sponsored by the World Phenomenology Association, Harvard University, April 1987.

1. Husserl, *Phenomenology of Internal Time-Consciousness*. See part 1, section 3, "The Levels of Constitution of Time and Temporal Objects," 40–97.

2. In fact, a part as experienced outside the whole is changed to some degree from the part as experienced within the whole. One of the essential attributes of our experience of any part is its position relative to the other parts and to the whole. In the successions described here, though, that relational attribute is a minimal component of the essence of our experience of the parts.

3. Husserl, *Internal Time-Consciousness*, 76.

4. Or line B–A^1; the two lines both represent the continuity of "just-having-been" now-phases.

5. Or dotted line A–cc; the two lines both represent the continuity of "as-yet-to-come" now-phases.

6. Any such absorption with emotions is an associative listening, as there is no emotion in the music, there is at most character. Emotions live in the subject; thus the structure of an emotional experience derived from listening to a musical performance is the structure of associative listening.

7. While the tones of the tuba have essential attributes resulting from their participation in a musical structure, this context does not render the object indivisible. The extension of the object is completely at the random option of the selective listener; thus the experience does not include the aspect of protention.

8. There is, to be sure, a non-sense about figures 6.5 and 6.6. Rather than schemata undertaken from a scientific stance, they are meant to be evocative of the aesthetic experience, in contrast to ordinary experiences of physical reality. Admittedly the experience of musical beauty, while sharing much with other experiences of ordinary temporally extended objects, strains Western logical investigation.

9. Note that no loss-of-self experience is available from either associative or selective listening. Associative listening requires a judgment to connect the musical object and the external object. Selective listening requires an act of judgment to separate the object from the remainder.

Chapter Seven

1. This is assuming a work that allows it. In fact a masterwork is a masterwork on the basis of its potential for singularity as a result of a global structure of energy such that impulse can be consequently resolved.

2. Groupings that are nested in larger groupings may or may not allow their performance so that the impulse created is completely resolved. A grouping that participates in a larger impulse may well create more energy than it resolves; likewise a grouping that participates in a larger resolution may well resolve more energy than it has created.

3. To participate in a broad-scale impulse, a new key must be established to the degree that the home key has been established. In the rare cases in which the home key is only faintly established as a tonic, only a similarly subtle implication of the new tonality may suffice to render it a new tonic, and thus to generate impulse on a broad scale.

4. With a minor-mode pitch field that includes the lowered 6th and 7th scale degrees, we tend in fact not to hear the minor mode as tonic but rather its relative major (for example with an operative pitch field of F, G, A♭, B♭, C, D♭, and E♭, we tend to hear A♭ major as the home key).

5. See the discussion of the Forlane from Bach's Orchestral Suite No. 1 in C Major, BWV 1066, in the appendix.

6. This hierarchy of activity can exist on multiple levels: if the crib were on a ship, the baby would have moved on the next level; if the ship were steaming in a circle, there would be no motion on the next higher level, and so on.

7. See further on in this section for a discussion of the relation of the mode of tonicized tonalities to that of the home key.

8. This may be associated with the impulse-giving tendency of the subdominant: in a progression from tonic to subdominant to dominant to tonic, the impulse is likely to climax with the subdominant chord.

9. See the appendix for detailed discussions of dance-form movements from Bach's Suite No. 1 in C Major, BWV 1066 (Gavotte II and Forlane); and from Beethoven's String Quartet, Op. 74, "The Harp" (mvt. 3, Presto).

10. See the appendix for detailed discussions of two theme-and-variation movements: Mozart, Quintet for Clarinet and Strings, K. 581 (mvt. 4, Allegretto con Variazioni); and Beethoven String Quartet, Op. 74, "The Harp" (mvt. 4, Allegretto con Variazioni). See also the discussion of the second movement (Adagio ma non troppo) of the "Harp" Quartet in chapter 8, "Dynamic Analysis."

11. The essence of the book depends on music being experienced, hence the directive "listen." Readers can listen to the example from the website, they can perform it and hear it, or they can "hear" it in their heads.

12. See the appendix for detailed discussions of the sonata-form first movements of Mozart, Symphony no. 38, "Prague" (mvt. 1, Adagio; Allegro), and Beethoven's String Quartet, Op. 74, "The Harp" (mvt. 1, Poco adagio; Allegro).

13. Sonata-form reveals its roots in the binary dance forms of the Baroque in the structure of repeats. Early, relatively short sonata-form movements had repeats indicated both for the exposition and for the development/recapitulation, like binary dance forms. As sonata-form movements grew in scope (and perhaps as the need for added length receded), the second repeat was eliminated. Eventually many composers eliminated both repeats.

14. In the expositions of sonata-form movements in the minor mode, when the B material is in a key other than the dominant it is usually preceded by a tonicization of either the dominant or the subdominant—one ascending or descending harmonic step. In this case the B material functions as a structural harmonic coloration of that first harmonic step of a fifth.

15. See the appendix for detailed discussion of two fugues: Bach, *The Well-Tempered Clavier, part I*, Fugue I; and Beethoven, String Quartet, Op. 131 (mvt. 1, Adagio ma non troppo e molto espressivo).

Chapter Eight

1. For further reading, see the annotated bibliography edited by Barolsky and von Foerster; for an insightful historical summary see Rink, review of *Musical Structure and Performance*, by Berry.

2. Pursuing the argument logically, a sequence of "Why?" questions would invariably end with either "I don't know" or "just because I like it that way" (for example: "You say that note should have emphasis. Why?" "Because it begins a new phrase." "Why should a note beginning a new phrase have emphasis?" and so on).

3. As expressed by Lee Rothfarb, "For Halm, forces are the content of music. They intensify and deintensify to produce a dynamic drama. Like Hanslick, Halm resisted the lure of emotive interpretations. He condemned program music as aesthetically corrupt and musically ruinous. . . . Analyses based on programs, emotive or otherwise, thus legitimize musical ruin. Accordingly, analysis should focus exclusively on what Halm . . . called the 'objective spirit' of the artwork—the dynamic system." Rothfarb, "Hermeneutics and Energetics," 61. And: "To him, analyzing a piece of music meant determining the dynamic functions of its events, their relationships and reciprocal influences, and revealing the logic of their succession." Idem, *August Halm*, 74.

4. Meyer, *Explaining Music*, 29.

5. For example, in *Rhythmic Structure* they write, "This book is in fact concerned throughout with grouping—for that is what rhythm is." Cooper and Meyer, *Rhythmic Structure of Music*, 8. This allows the authors another assumption that is problematic for our purposes: that any two or three successive tones necessarily form a grouping.

6. Lerdahl and Jackendoff, *Generative Theory of Tonal Music*.

7. Rink, Review of *Musical Structure and Performance*, 321.

8. See chaps. 4, "Gurus," and 6, "Remembrance of Things Future" on the attributes of tones.

9. Linear function is nested, too, as are scale degree and harmonic function in works with modulations.

10. A tone lower on the hierarchy that represents another tone is an "agent" for that "client" tone, which is higher on the hierarchy. See Thakar, *Counterpoint*, 154–69.

11. Of course no two performances will share the original attribute of temporal placement; they will occur at different times.

12. The point could be made that although the composer gives broad directions for tempo and volume, the performer has ultimate responsibility for both. Tempo *per se* is not an attribute, but a condition that allows the listener to absorb all the tones sounding in succession. The composer offers tempo indications (Allegro, Langsam, and so on), and sometimes metronome marks. The performer, however, has ultimate responsibility to the extent that a performance could reasonably be understood to comport with the tempo indication and still be too fast or too slow. As for metronome marks, they too are insufficient guides to a workable tempo, as metronomic speed is but one determinant of tempo. So similarly, a performance could match a metronome marking and still be too fast or too slow. (Consider the discrepancies—often dramatic—between metronome mark and tempo in composers' recordings of their own compositions.) Likewise, Italian dynamic indications (*piano, forte*) are unspecific, and thus insufficiently determinative: a performance could reasonably be understood to comport with the broad dynamic indication and be too loud or too soft.

13. Schenker made an aborted attempt toward a systematic consideration of local volume and tempo inflections. A dedicated pianist, he intuited that the performer had a responsibility in the creation of the phrase structure, with the use of tempo and dynamic inflections. As described by Rothstein in "Heinrich Schenker as an Interpreter of Beethoven's Piano Sonatas," Schenker's personal scores are filled with notations for the shaping of phrases with the use of crescendos, diminuendos, and rubato. In fact, he also had an inkling that these inflections had some implications at higher levels of the hierarchy. In "The Largo of J. S. Bach's Sonata No. 3 for Unaccompanied Violin, [BWV 1005]," Schenker writes: "In my forthcoming treatise, 'The Art of Performance,' it will be systematically shown for the first time that dynamics, like voice leading and diminution, are organized according to structural levels, genealogically, as it were. For each level of voice leading, background or foreground, and for each diminutional level, there is a corresponding dynamic level of the first order, second order, and so forth." The planned treatise on performances was never completed. Perhaps this was due at least in part to the obvious impossibility of dynamics being ever louder or ever more contrasting at ever-higher structural levels. Although he was very much on the right track, the essential consideration missed by Schenker was that it is not the dynamic inflection itself that operates on different levels of the hierarchy, but the pattern of energy that results (in part) from the dynamic structure. In other words, the phrasing—i.e., grouping—structure on the local level is articulated by the creation and playing out of energy, resulting in part from the dynamic inflections given by the performer. The grouping structure on higher levels is also articulated by the creation and playing out of energy, which also results in part from the contribution of the performer. But at higher structural levels, volume is not a controlling factor in the creation or release of energy; rather the performer's contribution to the pattern of energy is largely confined to building or decreasing tempo.

14. Unlike the analyst, the performing musician does not need to be able to articulate the structure necessary for the unfolding of those relationships, he only needs to unfold them. However that conductor or teacher who would guide musicians toward bringing about the highest possible aesthetic object needs a conscious understanding of the structure of relationships that allows the highest experience.

15. This is not to suggest that a dynamic analysis is ultimate, or the last word; doubtless we will come in time to understand works with increasing depth. And it seems unimaginable that we will ever approach what could be considered a complete understanding.

16. Tonicizations over a pedal have only a secondary effect on the structural harmonic motion: they can only be partial.

17. *Beethoven: String Quartets op. 74 & 95*, ed. Jonathan Del Mar (Kassel: Bärenreiter-Verlag, 2008).

18. Printing examples 8.3 and 8.4 on individual pages may facilitate comprehension.

19. The lines of triangle marks indicate the dynamic/grouping structure required at the associated level of reduction. The climax of a higher level grouping may or may not coincide with that of one closer to the musical surface. Where they differ, as between levels A and B at bar 32, it is because as an upper-level event is prolonged, additional energy is required to sustain the phrase.

Appendix

1. Chromatic inflections that suggest a new key but do not result in the complete operative pitch field of that key do not rise to the level of partial tonicizations.

2. The sounding of the B♭ results in an operative pitch field of F major as well a C dominant seventh harmony; F major is only partially tonicized because this occurs over the C pedal in the bass.

3. See chapter 7, "Patterns of Energy."

4. It is up to the performer to generate the overall dynamic structure of the work, such that the impulse climaxes with the climactic D minor in the first sounding of the Più presto quasi Prestissimo. The subsequent soundings extend the resolution. See chapter 8, "Dynamic Analysis."

Bibliography

Arnheim, Rudolf. *Art and Visual Perception: A Psychology of the Creative Eye.* 2d. ed. Berkeley and Los Angeles: University of California Press, 1974.

Barolsky, Daniel, and Richard von Foerster, eds. "Bibliography/Annotated Bibliography of Performance and Analysis," for the Performance and Analysis Interest Group (PAIG) of the Society for Music Theory. http://www.humanities. mcmaster.ca/~mcgowan/PAIGAnnotatedBib.html.

Beethoven, Ludwig van. *Beethoven: String Quartets op. 74 & 95.* Edited by Jonathan Del Mar. Miniature score. Kassel: Bärenreiter-Verlag, 2008.

Berry, Wallace. *Musical Structure and Performance.* New Haven, CT: Yale University Press, 1989.

Burkhart, Charles. "Schenker's Theory of Levels and Musical Performance." In *Aspects of Schenkerian Theory,* edited by David Beach, 95–112. New Haven, CT: Yale University Press, 1983.

Clarke, Eric. "Empirical Methods in the Study of Performance." In *Empirical Musicology: Aims, Methods, Prospects,* edited by Eric Clarke and Nicholas Cook, 77–102. Oxford: Oxford University Press, 2004.

———. "Expression in Performance: Generativity, Perception, and Semiosis." In *The Practice of Performance,* edited by John Rink, 21–54. Cambridge: Cambridge University Press, 1995.

Cone, Edward T. *Musical Form and Musical Performance.* New York: Norton, 1968.

Cook, Nicholas. "Analysing Performance and Performing Analysis." In *Rethinking Music,* edited by Nicholas Cook and Mark Everist, 239–61. Oxford: Oxford University Press, 1999.

———. "The Conductor and the Theorist: Furtwängler, Schenker, and the First Movement of Beethoven's Ninth Symphony." In *The Practice of Performance,* edited by John Rink, 105–25. Cambridge: Cambridge University Press 1995.

———. "Words about Music, or Analysis versus Performance." In *Theory into Practice: Composition, Performance and the Listening Experience,* 9–52. Collected Writings of the Orpheus Institute 2. Leuven, Belgium: Leuven University Press, 1999.

Cooper, Grosvenor, and Leonard B. Meyer. *The Rhythmic Structure of Music.* Chicago: University of Chicago Press, 1960.

Dunsby, Jonathan. "Guest Editorial: Performance and Analysis of Music." *Music Analysis* 8 (March–July 1989): 5–20.

———. *Performing Music: Shared Concerns.* Oxford: Clarendon Press, 1995.

Howell, Timothy B. "Analysis and Performance: The Search for a Middleground." In *Companion to Contemporary Musical Thought,* 2 vols., edited by John Paynter, Timothy B. Howell, Richard Orton, and Peter Seymour, 2:692–714. London: Routledge, 1992.

Husserl, Edmund. *The Phenomenology of Internal Time-Consciousness.* Edited by Martin Heidegger. Translated by James S. Churchill. Bloomington: Indiana University Press, 1964.

Lerdahl, Fred. *Tonal Pitch Space.* Oxford: Oxford University Press, 2001.

Lerdahl, Fred, and Ray Jackendoff. *A Generative Theory of Tonal Music.* Cambridge, MA: MIT Press, 1983.

Lester, Joel. "How Theorists Relate to Musicians." *Music Theory Online* 4/2 1998. http://mto.societymusictheory.org/issues/mto.98.4.2/mto.98.4.2.lester_essay.html.

———. "Performance and Analysis: Interaction and Interpretation." In *The Practice of Performance: Studies in Musical Interpretation,* edited by John Rink, 197–216. Cambridge: Cambridge University Press, 1995.

Meyer, Leonard B. *Emotion and Meaning in Music.* Chicago: University of Chicago Press, 1956.

———. *Explaining Music: Essays and Explorations.* Berkeley: University of California Press, 1973.

Narmour, Eugene. "On the Relationship of Analytical Theory to Performance and Interpretation." In *Explorations in Music, the Arts, and Ideas: Essays in Honor of Leonard B. Meyer,* edited by Ruth A. Solie and Eugene Narmour, 317–40. Festschrift Series 7. Stuyvesant, NY: Pendragon Press, 1988.

Ramirez, Rafael, Emilia Gomez, Veronica Vicente, Montserrat Puiggros, Amaury Hazan, and Esteban Maestre. "Modeling Expressive Music Performance in Bassoon Audio Recordings." In *Intelligent Computing in Signal Processing and Pattern Recognition: International Conference on Intelligent Computing, ICIC, 2006, Kunming, China, August 16–19, 2006.* 3 vols. Berlin: Springer, 2006.

Rink, John. "Analysis and (or?) Performance." Chap. 3 in *Musical Performance: A Guide to Understanding.* New York: Cambridge University Press, 2002.

———. *The Practice of Performance: Studies in Musical Interpretation.* Cambridge: Cambridge University Press, 1995.

———. Review of *Musical Structure and Performance,* by Wallace Berry. *Music Analysis* 9, no. 3 (1990): 319–39.

Rosenwald, Lawrence. "Theory, Text-Setting, and Performance." In *Journal of Musicology* 11 (Winter, 1993): 52–65.

Rothfarb, Lee. *August Halm: A Critical and Creative Life in Music.* Eastman Studies in Music 68. Rochester, NY: University of Rochester Press, 2009.

———. *Ernst Kurth as Theorist and Analyst.* Philadelphia: University of Pennsylvania Press, 1988.

———. "Hermeneutics and Energetics: Analytical Alternatives in the Early 1900s." *Journal of Music Theory* 36 (Spring 1992): 43–68.

Rothstein, William. "Analysis and the Act of Performance." In *The Practice of Performance: Studies in Musical Interpretation,* edited by John Rink, 217–40. Cambridge: Cambridge University Press, 1995.

———. "Heinrich Schenker as an Interpreter of Beethoven's Piano Sonatas." *19th-Century Music* 8 (Summer 1984): 3–28.

———. "Like Falling off a Log: Rubato in Chopin's Prelude in A-flat Major (op. 28, no. 17)." *Music Theory Online* 11/1 2005. http://mto.societymusictheory.org/issues/mto.05.11.1/mto.05.11.1.rothstein.html.

Sapp, Craig Stuart. "Hybrid Numeric/Rank Similarity Metrics for Musical Performance Analysis." Paper presented at the Ninth International Conference on Music Information Retrieval, Philadelphia, September 2008. http://74.125.47.132/search?q=cache:p8AtWXCzH-oJ:ismir2008.ismir.net/papers/ISMIR2008_240.pdf.

Schachter, Carl. "20th-Century Analysis and Mozart Performance." *Early Music* 19, no. 4, *Performing Mozart's Music I* (November 1991): 620–26.

Schenker, Heinrich. "The Largo of J. S. Bach's Sonata No. 3 for Unaccompanied Violin, [BWV 1005]." Translated by John Rothgeb. In *The Music Forum IV*, edited by Felix Salzer, 141–59. New York; Columbia University Press, 1976.

Schmalfeldt, Janet. "On Performance, Analysis, and Schubert." *Per Musi: Revista de Performance Musical* (published by the Music School of the Federal University of Minas Gerais) 5–6 (2003): 38–54; followed by "An Interview with Janet Schmalfeldt," led by André Cavozotti and Salomea Gandelman, 55–67. http://www.musica.ufmg.br/permusi/port/numeros/05-06/Num5-6_cap_03.pdf.

———. "On the Relation of Analysis to Performance: Beethoven's Bagatelles Op. 126, Nos. 2 & 5." *Journal of Music Theory* 29 (Spring 1985): 1–31.

Thakar, Markand. *Counterpoint: Fundamentals of Music Making.* New Haven, CT: Yale University Press, 1990.

Index